# Beyond the Battlefield

# Pergamon Titles of Related Interest

*Daniel* STRATEGIC MILITARY DECEPTION
*Douglass* SOVIET MILITARY STRATEGY IN EUROPE
*Shultz/Hunt* POLITICAL MILITARY LESSONS FROM AN
UNCONVENTIONAL WAR: Reassessing American Strategies in
the Vietnam Conflict
*Sherraden/Eberly* NATIONAL SERVICE: Social, Economic and
Military Impact
*Taylor/Olson/Schrader* DEFENSE MANPOWER PLANNING: Issues
for the 1980s

# Related Journals*

DISASTERS
HISTORY OF EUROPEAN IDEAS
INFORMATION TECHNOLOGY IN HUMAN AFFAIRS
TECHNOLOGY IN SOCIETY
WORLD DEVELOPMENT

*Free specimen copies available upon request.

PERGAMON
POLICY
STUDIES
ON INTERNATIONAL POLITICS

# Beyond the Battlefield
## The New Military Professionalism

Sam C. Sarkesian

**Pergamon Press**
NEW YORK • OXFORD • TORONTO • SYDNEY • PARIS • FRANKFURT

Pergamon Press Offices:

| | |
|---|---|
| U.S.A. | Pergamon Press Inc., Maxwell House, Fairview Park, Elmsford, New York 10523, U.S.A. |
| U.K. | Pergamon Press Ltd., Headington Hill Hall, Oxford OX3 0BW, England |
| CANADA | Pergamon Press Canada Ltd., Suite 104, 150 Consumers Road, Willowdale, Ontario M2J 1P9, Canada |
| AUSTRALIA | Pergamon Press (Aust.) Pty. Ltd., P.O. Box 544, Potts Point, NSW 2011, Australia |
| FRANCE | Pergamon Press SARL, 24 rue des Ecoles, 75240 Paris, Cedex 05, France |
| FEDERAL REPUBLIC OF GERMANY | Pergamon Press GmbH, Hammerweg 6, Postfach 1305, 6242 Kronberg/Taunus, Federal Republic of Germany |

Library of Congress Cataloging in Publication Data

Sarkesiam, Sam Charles
 Beyond the battlefield.

 (Pergamon policy studies on international politics)
 Bibliography: p.
 Includes index.
 1. United States--Military policy.  2. Sociology,
Military--United States.  3. United States--Armed
Forces--Officers.  4. Military service, Voluntary--
United States.  5. Military ethics.  I. Title.
II. Title: Military professionalism.  III. Series.
UA23.S27      306'.2      80-27027
ISBN 0-08-027178-2      AACR1

*Printed in the United States of America*

to

Jeanette

# Contents

# Preface

I have compiled this volume because I firmly believe that there is a serious need to again speak out against the increasing tendency for the military to view professionalism primarily in terms of military skills with only a cursory nod to the idea that military professionals must be more than battlefield technicians. Such a view not only creates compartmentalized competence, but limits intellectual horizons, reduces the professional ability to deal with political-social matters, and makes moral and ethical criteria a matter of tactical expediency.

Since the final years of the Vietnam involvement, there has been a great deal of discussion and debate regarding the nature and character of military professionalism. These ranged from biting criticisms of the conduct of the officer corps and charges that the American Army collapsed in Vietnam to the claim that the military did its job and any failures in Vietnam were due to civilian leadership. Serious reassessments were made of military honor, morality, and ethical behavior. Many examinations led to recommendations for the revitalization of military professionalism including such items as publishing a code of conduct, revamping military education, and restoring the concept of honor. Yet, many argued that the real problem lay in not following the traditional concepts of "Duty, Honor, Country." From all of these debates and examinations, one would expect to see a revitalized military professionalism emerge attuned to the challenges of the new decade. What appears to have evolved, however, is a concept of professionalism chained to the traditional view that <u>military</u> training and <u>military</u> skills produce the best professional. Translated into the realities of military life, this simply means that military officers should spend more time in on-the-job training, learning, for example, how to command companies and battalions, as

well as learning the technical skills required for various
positions associated with these units. There is little to
criticize about these efforts and goals. What is disturbing,
however, is the perpetuation of a narrow concept of professionalism which disregards almost two decades of change and
challenge. This reversion to a traditional professional posture
not only indicates the lack of an institutional memory, but
attempts to blot out the lessons of Vietnam and implies a
political-psychological isolation from the political-social environment. Carried to its logical conclusion, such a concept will
erode the very basis of military professionalism by ignoring
the humanistic and political-social character of the military
institution as well as the characteristics of the environment in
which the military must operate.

Let me illustrate this. At the Army Command and General Staff College at Fort Leavenworth, many hours are spent
over terrain boards of Europe with students maneuvering
American armor units against Soviet units. In these exercises
little if any attention is given to the responsibilities of unit
commanders to the "people" problem - what to do with hundreds and thousands of refugees or how to deal with the
problems encountered in trying to engage an enemy within the
territory and population of friendly countries.

Similar shortcomings are evident in FM 100-5, Operations. The thrust and substance of FM 100-5 have been
debated in a number of forums. In sum, this Field Manual is
primarily concerned with the land battle in Europe. The fact
that FM 100-5 is the operational bible for the U.S. Army
makes it appear that little operational attention will be given
to contingencies outside of the European area - contingencies,
it might be added, that in the view of a number of observers
are most likely to be the areas of future operations and the
most difficult to undertake. Most importantly, these shortcomings are a reflection of the traditional professional orientation and its educational and socialization processes.

The theme of the essays in this volume is that American
military professionalism, as it is presently conceived and
followed, is inadequate to meet the challenges of the coming
decade. Not only is this true with respect to the international security environment, but professional expertise is
woefully inadequate in its capacity to understand and respond
to political-social issues, making the profession unprepared to
interact harmoniously with its own political system. Nor is it
prepared for the political-social challenges of non-nuclear and
low intensity conflicts. It is argued that the concept of
military professionalism must be broadened and "humanized,"
intellectual preparation and military posture revised and in a
number of instances changed, if the military profession is to
be more than a "robot-like" mechanism designed for uncritical
and nonthinking utility.

Complementing this theme is one that focuses on the moral and ethical aspects of professionalism, arguing that the military professional must perceive these free from the confines of traditional perspectives. Moral and ethical criteria cannot be derived solely from within the military profession. They must originate from the broader community and from universal philosophical principles, echoing the essential thrust of the other theme in these essays.

Finally, underlying these themes is the view that the decade of the 1970s saw the end of American military posture and professionalism characteristic of the post World War II period, and the beginning of a new one marked by the end of the Vietnam War. This new era is characterized by at least four major factors: the volunteer military system; the impact of the Vietnam War; the loss of America's dominant position in international politics; and the rise of egalitarianism in American society.

The essays in this volume are linked to these factors in a number of ways and from a variety of perspectives. While several of these factors are studied in some detail, they are not treated as separate topics, but rather as part of the general study of professionalism and institutional change. Even in examining the impact of Vietnam (which is done in several chapters), the concern is not necessarily with the details of the War, but with the issue of professionalism.

Even though a number of the essays appeared earlier, I have placed them in this volume, together with several original works, in order to encourage a sharper focus and a more critical reassessment of military professionalism. In doing so, I have not attempted to place these works in chronological order. Rather, they have been organized around three major issues: the meaning of military professionalism; the problems facing the profession stemming from the Vietnam experience through the past two decades; and the character and nature of military professionalism necessary for the coming decade.

The essays represent a range of data, sources, and inquiry techniques. Some are based on survey data, others are based on my own military experience, and still others are an attempt to integrate the practicalities of military life with theoretical perspectives. Some of the issues facing the military and several institutional procedures have changed since the publication of the earlier articles; i.e., the establishment of alternate career patterns (secondary specialties) for Army officers. Little attempt has been made to revise the earlier articles to reflect current procedures, since these are tangential to the main themes. Finally, all of the work has taken advantage of the input of colleagues and friends from both the military and academic professions.

Most of the essays not only attempt to identify prevailing views of a particular aspect of professionalism, but also include an assessment of the implications of existing professional perspectives and what revisions, modifications, and/or changes are necessary. Nevertheless, this volume is not intended to serve as an operational manual to implement programs and training designed to correct professional shortcomings and weaknesses. While the final chapter does address the problem of "what needs to be done," this is viewed from broad operational principles aimed primarily at the philosophical and educational underpinnings of the military profession. Thus, one will not find in this volume, for example, what changes of curricula are needed in senior military schools to develop proper dimensions of professionalism. Nor will one find a training plan to train professionals in the proper strategy for low intensity conflict. To be sure, specific programs and plans are necessary to convert the theoretical into the practical and operational. I argue, however, that this cannot be done correctly without first recognizing the nature and extent of the problem, understanding the philosophical principles and values of the military in a liberal democracy, and developing the intellectual capacity and critical inquiry needed to deal with the complexity of issues facing the military profession. Programmatic templates are simply the visible reflection of these fundamental concepts.

My own interest and research has been primarily on professionalism in the U.S. Army. The articles reflect this perspective. Yet, a number of assessments apply equally to all services and hopefully provide insights into the general concept of the military profession. There are overlaps in these works (as one would expect) - even the use of identical sources. This not only reflects my continuing concern and focus on a broadly based military professionalism, but also my recognition of the complexity of the subject and its multidimensional considerations, particularly its political dimension.

In the final analysis, however, the conclusions and policy recommendations are my own. These do not profess earth-shaking revelations or completely new views divorced from the long line of scholarship on the subject. What I do claim, however, is persistence in advocating a political-military dimension to the profession. Without such a dimension, I fail to see how the military profession can cope with its own system and with American society, much less with the international environment.

Sam C. Sarkesian
Chicago, Illinois

# Acknowledgments

The following works by the author of this volume have been included by permission of the publishers:

"Political Soldiers:  Perspectives on Professionalism in the U.S. Military," Midwest Journal of Political Science, Vol. XVI, No. 2, May, 1972, pp. 239-258.

"Vietnam and the Professional Military," Orbis, Vol. XVIII, No. 1, Spring, 1974, pp. 252-265.

"Revolution and the Limits of Military Power:  The Haunting Specter of Vietnam" Social Science Quarterly, March, 1976, Vol. 56, No. 4, pp. 673-688.

"Professional Problems and Adaptations," in Ellen Stern (Ed.), The Limits of Military Intervention.  Beverly Hills, Cal.: Sage Publications, 1977.

"Reassessment of Military Professionalism:  Military Review, Vol. LVII, No. 8, August, 1977, pp. 3-20.

"Changing Dimensions of Military Professionalism:  Education and Enlightened Advocacy," Military Review, Vol. LIX, No. 3, March, 1979, pp. 44-56.

"Military Leadership:  Time for a Change?"  Military Review, Vol. LX, No. 9, September, 1980, pp. 16-24.

"Low Intensity Conflict:  An Overview."  Published by permission of Transaction, Inc. from U.S. Policy and Low Intensity Conflict, edited by Sam C. Sarkesian and William Scully.  Copyright (c) 1981 by Transaction Books.

# I

# The Dimensions of Military Professionalism

# Part I
# An Introduction

This part examines the various concepts and definitions of military professionalism. The first selection defines military professionalism using the general notion of professions and how these apply to the military profession. The following two selections examine military professionalism from the perspective of military men. Data from several surveys are compared and major ingredients of military professionalism identified, ranging from views about the political system to the military mind. The final selection is an examination of scholarly concepts on military professionalism and an assessment of how these apply to the modern environment. Several conclusions can be drawn from these discussions. The experience of the past two decades has considerably eroded the relevancy of traditional professional criteria. In this respect, the military profession, whether it likes it or not, has been drawn inextricably into the political-social environment. Moreover, it is clear that scholars disagree not only with respect to the meaning of profession, but also as to the long-run professional implications of the domestic socio-political and international changes of the past two decades.

# 1 Professions and Professionalism

In any modern political system, the designation of the label professional is a mark of distinction. Not only does it indicate an exceptional competence, but also a commitment to a particular lifelong career. A profession, therefore, means something more than an occupation. It presumes that the institution or group that is identified as a profession has a purpose that is linked to the public good - above and beyond monetary considerations. Thus, professionals and professions gain their status by rising above the day-to-day mundane activities of the marketplace, by recognition that they are involved in an essential public need, and by motivations of professional morality and ethics. Finally, an important part of the status of a profession is based on the public's acceptance of the label and the perpetuation of the title by members of the group or institution proclaiming such status.

While most professions and professionals are not greatly introspective or self-analytical of their status, the military has gone to great lengths to assess the meaning of military profession and professionalism. This is probably to be expected. It is an anomaly, both in terms of the institution and the individual, to reconcile the purpose of the military to the higher ideals of public good, morality, and ethics. Killing, even when ordered by the state, is hardly a goal or mission that engenders high ideals of professionalism or is necessarily associated with the public good. Important debates regarding the military profession, its components, and the character of the professional ethos are not generally addressed in the public realm. They are, however, perennial issues within the military profession.

The purpose of this introductory chapter is to explore the various concepts and definitions of profession and professional, apply these to the military, and analyze the implications

5

of these concepts to the military. It is not intended to dwell at any length on the considerations of profession or professional in the abstract. Yet, it is necessary at the outset to address theoretical concepts and definitions of profession and professionalism in order to establish a framework to use for further analysis.

## AN OVERVIEW

A profession, according to Greenwood, is characterized by authority, a systematic body of theory, sanction of the community, a regulative code of ethics, and the professional culture.(1) Moreover, professional competence is based on a "fund of knowledge that has been organized into an internally consistent system, called a body of theory."(2) This broad education based on systematic theory provides the professional with a "type of knowledge that highlights the layman's comparative ignorance. . . . In a professional relationship . . . the professional dictates what is good or evil for the client, who has no choice but to accede to professional judgment."(3) Thus the professional's authority and expertise give the professional a virtual monopoly of power and responsibility in a particular area of social need within the political system. This characteristic leads directly to community sanction. It is the community that gives the profession powers and privileges in certain areas. This may include such things as control over recruiting, training, and licensing. To maintain professional authority and community support, professions also develop a regulative code of ethics. This establishes professional norms of behavior in client-professional and colleague-colleague relationships. Finally, the concept of profession envisions a professional culture in which the values, norms, and symbols of the profession are transmitted through a network of formal and informal groups.

Cogan sums up the characteristics of the profession as follows:

> A profession is a vocation whose practice is founded upon an understanding of the theoretical structure of some department of learning or science, and upon the abilities accompanying such understanding. This understanding and these abilities are applied to the vital practical affairs of man. The practices of the profession are modified by knowledge or a generalized nature and by the accumulated wisdom and experience of mankind, which serve to correct the errors of specialism. The profession, serving the total needs of man, considers its first ethical imperative to be altruistic services to the client.(4)

These professional characteristics apply to the military profession with a fundamental difference. The purpose of the military profession differs from civilian professions. In examining the meaning of military professionalism, therefore, certain qualifications must be made. Not only must we incorporate the unique purpose of the military, but an added dimension must be considered which stems from the concept of "honor."

## THE UNIQUENESS OF MILITARY PROFESSIONALSIM

A number of scholars have suggested that the uniqueness of the military profession is summed up by its purpose: "management of violence in the service of the state." In this respect two definitions articulated by men a generation apart are useful starting points. Sir John Hackett defined the function of the profession of arms in a democratic society as "the ordered application of force in the resolution of a social problem."(5) Donald Bletz writes that "the military professional is defined simply as the career officer who devotes himself to the expertise, responsibility, and corporateness of the profession of arms."(6)

According to Brown and Bradford, however, professionalism is a much more encompassing concept:

Professionalism is more than simply belonging to the officers corps. It is a status determined jointly by the officer and his government. Neither the state nor the officers corps will grant professional standing to the man who lacks the necessary competence or who will not agree to make an unconditional commitment to duty if he is in the combat army. The unconditional quality of his commitment is signified by the career length and life of selfless sacrifice, ranging from Melville Goodwin's "genteel poverty" to the Gettysburg "last full measure of devotion." Professionalism thus has both objective and subjective content. It is objective in that professional status is granted by the state if certain performance criteria are met by the officer. It is subjective in that the officer must feel a sense of duty to serve the lawful government "for the full distance," even at the risk of his life. Mentally, he does not condition this obligation.(7)

Janowitz writes that military professionalism includes a basic concern with military honor. This includes:

Gentlemanly conduct. As long as members of the military elite consider themselves to be special because they embody the martial spirit. It is indispensable that they consider themselves gentle-men. . . .

Personal Fealty. Personal allegiance, as a component of honor, has had to be changed to fit the growth of bureaucratic organization. . . .

Brotherhood. In its contemporary form a major aspect of military honor comprises a sense of brotherhood and intense group loyalty. . . the sense of fraternity in the military is more than instrumental, it is an end in and of itself and for this reason it becomes suspect of the out-sider. . . .

Pursuit of Glory. The code of professional honor has had to be self-generating by drawing on its own historical achievement . . . the military in the United States have had to develop a sense of honor rooted in the practical contributions of the profession, rather than in the survival of feudal notions of military glory.(8)

Thus, the basic characteristics of professions in general identified by Greenwood and Cogan are given military sub-stance by the uniqueness of the military's purpose, a sense of duty and honor, and ultimate liability.(9)

## SPECIAL KNOWLEDGE AND COMMUNITY SANCTION

Moreover, the military's professional authority rests on a special knowledge whose wellsprings are skills at war. Over the years, through the system of military skills, historical experience, and a pervasive socialization process, the military profession not only perpetuated such knowledge but has been conditioned to look at the world through a particular lens. In this way, the uniqueness of the profession vis-a-vis other professions is perpetuated and a professional isolation is maintained from the broader community. However, since the military's authority and identity as a profession is sanctioned by the community, the military must continually reinforce a linkage with the community. Not only must the military demon-strate its expertise at war, but also its acceptance of the community's value system and "rules of the game." Clearly, in times of peace this becomes more difficult: The community is prone to be more sensitive to value systems and "rules of the game." In any case, society must be continually assured that its military professionals are competent war makers, within the general value system of society. The most important point is that the professional role and authority is directly linked to the community.

Some of these considerations are summed up by Huntington who writes:

> The military vocation is a profession because it has accumulated experiences which make up a body of professional knowledge. In the military view, man learns only from experience. . . .Hence, the military officer studies history . . . the military is . . . pessimistic, collectivist, historically inclined, power-oriented, nationalistic, militaristic, pacifist, and instrumentalist in its views of the military profession.(10)

Huntington goes on to say that the military perspective and its collective knowledge gives the military responsibility for the security of the state and this in turn causes the military:

> (1) to view the state as the basic unit of political organization; (2) to stress the continuing nature of the threats to the military security of the state and the continuing likelihood of war; (3) to emphasize the magnitude and immediacy of the security threats; (4) to favor maintenance of strong, diverse, and ready military forces; (5) to oppose the extension of state commitments and the involvement of the state in war except when victory is certain.(11)

Because the profession has a virtual monopoly on a systematic body of knowledge concerning the actual conduct of war, it not only has the sanction of the community, but is able to dictate the norms of the profession with little community interference. Thus, the military profession has its own system of law, social structure, education, recruiting, and rewards and punishments. Admittedly, most civilian professions have similar characteristics, but given the purpose of the military and the fact that it is an integral part of the political system, such considerations become crucial with respect to the military profession.

## THE STUDY OF MILITARY PROFESSIONALISM: DIMENSIONS AND SUBSTANCE

The definition of professionalism, however, does not necessarily provide an adequate framework for its study. Indeed, even with some consensus regarding the meaning, one can identify a number of approaches to the study of military professionalism. These can be clustered around three major perspectives: community, institutional, and individual. The scope and dimension range from the macro at the community level to the micro at the individual level. In each case the substantive issues of professionalism include technical skills, professional ethics, and political perspectives. And in each case, the scope and dimensions of these issues, from the more technical to the more broadly based political perspective, must be assessed at each level; i.e., community, institution, individual. Thus, at the level of the individual, one can study professionalism in terms of the individual officer's competence as a military technician, his particular attitude and conduct regarding professional ethics, and his political attitudes and perceptions. It is the total of these substantive issues that provide the quality of professionalism at the individual level. On the other hand, the professional ethos is not limited to the individual level, but must include the institutional requirements and community expectations and images.

This may be better understood by viewing the relationships as a system of concentric circles, in the center of which stands the professional officer. His immediate concern and sensitivity is to the core value system which personally affects him. These concerns directly influence the officer's own view of himself and his immediate world. Such concerns stem from questions of personal honesty, integrity, conduct, honor, and competence. Although these may be of immediate personal concern, this aspect of professionalism is least coherent since it has an inherently individualistic dimension. That is, each individual officer perceives these values from his own conscience and applies them accordingly, rationalizing their validity and his own performance. This individual perspective, however, is strongly influenced by institutional socialization.

The officer perceives his relationship to the institution as directly linked to his personal value system and performance. Thus, the institution sets the criteria for performance, establishes rules for conduct, and manifests basic professional principles which is the context within which most of the officer's own professional value system operates. Although the institution is wider in scope than the individual officer's perspective, it is inextricably linked to the personal value systems. Nevertheless, the institution does not subsume, nor is it perfectly coincident with, the personal perspective of the individual officer.

It is at the community level that the political perspective becomes increasingly important. Here the concern is civil-military relations and a whole range of considerations regarding the political role of the military in democratic society, the

military value system vis-a-vis civilian values, and the linkages between the military and society. This level, however, is
removed from the real concerns of the individual officer, but
is important at the institutional level. The average professional officer is not consciously striving for a systematic
impact on community-military relationships. Only a small group
of officers at the highest levels of the hierarchy are directly
involved, yet the individual value system and institutional
performance as perceived by the community have a direct
bearing on the community's image of the military and on the
professional's own sense of performance and competence.

One of the major considerations that can be drawn from
this assessment of military professionalism is that there is no
single, clearly articulated view of the military profession that
evolves from actors in the political system. This view was
further confirmed by the work of two scholars. Using a
national sample of civilians in 1973, they concluded:

> . . . public views of the military were indeed a
> mixture of positive and negative feelings, depending
> upon the dimension being considered. The evalua-
> tion of the military organization was generally favor-
> able; yet there was considerable reluctance to
> support the use of military force except in self
> defense (even though those individuals most favor-
> able toward the military organization were also more
> willing to support the use of military force under a
> wider range of circumstances). In the area of
> civil-military relations, we found mostly positive
> ratings of the role of the military in society and the
> level of military versus civilian influence; never-
> theless, a majority of respondents were critical of
> waste, inefficiency, and excess spending in the
> military.(12)

## ABSOLUTE-RELATIVE VALUES

What makes the examination of military professionalism considerably more difficult is the concept of absolute and relative
values. There are certain core principles of professionalism
that are rarely questioned. These include honesty, integrity,
loyalty, honor, and gentlemanly conduct. They apply in their
most clearly articulated form at the personal level and in
colleague-to-colleague relationships. These principles become
more diffuse as an increasing variety of forces and relationships develop. Thus, at the institutional level, a dimension
is added to each of these principles which are primarily rooted
to institutional considerations. At the community level, these

same principles become even more diffuse and obscure in their operational applicability because of the increased dimensions to their meaning and interpretation.  Indeed, one can argue that, in the main, professional principles at the personal level tend to be accepted as absolute; that is, one does not lie to and cheat fellow officers, for example.  This remains true at the institutional level, but is conditioned by institutional requirements which subsume and may subordinate individual considerations.  For example, as individuals we may accept the absolute value that one does not kill.  Within an institutional context, however, killing becomes part of the professional ethos sanctioned by the institution and community.  This absolute-relative dichotomy applies to a variety of professional considerations.

In examining military professionalism, therefore, we must not only account for the perspectives at the individual, institutional, and community level, but also understand the focus of the substantive issues.  A highly competent officer in terms of technical skills may be a professional renegade in terms of institutional requirements.  Institutional requirements may demand compliance with rules and regulations personally abhorrent to the individual professional.  Institutional criteria for promotion, which so many professionals objected to during the Vietnam involvement, may foster careerism which is at cross-purposes to honesty, integrity, and gentlemanly conduct at the personal level.

Clearly, personal value systems, institutional requirements, and community perspectives will never be in perfect harmony in terms of military professionalism.  The greater the discord, the less professionalism one finds in the military.  This may well be the reason that there are differing points of view regarding the professionalism of the U. S. military and varying interpretations regarding the substance of military professionalism.

## MILITARY-COMMUNITY LINKAGE

These substantive and dimensional considerations of military professionalism take their cue from the values and expectations of the society from which the military evolves.  Scholars are prone to state that the military must have links with society and provide an institution through which the core values of society can be transmitted and incorporated into the professional system.  In American society, therefore, the military is thought to be supportive of democratic values, even though the military is presumed to be more of an authoritarian structure.  More important, society expects military men to be committed to the basic "rules of the game" of the political system.  Civilian control of the military, individual dignity and worth, and justice before the law, for example, are expected to be ingrained in the military professional perspective.

Equally important, technical skills and professional ethics are expected to sustain the ability of the military to perform its primary role without doing violence to the concept of democratic values.  In this sense then, the total value system of military professionalism must be linked to society - in turn, society provides the context within which the military is assessed regarding credibility and legitimacy.

Professional perspectives and values cannot be developed in a vacuum, however.  Military systems, to remain legitimate, reflect society and, thus, professional ethics, attitudes, and beliefs develop from roots within the political-social system. This is a particularly important consideration in a democratic environment.  This is not to suggest, however, that professionalism does not develop its own dimension.  For example, the fact that society declares no more Vietnams does not mean that the military should not study counter-insurgency.

The one fundamental and singular concern in the study of professionalism, therefore, is societal values and the extent to which these influence the military professional value system and the "parallelism" between the two systems.  A military system in a democratic society cannot long exist without some reference to civilian values.  Equally important, the values of society, whether they be considerations of technical skills, professional ethics, or "proper" political perspectives, must have some visible and meaningful connection with these same values within the military.

## THE FUNDAMENTAL ISSUE

It is this issue - societal values and the military - that lies at the root of the prevailing professional restiveness and is the basis for the philosophical debate regarding the meaning of military professionalism.  Moreover, we feel that much of the debate regarding the substantive issues, whether they be at the community, institutional, or individual dimension, draws its sustenance from civilian value systems.  This is reflected in much of the existing literature.

Our concern with community-military relationships should not, however, overlook the fact that within the profession there is also a deep concern regarding the institutional and individual dimension.  One of the most illuminating views on such matters comes from a study on military professionalism conducted at the U.S. Army War College.  This states in part:

. . . It is impossible to forecast future institutional
climates with any degree of reliability. Nevertheless, it is not unreasonable to state as consequences
of the present climate: it is conducive to self-
deception because it fosters the production of in-
accurate information; it impacts on the long term
ability of the Army to fight and win because it
frustrates young, idealistic, energetic officers who
leave the service and are replaced by those who will
tolerate if not condone ethical imperfection; it is
corrosive of the Army's image because it falls short
of the traditional idealistic code of the soldier - a
code which is the key to the soldier's acceptance by
a modern free society; it lowers the credibility of
our top military leaders because it often shields them
from essential bad news; it stifles initiative, innovation, and humility because it demands perfection
or the pose of perfection at every turn; it down-
grades technical competence by rewarding instead
trivial, measureable, quota-filling accomplishments;
and it eventually squeezes much of the inner satisfaction and personal enjoyment out of being an
officer.(13)

This conclusion by a group of military professionals
looking at their own profession has deep ramifications for the
meaning of profession in the community context. It suggests
the prevalence of a particular kind of professional who will be
at some of the highest levels of the military hierarchy, sym-
bolizing the profession to the community, and dictating the
nature of the military value system and community-military
relationships.

Regardless of the self-assessments of military men regarding their own profession, one underlying weakness has not
been seriously addressed. There is lacking a professional
dimension that clearly distinguishes military professionals from
skilled occupations in terms of intellectual horizons. It is our
contention that such an intellectual distinction is necessary if
professional status and conceptual clarity is sought between
profession and occupation. It is necessary that professionals
and the profession develop intellectual horizons that free the
professional from exclusive concern with professional competence and skills. The true professional's world view must
go beyond the specific role of the profession and include a
concern with the state of society and the nature of man. This
perspective was best summed up by Kingman Brewster, Jr.,
who stated, "perhaps the most fundamental value of a liberal
education is that it makes life seem more interesting. . . . It
allows you to see things which the undereducated do not see.
It allows you to think things which do not occur to the less

learned. In short, it makes it less likely that you will be bored with life."(14)

An even more apt statement regarding the professional horizon appeared in a book of fiction. The author stated:

> Education is something which should be apart from the necessities of earning a living, not a tool thereof. It needs contemplation, fallow periods, the measured and guided study of the history of man's reiteration of the most agonizing question of all: Why? Today the good ones, the ones who want to ask why, find no one around with any interest in answering the question, so they drop out, because theirs is the type of mind which becomes monstrously bored at the trade-school concept. A devoted technician is seldom an educated man. He can be a useful man, a contented man, a busy man. But he has no more sense of the mystery and wonder and paradox of existence than does one of those chickens fattening itself for the mechanical plucking, freezing, and packaging.(15)

Without such a perspective, it is difficult to see how a profession can claim it serves the public good. To do so requires an understanding of society, its political system, and the ideology that provides purposeful political action. Professions cannot understand and carry out their own role without first understanding the political-social context within which this role must be played.

## CONCLUSIONS

The fundamental issue for the military in the post Vietnam era is how to revise the professional ethos and adapt it to the new international security environment and the nature of liberal democratic society. Regardless of the number of administrative and procedural changes made over the past decade, it appears that the military remains wedded to a narrowly defined professionalism, dominated by the goals of military skills and training, almost to the exclusion of "education." The argument that military professionals need to be more than battlefield specialists is generally countered by the argument that professionals are military men first, committed to "success in battle." Nevertheless, the military is part of the American political system and functions in a political-social environment. Not only does this require a commitment to democratic ideology and to the core values of a liberal democratic system, it also means that professionals must perceive modern conflicts in

their totality - political-social dimensions as well as military
tactical considerations. This is particularly true with respect
to the Third World. To strive to reach the highest professional standards, therefore, requires serious and systematic
study; in brief, it means "education".

If we accept the premise that employment of force in the
future will be a highly complicated and difficult matter, and
that the ability of human beings to handle a variety of inputs
is limited, then we can easily accept the prevailing view
regarding the military profession. Indeed, according to some,
such a view is supported by the characteristics of a technological society.

In such an environment, human judgment is easily re-
legated to mechanical decision making - management by computer. The increasing specialization and division of labor
characteristic of technological systems has its parallel in the
military with a concomitant deprecation of heroes and leaders,
and the glorification of managerial and technological expertise.
Sophisticated weaponry and the electronic battlefield tend to
create an increasing gap between the military elite and the
"humanistic" elements in the military, as well as in society.
The expertise of the military professional whose main concern
is technological supremacy and efficient application of force is
fundamentally antagonistic to the humanistic impulses of a
democracy - even one in the context of the technological era.
The question is whether the profession can properly serve the
democratic state with such an orientation. We believe that it
cannot.

What needs to be done is addressed in the final chapter
of this volume. Suffice it to say here that the profession must
include a political-social dimension and substantive ingredients
that stimulate a critical inquiry: a capacity to judge the
quality of contending perspectives, a socio-psychological
appreciation of human nature, and an appreciation of the
consequences of policy - particularly military policy. Without
such a professional dimension, the "real" professional will
eventually be replaced by managerial and technological men
who are better suited in an organization labeled, "Association
of Military Technicians," prepared for all of the intricacies of
electronic warfare with little sensitivity to the human environment.

The following chapters are an exploration of the various
facets of American military professionalism. There are two
fundamental premises to each of these chapters. First, the
military profession cannot divorce itself from the American
political system. Second, the profession cannot ignore the fact
that wars are more than the application of force in the most
efficient way possible. Unfortunately, it does not appear that
the military profession has either the necessary orientation or
intellectual "grasp" to accept and integrate these fundamental
premises.

NOTES

1.  Ernest  Greenwood,  "Attributes  of  a  Profession,"
Social Work,  Vol.  2,  No.  3,  July,  1957,  p.  45.   See also
Geoffrey  Millerson,  The Qualifying Associations; A Study in
Professionalization  (New  York:   The  Humanities  Press,  1964),
p. 10.
2.  Ibid., p. 46.
3.  Ibid., p. 48.
4.  Morris  L.  Cogan,  "Toward  a  Definition  of  Profession,"  Harvard Educational Review,  Vol.  23,  Winter 1953,  pp.
48-49.  See also Howard M. Vollmer and Donald L. Mills, (Eds)
Professionalization.   Englewood  Cliffs,  N.J.:   Prentice-Hall,
Inc., 1966.
5.  Homer  Lea,  The Valor of Ignorance.   New  York:
Harper, 1909, p. 254.
6.  Donald  F.  Bletz,  The Role of the Military Professional in U.S. Foreign Policy.   New  York:   Praeger,  1972,
Praeger  Special  Studies,  p.  6.   See also Sam  C.  Sarkesian,
The Professional Army Officer in a Changing Society.  Chicago:
Nelson-Hall,  1974,  pp.  8-21;  and Bengt Abrahamson,  Military
Professionalization and Political Power.   Beverly  Hills,  Cal.:
Sage Publications, 1972, pp. 59-70.
7.  Zeb  B.  Bradford,  Jr.,  and  Frederic  J.  Brown,
The United States Army in Transition.   Beverly  Hills,  Cal.:
Sage Publications, 1973, p. 223.
8.  Morris  Janowitz,  The Professional Soldier.   New
York:  The Free Press, 1960, pp. 218-220.
9.  While  arguments  can  be  made  regarding  the  finer
points  of  defining  profession,  professional,  professionalism,
and  professionalization,  we  feel  that  these  are  not  the  main
issues  here.   Fundamentally,  all  of  these  terms  rest  on  the
basic concept of military profession discussed in this chapter.
More  simply,  profession  is  based  on  the  definition  of  criteria
and  requirements;  professional  is  one  who  is  in  the  profession;
professionalism  is  the  degree  to  which  the  professionals  and
the  profession  achieve  the  criteria  and  requirements  of  the
profession  (ideally);  and  professionalization  is  the  process
through  which  the  professional  acquires  the  values  and  skills
of  the  profession.   See  the  discussion  in  Abrahamson,  pp.
13-17.
10.  Samuel  Huntington,  The Soldier and the State.   New
York:  Vintage Books, 1964, pp. 64-65 and 79.
11.  Ibid.
12.  John  D.  Blair  and  Jerald  G.  Bachman,  "The Public
View of the Military,"  paper  presented  at  the  Research  Seminar
on  Social  Psychology  of  Military  Service,  April  23-25,  1975,  at
the  Center  for  Continuing  Education,  University  of  Chicago.

13.  U.S.  Army  War  College,  Study on Military Professionalism.  Carlisle  Barracks,  Pa.,  June 30,  1970,  pp.  28-29.
    14.  Kingman  Brewster,  Jr.,  "The  Report  of  the  Presi-
dent,  1975-76."  New  Haven:  Yale  University  Printing  Service,  1976.  Mr.  Brewster  is  the  former  President  of  Yale
University  and  (in  1978)  the  U.S.  Ambassador  to  the  Court  of
St.  James.
    15.  John  Macdonald,  A Purple Place for Dying.  New
York:  Fawcett,  1978,  p.  47.

# 2 An Empirical Reassessment of Military Professionalism

The issue for the U.S. military in Vietnam was not whether the war was just or unjust, nor whether they should serve there, but rather how well the job was done to defeat the enemy, and what impact the total experience would have on the military institution and the profession.(1) It is this last concern that has caused much debate and discussion in the aftermath of Vietnam. To be sure, the Vietnam war cannot be blamed for all of the ills of the military establishment nor is it responsible for all of the issues of professionalism. Nevertheless, it was a precipitating factor that created the environment and provided the experience which rapidly stimulated a major reassessment of military professionalism.

The purpose of this chapter is to reexamine military professionalism in the post-Vietnam era with respect to perspectives on value convergence and empathy between military and society and perceptions of the military institution and profession. The concern is not with a particular disciplinary focus, but rather with an approach that examines the major themes evolving from empirical studies and the relationship of these themes to general propositions regarding the military profession.

General propositions regarding the military are well known to most scholars of the subject and need not be reviewed here.(2) While it is recognized that such works are important in the study of armed forces and society, the purpose here is to examine the subject based on recent empirical studies.(3)

There are five studies of particular relevance to the purposes of this essay. These include the following: Study on Military Professionalism by the Army War College, 1970; Moellering, 1973; Russett, 1974 (Russett and Hanson, 1975, which is a more detailed presentation of the material in Russett, 1974. It is included as part of the 1974 study);

Bachman and Blair, 1975; and Margiotta, 1976.(4)  While there
are other useful empirical studies, the works noted here are
particularly relevant to the study of professionalism.

The Study on Military Professionalism conducted by the
Army War College (hereafter the Army War College Study) in
1970 was designed to "assess the professional climate of the
Army, to identify any problem areas, and to formulate cor-
rective actions."  Approximately 250 officers from six Army
schools and 165 members of the Army War College class of 1970
and Army members of the faculty were involved.  Questionnaires were used, supplemented by interviews (at schools
outside the Army War College) and seminars.  Officers involved in the sample ranged in grades from Second Lieutenant
to General, with most of the respondents in the Captain to
Colonel grades.

Moellering conducted his study in February, 1972.  Using
questionnaires, he surveyed about 935-970 Army Command and
General Staff College students and faculty regarding perceptions of the profession and civil-military relations.  Moellering's
purpose was to assess the relevancy of the presumption that
the Army was turning inwards as a result of the Vietnam
experience.

Bruce Russett examined the perspectives of U.S. military
and business elites in 1973 by assessing survey data from 567
vice-presidents and senior vice-presidents from "Fortune 500"
industrial corporations and leading financial institutions.  He
also surveyed by questionnaire 619 American military officers
enrolled in the five U.S. War Colleges (Air, Army, Navy,
National, and Industrial College of the Armed Forces).  The
survey dealt with various U.S. foreign and domestic policy
matters, international relations, and issues of peace and war.
(The material was published later in a book by Russett and
Hanson).

Bachman and Blair examined samples from the Army,
Navy, and the civilian population regarding value preferences
and perceptions about the military.  The data-sampling years
were from 1972 to early 1975.  Data were collected from 38
different Navy sites and included 2522 Navy officers and
enlisted personnel.  Civilian data were collected in February
and March, 1973, as part of a larger interview study conducted by the Survey Research Center.  This included 1327
dwelling units in which a trained interviewer conducted an
interview with a designated respondent, male or female, age 18
or older.  This resulted in a 75 percent response rate from
interviews and about 90 percent from questionnaires.  The
Army sample was collected during the period November 1974-
April 1975 and included a population of 2286 Army officers and
enlisted personnel from a cross-section of units.

Margiotta's study was based on an analysis of the biographic, demographic, and carrer information of 351 line Air

Force general officers in active duty on January 1, 1974. Also, 23 items of biographic, demographic, and career data were collected in a computer search of personnel files. The major part of the study was based on responses from 675-680 students who were enrolled at the Air War College and the Air Command and General Staff College in 1974. A series of questions was asked about the Air Force career and perceived social status. These were supplemented by interviews.

Although these studies cover a variety of matters, there are several themes that emerge. These include professional ethics and behavior, considerations of military and civilian value systems, and the nature of professional perceptions regarding society, the military institution, and the profession. It should be made clear at the outset, however, that the examination of professionalism, its boundaries, and substantive elements lack a generally accepted and coherent perspective. The elusiveness of professional boundaries and the imprecise definitions and measures of substantive professional matters such as honor, ethics, and morals, invite an intuitiveness and subjectivity into the study of professionalism. Nevertheless, what is significant in these studies is the amazing consensus around substantive issues that appear - and this with different populations, services, and times!

Identifying ethical criteria and their underlying moral content is difficult enough for most scholars, but for professional officers it is a dilemma that most resolve by reference to organizational behavior and institutional loyalty. Equally important, behavior and professed ethical standards do not necessarily coincide. Indeed, as many will argue, even the best military professionals are rationalizing individuals. It is also not clear what impact socialization and institutional behavior have on professionalism. These matters in themselves are difficult analytical concepts. The difficulty in assessing cause-and-effect relationships compounds the problem. Finally, the gap is wide between macroanalytical and microanalytical perspectives on professionalism; that is, the translation of concepts of "Duty, Honor, Country" to day-to-day behavior is at best an ambiguous undertaking and filled with ethical pitfalls and analytical roadblocks. Yet the issue persists - what is the new professionalism in the post-Vietnam era? Indeed, is there a new professionalism? What impact does this professionalism have on the character of the military system?

## THE VIETNAM HERITAGE

Although the Vietnam era cannot be blamed for all of the problems and dilemmas facing the military profession in the late 1970s, most scholars would agree that the war provided the catalyst for the surfacing of a number of substantive professional issues including civil-military relations. Nowhere is this more evident than in the matters of professional integrity and institutional demands. One of the consistent themes evolving from the Vietnam War is the clearly visible gap between the ideals of the profession and the actual behavior of professionals. Another major concern attributed to the Vietnam War is the volunteer military - a result, according to many, of the public resistance to the selective service system. The antimilitary sentiments and anti-war attitude of important segments of the populace have also been viewed by many scholars and military men as a crucial element in the depreciation of the military service in terms of status and prestige. Thus, there is sufficient persuasion to conclude that the American military, coming out of a major conflict in which virtually the entire office corps of the time was involved, has been affected institutionally and professionally, and also in its relationship to society.

My Lai, as perhaps no other incident, is illustrative of these professional matters. The details of the incident are too well known to relate here. In brief, Lieutenant William Calley and other members of Charlie Company, Task Force Baker of the American Division, were accused of murdering Vietnamese - old men, women, and children - in March, 1968.

What compounded the issue was the behavior of a number of officers in response to My Lai. Rather than aggressive investigations and positive procedures to preclude future incidents, there is ample evidence to suggest procrastination, delay, self-protection, and all of the characteristics of an institutional loyalty and career concerns that are at the basis of current criticism of professionalism.(5) These are best summed up by one scholar who writes:

> All the bureaucratic tendencies visible in the Army
> are characteristic of all organized power in America.
> But the Army accentuates and exaggerates bureau-
> cracy because it is a bureaucracy without com-
> petitors; conformity, careerism, cultivation of the
> right attitudes and the safe style become almost
> necessary obsessions, difficult for any but a very
> few to resist.(6)

There are other incidents associated with Vietnam that have been part of the catalyst of professional self-examination and criticism. These need not be repeated here since they are also generally well known - ranging from the "Khaki" Mafia and the unauthorized bombing raids over North Vietnam (and the subsequent falsification of reports), to the refusal of officers to engage in bombing missions. The issues raised by such events are not limited to the military profession, of

course.  Professions in general are faced with similar problems.  Nevertheless, the importance of this matter to the
military is clear - given the uniqueness of the profession, its
purpose, and the nature of its relationship to society, the
profession is placed in a dilemma regarding its ethical behavior, professional ideals, and civil-military linkage.

## MILITARY VALUES AND SOCIETAL NORMS

### An overview

Concerned that military and civilian systems should have
a close linkage, some scholars and military men argue that it is
the community that bestows legitimacy upon the military.
Thus, to reinforce and maintain this legitimacy, there must be
a congruence of values between the two systems.  The community's perceptions of professional ethics and norms are
essential in developing esteem, prestige, and credibility.  The
important point is that the military profession is relevant only
in terms of the community.  The community is the sole client.
However, the profession's authority and identity, although sanctioned by the community, must be continually
nurtured and reinforced by military-civilian linkages.  Not
only must the profession demonstrate its expertise at war, but
also its acceptance of the community's value system and "rules
of the game."  As Barnes has written:

> How, then, are we to assess the vast powers that
> the military has come to hold over millions of
> American citizens?  Simply, the military's powers are
> legitimate to the extent - and only to the extent -
> that they are in the first instance, consonant with
> contemporary standards of justice and humanity, and
> then only when the foreign policy which the military
> carries out is both (1) directly related to the de-
> fense of the nation or its closest democratic allies,
> and (2) by elected officials whose decisions are
> guided by the will of the people as expressed
> through the political process.(7)

The response by a soldier-scholar takes issue with this
view.  "One would be hard pressed to find a mature professional soldier who would accept Barnes' premise."(8)
The distinction between the civilian and the professional
represented in these views stems out of different perspectives:
one focusing on political and the other on operational considerations.  It is this difference in perspective that is at the
root of the distinctions between society's view and the military

view of ethical behavior - indeed, this is one of the important distinguishing factors between the military and society.

Scholars are prone to state that the military must have links with society and provide an institution through which the core values of society can be transmitted and incorporated into the professional system. In American society, therefore, the profession is thought to be supportive of democratic values, even though professional values are presumed to be more of an authoritarian and bureaucratic nature. More important, society expects military men to be committed to the basic precepts of the political system. Civilian control of the military, individual dignity and worth, and justice before the law, for example, are expected to be ingrained in the military professional perspective.

Professional perspectives and dimensions cannot be developed in a vacuum. Military systems are presumed to reflect the society; and thus professional ethics, attitudes, and beliefs develop a close identification with those of society. Moreover, the socialization process of the military professional is not completely divorced from society. This is not to suggest that professionalism does not develop its own dimensions. For example, the fact that society declares no more Vietnams does not necessarily suggest that the professional should not study counter-insurgency. But what it requires is a shift of professional emphasis to those compatible with society.

A fundamental concern in the study of professionalism, therefore, is societal values and the extent to which these influence the military professional value system and the degree of congruence between the two systems. A military system in a democratic society cannot long exist without some reference to civilian values. Equally important, the values of society - whether they be considerations of technical skills, professional ethics, and "proper" political perspectives - must have some visible and meaningful connection with these same values within the military.

Yet, there is much disagreement regarding the proper relationships between the profession and society. While some argue for a distinct separation, others press for a civil-military fusion.

Hauser, for example, writes:

> It seems almost simplistic to conclude that a dis-
> juncture between the Army and society has brought
> about this long litany of troubles, but that is what
> the evidence suggests. The Army has been unable
> to isolate itself from society sufficiently to maintain
> its authoritarian discipline or to prevent the in-
> trusion of such social ills as racial discord and drug
> abuse. . . .(9)

Thayer, on the other hand, notes that:

The concept of professionalism seems to demand that
professionals themselves be constantly aware of the
delicate balance they must maintain in their own
behavior between autonomy and fusion. They cannot
be so totally separated as to become the proverbial
"society within a society," but neither can they
afford total integration within the civilian over-
head. (10)

Thus, the debate focuses on theories of convergence,
divergence, or cautious but limited linkage. While convergence
presumes that domestic pressures and institutional requirements are causing a convergence of military and civilian value
systems, divergence presumes a return to a professional
isolation of pre-Vietnam years, encouraged by the volunteer
system. On the other hand, a middle perspective rests on the
presumption that the profession recognizes the need for closer
association with society and a commitment to societal values.
Yet the military, according to this approach, needs to maintain
its separateness and uniqueness.

## Separateness and alienation

The evidence suggests that military men are ambiguous
about the proper relationships between the military and society, although they are clear about such relationships in
certain specific areas. On the one hand, military men accept
as legitimate control by society and desire a close linkage
between democratic values and the military. On the other
hand, most military men feel that military influence, vis-a-vis
civilians, should increase in specific areas concerning military
matters. Moreover, the evidence shows an underlying dissatisfaction with civilian perceptions of the military and the
lack of civilian appreciation of the demands of the military
profession.

With respect to military-civilian convergence, Moellering,
for example, found that 74 percent of the officers, in response
to the question regarding the best course for the Army to
follow in present troubled times, stated that the Army should
"take more cognizance of American civilian society, its values,
and its criticism."(11) Both Margiotta and Moellering also
found a concern among officers regarding the representativeness of the volunteer military – a concern that reflected a
feeling that the volunteer military should be representative of
society lest it become isolated from society.

It is also interesting to note that Margiotta found that
two-thirds of the officers surveyed were opposed to secondary
roles for the military; i.e., remedial education, engineering

projects, ecological reclamation, highway rescue, etc. He
states that "Younger, lower-ranking ACSC officers expressed
less resistance to changes in traditional Air Force roles.
Although most officers opposed the suggestion of an expanded
role, 40 percent of the ACSC officers expressed at least a
qualified agreement."(12) Russett's data also show that most
officers would prefer a focus on social problems within the
military prior to focusing on problems external to the military.(13) And in external problems, most military men,
according to Russett's findings, would prefer not to become
involved in the broader range of social issues.

The clearest manifestation of professional attitudes,
however, was found in the views regarding the uniqueness of
the profession. These show an underlying desire to be
separate from society and a recognition that the profession is
unique from all others.

The Army War College Study, reporting the results from
one interview team, found that officers felt that the military
ought to "accept the fact in the Army that the rights, privileges and responsibilities of the military are not and cannot be
the same as the rights, privileges, and responsibilities in
civilian life . . . we have a democracy in this country but we
have an autocracy in the military. And the public ought to be
educated along these lines and the military ought to stand up
for what it has to have - and that is a disciplined force of
people."(14) Of the officers surveyed at the Army Command
and General Staff College, 68 percent felt that the virtues of
discipline, sacrifice, and patriotism are found "to a greater or
much greater extent in the U.S. Army" than in American
society.(15)

The professionals' perceived gap between the military and
society, as well as the attitude that the military is distinct, is
also reflected in their views regarding society's perception of
the profession. Margiotta states that "at least three-fourths of
our interviewees cited specific instances in which their friends
and families either misunderstood their careers or undervalued
the highly competitive criteria for advancement in the Air
Force."(16) In other words, immediate friends and relatives
outside the military have little understanding of the military
profession and in turn place little value on it.

Margiotta concluded from his study that:

> Officers believe that the public neither knows nor
> understands their educational achievements, their
> lifestyle based on upper middle-class pay and al-
> lowances, the competitive promotion system in the
> Air Force, and the variety and complexity of jobs
> that may be required of them. When we added
> officer experiences in Southeast Asia, their dis-
> satisfaction with media coverage of the military and

their feeling that they safeguard important national values, then perceived patterns of status and alienation are more understandable, if not completely realistic.(17)

Linked with perceptions on the Vietnam experience, professionals seem to have indeed developed a concern regarding society's perception of the military role in the war and a great deal of suspicion of the press. These attitudes seem to reinforce the feeling of separateness from society and may also indicate a latent but deeply felt resentment regarding society's treatment of the military.

For example, Moellering found that 67 percent of the officers surveyed felt that "the American public's view of U.S. Army involvement in Vietnam was negative."(18) Supporting this perspective is the feeling by 40 percent of the officers surveyed that antiwar and antimilitary attitudes evolved from within American society because "politicians got the Army into a war it didn't want to fight and placed undue restrictions on it which precluded its proper mission accomplishment." Another 20 percent felt that antiwar and antimilitary sentiments stem from "the general lack of commitment to traditional values by the youth of our country." Less than 5 percent thought the Army was at fault.

In answer to the question, "Do you personally think it was correct for the U.S. to send ground troops to Vietnam?" Russett found that over 52 percent of the business elite surveyed responded "No." On the other hand, over 70 percent of the military officers said "Yes." Slightly over 38 percent of the business elite said "Yes" to the question, while about 27 percent of the military officers responded "No."(19) Equally instructive is the conclusion by 95 percent of the Air Force officers in Margiotta's study that the "recent media coverage of the military was biased against the military, and fully 48 percent selected the extreme response 'strongly biased against the military.'"(20) In reference to the attitudes regarding the media, Margiotta noted that "officers comprising the future military elite have, at this moment, a basic distrust of a major and influential national institution." This perspective was reinforced by Moellering's study in which he found that over 19 percent of the Army officers surveyed "considered the press highly biased and antagonistic." Over 67 percent considered the news media "usually biased against the Army."(21)

The Army War College Study reported the results of a series of interviews, stating that "A frustration - a real feeling of frustration - and this is expressed all the way up to the most senior officers we talked to - the senior officers expressing a strong frustration - just as strong as the young captains, that the media is biased."(22)

Although alienation from society is a relatively strong word to use in describing the military and society in the 1970s, the evidence seems to suggest that it has some relevance. Focusing specifically on this issue, Bachman and Blair noted that career military men have a "profound sense of dissatisfaction."(23)    The study indicated that they have a "...feeling that their own kind, the top military leaders, should have a good deal more power over most national military policy than civilian leaders do."

Margiotta observed that "Our officers, however, did not feel valued by society . . . Fully 80 percent of our potential future elite view their status as low or declining."(24)    Moreover, according to Margiotta, ". . . we found that two-thirds of our respondents felt that 'alienation' is the best way to characterize present civil-military relations."(25)

There is evidence of a great degree of professional ambiguity regarding the relationship between the military and society. There is a recognition that some degree of congruence between military and civilian systems is needed, yet this stops far short of accepting any linkage which would dilute the uniqueness of the profession and the profession's military focus. The underlying suspicion of society's intentions and attitudes, partly stemming from the Vietnam war, seems to have become ingrained in the profession - a factor that may have serious civil-military repercussions in future crises. The fact remains, however, that the profession is not sure of how to reconcile its desires to maintain congruence with society while insuring its professional distinction.

## The military mind

The distinctions between society and the military, although reflecting an ambiguity within the profession, help to explain a similar phenomenon regarding the concept of the "military mind." There is, of course, considerable doubt regarding the existence of a "military mind" and the notion of a monolithic professional perspective. Indeed, a number of scholars argue that there is no great divergence between the attitudes of military men and other elites within society.(26) Nevertheless, there is evidence to suggest the existence of commonly held professional attitudes regarding the nature of professionalism and military purpose.(27) Moreover, these distinctions when viewed within the general context of professional lifestyles and professional purpose do provide a persuasive argument that the professional perception of the environment and society is in clear contrast to other elites in society.

This view seems to be supported by the evidence presented in Moellering and in Bachman and Blair. Moellering found that over 82 percent of the respondents felt that the

American public viewed the military as possessing a "military mind."(28)   On the other hand, in response to a question regarding professional self-perceptions, only 15 percent felt that the officer corps possessed a military mind.   Bachman and Blair reach similar conclusions:

> . . . there is considerable evidence that the belief system of career military men - officers and enlisted - is distinctive from that found among comparable civilian groups.  Career men were considerably more pro-military substantively and showed greater homogeneity or consensus in these beliefs. . . .
> One of the arguments raised in the debate about the all-volunteer force was the danger of a "separate military ethos" or distinctive "military mind" brought about by a military force made up largely of career men.  The findings presented above suggest some basis for concern in this area.(29)

Bachman and Blair also found that in comparison to college graduates,

> Career officers are a great deal more favorable toward the military organization, more eager for U.S. military supremacy (rather than parity with the Soviet Union), more willing to make use of military power, and much more in favor of enlarged military (vs. civilian) influence over U.S. policy affecting the military.(30)

Although attempts at categorizing political ideologies can easily distort conclusions regarding attitudes, it is important to note the general dominance of conservative or "hawkish" attitudes of military officers.  While not surprising, such attitudes do lend weight to the argument that there is a distinctly military view of the world.

Margiotta found what he calls a "pluralist conservativism," in which 64 percent of the respondents identified themselves as conservative or somewhat conservative.(31)   Additionally, he concluded that "Conservative ideology in the military increased with rank and age."  He also noted that although there was no clearly definable political ideology that differentiated military from civilian elites, ". . . issues related to national defense produced the most 'hawkish' or 'conservative' discussion."(32)

Moellering's survey of officers' self-characterization of political ideology found over 48 percent identifying themselves as "conservatives," 2 percent as "right," 34 percent "middle-of-the-road," with only 15 percent "liberal" and 3 percent "left."  He also concluded that this indicated some credence to

the view that the conservatism of the officer corps is a potential basis for alienation from a more "dynamic" society.(33)
   Although eschewing the concept "military mind," Russett
found an ideological distinction in military men - labeling them
"hawks" - from business elites. He concluded that:

> On many matters that might be construed as in the
> sphere of professional military expertise, but where
> constitutional authority is vested in civilians, the
> civilian-military differences in policy preferences are
> great. Especially on matters of weapons acquisition
> and defense spending levels, conflicts would be
> further compounded by any military effort to protect
> bureaucratic interests of their organization.(34)

Furthermore, Russett found that in response to the question,
"Do you think a 25% reduction in defense spending would have
an adverse effect upon the American economy?", slightly over
33 percent of the business elite said "Yes" and over 59 percent said "No." Responding to the same question, over 61
percent of the military officers said "Yes;" slightly over 31
percent said "No."(35)
   While in themselves, conservative versus liberal distinctions may not be an indication of a "military mind," a distinct
military perspective is clear, particularly when combined with
separateness and alienation, and the general views regarding
the values of society. Moreover, if one presumes that socialization does provide reinforcement to the military perspective
and that there is a self-selection process, as Bachman and
Blair conclude, then a distinctively conservative or highly
pro-military perspective is engrained in the institution.(36)
While each institution and profession can be expected to
develop its own perspective, in the military profession this is
manifested in dissatisfaction over the perceived lack of military
influence; it encourages a "we-they" syndrome and perpetuates
a separateness from society that can easily lead to alienation
and a motivation to protect military interests under all circumstances.


## THE INSTITUTIONAL AND PROFESSIONAL CONTEXT


### The volunteer system

   The question of the volunteer military has evoked wide
ranging debate since the publication of the Gates Commission
report.(37) The first debates centered on the availability of
proper levels of manpower for a volunteer system. A new
vocabulary developed with such terms as "shortfall," "first

term ascensions," and "true volunteers." Later, the debate focused on the black-white ratio with some arguing that a high black percentage would occur in the volunteer system and would tend to make the military less attractive for whites. Moreover, there was concern regarding the representativeness of the force.(38) Additionally, there is currently an increasing concern with the total force concept (active military, National Guard, and Reserves), of which the combat readiness and combat capability of the volunteer force is a component. Generally speaking, in the aggregate the issues of manpower quantity, quality, racial and sex percentages, combat readiness, and military posture have negatively affected professional perspectives regarding military capability. Undoubtedly, this is partly attributable to the relative lack of experience with a volunteer system and the fact that the system has not as yet been tested.

An observer and participant in the Gates Commission made this astute observation in 1971:

> Although the broader issues have received extensive airing in the media, it is not clear, because of the highly charged rhetoric frequently involved, that all of the probable long-range implications of moving toward an all-volunteer force have been clearly and forcefully set before the American public. Most of the detailed discussions and analyses have dealt with the draft and its individual virtues and shortcomings. While a good case can probably be made, costs aside, for preferring the all-volunteer concept over the draft, it would be imprudent at best to adopt the all-volunteer force without full consideration of the relevant costs and their possible long-term implications for national security policy.(39)

The evidence seems to suggest that the professional officers are still groping for clear-cut assessments of the impact of the volunteer force on the profession and on the ability of the military to carry out its combat mission.

Army officers appear to be the most ambiguous and skeptical about the volunteer system. Almost 40 percent of those surveyed by Moellering felt that the volunteer Army "will be worse than today's Army because it will have been cut off from American society."(40) (Five percent of this group felt that the Army would be worse because it would be less efficient.) Over 27 percent felt that it would not be much different from today's Army. It is interesting to note that only 1.8 percent felt that the volunteer Army would be an improvement because it could be cut off from American society and thus be more professional. (These observations are also relevant to the examination of military-civilian value convergence).

According to Margiotta's study, "Only a limited number of officers accept the all-volunteer concept, even though the Air Force should be influenced least by this new manpower policy. Two-thirds of the respondents felt that the all-volunteer force would be "worse than today's military." Almost one-half were concerned that the volunteer system would create a military that did not represent a cross-section of American society.(41)

## Individual ethics and professional norms

Military men are prone to view the dilemma between individual conscience and institutional demands as unique to their profession. Yet the study of history and political philosophy shows that this dilemma has been characteristic of men in various walks of life throughout Western civilization.

No one would argue that institutional demands and societal order are not important considerations. Yet what weight should be given to individual values and conscience? As individuals, we are responsible for our own actions and decisions. If there is a conflict between institution and the individual, what is to be done? In an institution such as the military, this becomes particularly troublesome.

Professional stress on the requirements of integrity and institutional goals has normally shaped individual behavior so as to subordinate dissent or resistance. In other words, integrity and instant obedience are the sine qua non of military institution. Yet the question of conscience contradictory to institutional demands has become a crucial issue of professional legitimacy.

While these issues have always been a part of the professional dimension, the nature of the Vietnam experience not only exacerbated the civil-military tensions, but also fostered alienation between professionals and the political system and developed some professional antipathy toward professional behavior. This is primarily a perceived professional issue, rather than one in society-at-large.

Professional perceptions of the profession are linked to perceptions regarding society's view of the profession. The most articulate groups in society are from the more educated elements, including young college graduates, some sectors of the liberal intelligentsia, and many important representatives of the mass media. Given the general antimilitary attitudes of these groups and the professionals' reaction and perception of such groups, there is a consistent danger of equating societal views of the military to such groups. The ultimate result is a negative professional view, depreciating the esteem and prestige of the military and with it, professional legitimacy.

With respect to the dilemma between the individual officer
and that of the profession, the Army War College Study concluded that "Officers of all grades perceive a significant
difference between the ideal values of the actual or operative
values of the officer corps. This perception is strong, clear,
persuasive, and statistically and qualitatively independent of
grade, branch, educational level, or source of commission..."(42)

The same study examined an in-house report by the
USMA Office of Research regarding the reasons for resignation
by several officers from the USMA class of 1966. According
to these officers, many senior officers (particularly Colonels
and Lieutenant Colonels who were in command positions)
". . . were forced to abandon their scruples and ignore the
precepts of duty and honor; and if necessary to lie and cheat
in order to remain successful and competitive . . ."(43)   This
was primarily attributable to the demands of the "system."

To underscore the point regarding professional integrity,
the Army War College Study noted the results from four teams
who had interviewed officers at all grades at different Army
posts. One team reported that "Dishonesty is across-the-
board."(44)   Another team noted that "This was a general
opinion of all these groups. . . . They brought out the fact
that in their judgment, integrity was a luxury that a junior
officer could not afford in today's Army and survive."(45)
The report from a third team concluded that "The word that
was used by every one of our four seminar groups, I think
it's the key word here, survivability. Unless you are willing
to compromise your standards, even ever so slightly, you will
not survive in the Army system."(46)   The fourth team observed that "Junior officers felt that the barrier to their
integrity was the senior officers' lack of integrity."(47)

The "West Point Scandal" (as one national magazine called
it) in 1976 is another reflection of the issues of honor –
professional ideals and actual behavior.(48)   Without engaging
in a long dissertation regarding the merits of the honor system
at West Point, it should be noted that the "operationalizing" of
the ideals of the profession remains an elusive matter, whether
at the service academies or in the profession. An officer is
not suppose to lie, cheat, or steal. This has been a fundamental element of professional behavior; and rightly so – but
the fact remains that there is a gap (perhaps an unbridgeable
gap?) between ideals and reality.

An important insight about professional views regarding
professional integrity and the gap between ideals and behavior
comes from the Army War College Study. Reporting the
comments of one interview team the study noted that "Every
group pinpointed the fact that the Army would not tolerate a
wave-maker or a boat-rocker regardless of how high the
officers' personal standards were."(49)   The study also ob-

served that "Pressures to achieve unrealistic goals, whether
imposed by design or generated through incompetence, soon
strain the ethical fiber of the organization."(50)
  The study concluded in part:

> The climate . . . is one in which there is dishar-
> mony between traditional, accepted ideals and the
> prevailing institutional pressures. These pressures
> seem to stem from a combination of self-oriented,
> success-motivated actions, and a lack of professional
> skills on the part of middle and senior grade of-
> ficers. A scenario that was repeatedly described in
> seminar sessions and narrative responses includes an
> ambitious, transitory commander - marginally skilled
> in the complexities of his duties - engulfed in
> producing statistical results, fearful of personal
> failure, too busy to talk with or listen to his sub-
> ordinates, and determined to submit acceptably
> optimistic reports which reflect faultless completion
> of a variety of tasks at the expense of the sweat
> and frustration of his subordinates.(51)

  These observations have deep ramifications regarding the
professionals' perspective on the military institution. They
suggest an institutional orientation which places high value on
institutional loyalty and doctrinal orthodoxy. Moreover, they
suggest that the institution rewards those who accept existing
institutional norms, thereby frustrating those who tend to be
more liberal and flexible. It might be added that such a
conclusion is supported to a degree by the professionals'
perception of their own ideology: a basically conservative
orientation which inherently supports the status quo and a
"don't rock the boat" attitude. As the Army War College
Study noted, "The layers of bureaucracy stifle innovative
ideas and intuitive thinking. Senior officers shy away from
new ideas, fear mistakes. The supervisory mode of the 'squad
leaders in the sky' is prevalent."(52)
  Moreover, the evidence seems to indicate an acceptance of
situational ethics in which individual ethics are subordinated to
the requirements of the institution, the demands of the mission, and career at any given time. In such circumstances,
the pressures of institutional loyalty, organizational requirements, and current professional practices impose a standard of
operation and an ethical norm which, in the view of many
professionals, are far removed from the idealistic notions of
"Duty, Honor, Country" in the context of gentlemanly conduct
and selflessness.

## CONCLUSIONS

That the profession is engaged in serious soul-searching is clear - although this does not appear to have a coherent focus. The ramifications of this soul-searching, however, are not clear. Nevertheless, two themes emerge from this examination. First, there is an underlying professional dissatisfaction with the military's status and influence in society. The Vietnam experience may well be at the root of the current professional dissatisfaction. Not only do professionals blame society for the Vietnam involvement, they feel the military is being made the scapegoat for society's mistakes. This is also reflected in the low marks given to the mass media by a great majority of professionals. The attitude of professionals is also reflected in the cautious and quite limited acceptance of the convergence of military-civilian value systems, which is probably indicative of the professional's desire to remain separate from society. This does not necessarily mean complete isolation, but rather a desire to retain a professional lifestyle unique to the military and strengthen the autonomy of the profession in its own sphere.

If by the military mind, one presumes a rigid, uncompromising perspective that focuses on problems through a primarily military intellectual (or semi-intellectual) view of the world and seeks essentially military solutions, then there is some doubt as to its existence in the U.S. military. This is not to deny that there may be such "minds" in the system, but these are probably in a distinct minority. But if a military mind means that the profession seeks to insure its autonomy over a unique way of life, then there is a military mind - at least according to the evidence presented here. This autonomy further motivates professionals to seek an effective voice in policies that have an impact on the military system and reflects a homogeneity of views when it comes to military matters. Finally, the military perspective reinforces and perpetuates those values that are distinct from civilian life.

The second major theme is the professional's concern over professional ethics, institutional demands, and individual values. This is reflected in the perceived gap between professional ideals and professional behavior. Indeed, one can reasonably conclude that professional ethics in the broadest terms, are at the base of professional restiveness concerning professional relationship to society, the capability of the military institution, and the general character of the profession itself. Professionals in the main feel that institutional demands and organizational behavior encourage "careerism," subordinate individual ethics, erode professional ideals, and develop a career orientation based on unquestioned acceptance of institutional requirements - regardless of the ramifications to the profession and the individual professional.

The profile that emerges from these studies is that of a profession that is generally conservative (in the sense of commitment to existing institutions, being distinctly pro-military, and being "hard line" in military matters), and becomes even more so as one moves up the rank pyramid. While there does not appear to be a visible divergence between military and civilian values in the abstract - i.e., in the broader sense of democracy and domestic policies - there is a distinctly different perspective on matters relating to war, military policy, and influence of military leaders. This difference is exacerbated by the professional perception of society's negative and deprecative attitudes regarding the military and military lifestyles.

This separateness between society and the military is crystalized into a more perceptible form by the homogeneity of professional views on specific matters dealing with the military, views of the institutional context, and self-depreciation. Indeed, one can see evidence of the existence of a type of "military mind" which insists upon professional autonomy, separateness from society, and greater influence in policy decisions affecting the military.

Although there does not appear to be great cause for alarm regarding professional perceptions of their roles and status in society, some attention should be focused on the root causes, since these may well have a direct link to a deeper professional concern. Perhaps the most relevant explanation lies in the succinct observations of de Tocqueville:

When a nation loses its military spirit, the career of arms immediately ceases to be respected and military men drop down to the lowest rank among public officials. They are neither greatly esteemed nor greatly understood . . . it is not the leading citizens, but the least important who go into the army. . . . The elite of the nation avoid a military career because it is not held in honor, and it is not held in honor because the elite of the nation do not take it up.

There is therefore no reason for surprise if democratic armies are found to be restless. . . . The soldier feels that he is in a position of inferiority and his wounded pride gives him a taste of war which will make him needed, or a taste of revolution, in the course of which he hopes to win by force of arms, the political influence and personal consideration which have not come his way.(53)

One need not unconditionally accept de Tocqueville's observations to recognize their relevance to current professional restiveness. While it is unlikely that the profession will deliberately seek "combat" to restore its perceived lost status and influence, evidence of lost honor and self-depreciation reveal a serious dilemma within the profession - a dilemma that is a result of a perceived gap between professional ethics and behavior, manifesting itself not only in a critical assessment of military purpose, and in the nature of civil-military relationships, but also in a continuing professional self-analysis. While one may argue that professional self-analysis is a healthy condition and a consequence of a dynamic profession, one may also argue that it may be a manifestation of a more serious problem within the profession.

Reinforced by institutional demands and professional loyalty, this professional condition, although not necessarily fostering a monolithic military, can easily lead to a profession preoccupied with its status, jealous of its prerogatives, harsh in its response to divergence, and relentless in its pursuit of professional purity. It is this "military mind" - unresponsive to society, rationalizing its actions as servants of the state, and cloaked in the barrier of military expertise - that is most dangerous to professional ideals and to professional compatibility with democratic society.

There are a number of alternatives available to the profession.(54) First, the traditional and narrow perception of professionalism can be perpetuated, based on the premise that military men are unconditional servants of the state. Not only does this suggest a "robot-like" response to political leadership, but a rationale for uncritical response with limited intellectual perspectives. Second, the profession can assume an occupational model which is based on a civil service role in which civilian politics, unionization, salary concerns, and fringe benefits become the underlying professional motivation. This can lead to erosion of the professional ethos and expose the profession to political manipulation, creating dangers not only for the profession but for the entire political system. Finally, the profession can strive to develop a new rationale in which the military is seen as something more than unconditional servants of the state. This would necessitate the profession to acquire political understanding and expertise, a sense of realistic and enlightened self-interest, and professional perspectives transcending boundaries that we have traditionally associated with duty, honor, country.

It is this third alternative that provides the greatest opportunity for the profession to establish a realistic and effective voice in the political system within the accepted "rules of the game." Moreover, it is this alternative that will allow some "individuality" in the search for professional satisfaction and purpose with a degree of recognition that individual ethics and values are a component of professionalism. The institutionalization of healthy skepticism, reasonable inquiry, and legitimate dissent would do much to reinforce the "worth" of the individual while providing a momentum to innovation, imagination, and self-examination. Finally, such an approach provides the greatest opportunity for the profession to respond to professional restiveness and to establish a civil-military relationship that can maintain value systems mutually enriching and supportive of professional ideals and democratic expectations.

## NOTES

1. See Sam C. Sarkesian, The Professional Army Officer in a Changing Society. Chicago: Nelson-Hall Co., 1975, p. 188.

2. For an excellent overview of the literature see Charles C. Moskos, Jr., "The Military" in Annual Review of Sociology, Vol. 2, 1976. See also, John C. Lovell, "No Tunes of Glory: America's Military in the Aftermath of Vietnam," in Indiana Law Journal, Vol. 49, No. 4, Summer, 1974.

3. See, for example: Morris Janowitz, The Professional Soldier, New York: The Free Press, 1971; Samuel P. Huntington, The Soldier and the State, Cambridge: Harvard University Press, 1957; Stuart Loory, Defeated, New York: Random House, 1973; William L. Hauser, America's Army in Crisis, Baltimore, Md.: Johns Hopkins University Press, 1973; and Zeb B. Bradford and Frederic J. Brown, The United States Army in Transition, Beverly Hills, Cal.: Sage, 1973.

4. U.S. Army War College, Study on Military Professionalism, Carlisle Barrachs, Pa.: June 30, 1970; John H. Moellering, "Future Civil Military Relations; The Army Turns Inward?" in Military Review, Vol. LIII, No. 7, July 1973; Bruce M. Russett, "Political Perspectives of U.S. Military and Business Elite" in Armed Forces and Society, Vol. 1, No. 1, Fall, 1974; Bruce M. Russett and Elizabeth C. Hanson, Interest and Ideology; The Foreign Policy Beliefs of American Businessmen, San Francisco: W.H. Freeman and Company, 1975; Jerald G. Bachman and John D. Blair, Soldiers, Sailors and Civilians; The "Military Mind" and the All-Volunteer Force, Ann Arbor, Mich.: Institute for Social Research, The University of Michigan, November, 1975; Franklin D. Margiotta, "A Military Elite Transition: Air Force Leaders in the 1980's" in Armed Forces and Society, Vol. 2, No. 2, Winter, 1976.

5. Seymour M. Hersh, My Lai 4; A Report on the Massacre and Its Aftermath. New York: Random House, 1970.

6. Wilson Carey McWilliams, Military Honor after My Lai. New York: The Council on Religion and International Affairs, 1972, Special Studies #213, p. 28.

        7.   Peter Barnes, Pawns:  The  Plight  of  the  Citizen-
Soldier.  New York:  Alfred A. Knopf, 1972, p. 8.
        8.   Hauser, p. 88.
        9.   Ibid., p. 186.
        10.  Frederick C. Thayer, "Professionalism:    The Hard
Choice," in Frank Trager and Philip S. Kronenberg (Eds.),
National Security and American Society.  Lawrence:   The Uni-
versity of Kansas Press, 1973, p. 568.
        11.  Moellering, p. 81.
        12.  Margiotta, pp. 177-178.
        13.  Russett and Hanson, p. 281.
        14.  Army War College Study, p. B-1-16.
        15.  Moellering, p. 80; Margiotta, p. 168.
        16.  Margiotta, p. 168.
        17.  Ibid., p. 180.
        18.  Moellering, p. 79.  The quotes in this paragraph are
from the same source.
        19.  Russett and Hanson, pp. 277-278.
        20.  Margiotta, p. 168.
        21.  Moellering, p. 80.
        22.  Army War College Study, p. B-1-15.
        23.  Bachman and Blair, p. 15.
        24.  Margiotta, p. 165.
        25.  Ibid.
        26.  Russett, p. 97.
        27.  David M. Krieger, "A Developmental Model of the
Military Man" in Steffen W. Schmidt and Gerald A. Dorfman,
Soldiers in Politics.  Los Altos:   Geron-X, Inc., 1974.   See
also, Huntington, The Soldier and the State.
        28.  Moellering, p. 78.
        29.  Bachman and Blair, p. 100.
        30.  Ibid., pp. 12-13.
        31.  Margiotta, p. 169.
        32.  Ibid., p. 172.
        33.  Moellering, p. 77.
        34.  Russett, p. 98.
        35.  Russett and Hanson, p. 277.
        36.  Bachman and Blair, p. 15.
        37.  Gates Commission, The  Report  of  the  President's
Commission  on  an  All-Volunteer  Armed  Force.  Washington,
D.C.:   Government Printing Office, February, 1970.
        38.  See for example, Morris Janowitz and Charles C.
Moskos, Jr., "Racial Composition in the All-Volunteer Force,"
Armed Forces and Society, Vol. 1, No. 1, November 1974, p.
109-123.
        39.  Ames S. Albro, Jr., "Observations on the Costs of
an All-Volunteer Armed Force," August 26, 1971, Unpublished
Manuscript.
        40.  Moellering, p. 80.
        41.  Margiotta, p. 175.

42. Army War College Study, p. iii-iv.
43. Ibid., p. 17.
44. Ibid., p. B-1-10.
45. Ibid., p. B-1-17.
46. Ibid., p. B-1-19.
47. Ibid., p. B-1-23.
48. Time, June 7, 1976.
49. Army War College Study, p. B-1-20.
50. Ibid., p. 24.
51. Ibid., pp. iii-iv.
52. Ibid., p. B-29.
53. J.P. Mayer, Alexis de Tocqueville, Democracy in
America. New York: Doubleday and Co., 1969, p. 648.
Translated by George Lawrence.
54. A fuller explanation of these alternatives are con-
tained in Sam C. Sarkesian and Thomas M. Gannon (Eds.),
"Introduction:    Professionalism," Military Ethics and Professionalism, American Behavioral Scientist, May/June, 1976, Vol.
19, No. 5.

# 3 The Dimensions of American Military Professionalism: Two Scholarly Viewpoints

Changes in the international security environment and the complexity of national security policy always raise questions regarding the military institution and military professionalism. It is no surprise therefore that the most important assessments of military professionalism have occurred over the past two decades. These were decades in which the United States moved from a situation of virtual monopoly of nuclear weaponry to an era of increasing nuclear proliferation; from relatively clear national security interests to a period in which national security issues have become obscure; from a relatively clear military posture and capabilities to one in which serious questions have arisen regarding military effectiveness; and from riches to poverty in terms of military manpower. All of these issues coincide with the increasing interest in and study of military professionalism.

A number of those engaged in the study of military professionalism have published important works focusing on such concepts as convergence-divergence, managerial skills, to a call for professionals who have political skills. All of these studies notwithstanding, two influential works remain Samuel Huntington's The Soldier and the State and Morris Janowitz's The Professional Soldier.(1) Most scholars are familiar with both of these works and little needs to be said regarding their substance. Our concern here is the applicability and insights of their particular perspectives to the environment of the late 1970s and beyond. The purpose here is not another comparison of the substantive differences and similarities, but rather an assessment at the macro-level, examining the central themes of military professionalism. Examining scholarly theses from a "universalistic" perspective is a useful intellectual undertaking since it focuses attention on the underlying philosophical premises and provides reference points for critical inquiry

41

based on a disciplinary landscape. In this respect, the Huntington and Janowitz theses are examined in light of the changing nature of international security, the domestic political environment, and the military posture of the United States. At the outset, there is a need to clarify some of the concepts and definitions relevant to military professionalism since a number of criticisms about the contributions of Huntington and Janowitz appear to be based on misinterpretations and perspectives not considered by either scholar. The label of military professional has, by-and-large, been reserved to the officer corps. This is not to denigrate other professionals; i.e., the professional warrant officer or non-commissioned officer. However, as Huntington notes and most scholars recognize, the nature of civil-military relations and the character of the political dimension of military professionalism, as well as the spirit and morale of the military, is in no small measure the result of the character of the professional officer - his education and socialization, and the relationship of the state to the officer corps. Equally important, the concept of officership makes the officer an agent of the executive department of the government, providing him with a legitimacy to control and supervise an important institution within the political system.

In examining both the Huntington and Janowitz theses in relation to the international security environment, the domestic environment, and military posture, therefore, we must note the direct relationship between professionalism and the officer corps. Similarly there is a need to examine these works from the perspective of the scholars concerned; i.e., political science and sociology. Some of the criticism regarding these works neglects consideration of the purpose and disciplinary orientation of the authors, raising questions about the validity of such criticism.

Huntington's political science perspective is concerned with civil-military relations and control of the military. Underlying his study is a political scientist's concern with state control over coercive instruments, legitimacy, and the proper functioning of the political system.(2) Janowitz's sociological perspective is primarily concerned with the political-social system within the military, the socio-economic characteristics of those who are professionals, and the impact these have on the character of professionalism.(3)

Using such an analytical framework, Janowitz examines attitudes and values to draw conclusions regarding the military professional - the now well-known "absolutist-pragmatic" categories. Beginning with different perspectives, both scholars focus on the state of the profession, projecting their concepts into the future as the basis for professionalism. Whereas Huntington concludes that the best professional is an apolitical one, well entrenched in the specifics of military skills, Janowitz argues that the professional must also develop political-social insights to deal with political-military issues and the ambiguous nature of the security environment.

## THE INTERNATIONAL SECURITY ENVIRONMENT

It is not commonly accepted that the nature of the international environment has changed significantly since the late 1950s. Yet this was not immediately reflected in the literature. Following the Korean War, a number of scholars began to examine the concept of limited war. These assessments rested on the view that politics established constraints on military operations and indeed, limited strategy and battlefield tactics which were difficult to reconcile to professional purposes. More astute observers recognized the political leverage gained by the Soviet Union in combining political advantage with military operations in World War II. Whereas the American concern remained primarily military, the Soviet and British concerns were political as well as military; i.e., the shape of the post-war world, and the relationships of military operations to the emerging control of Europe. The demand for unconditional surrender was a manifestation of the military view that "there is no substitute for victory." One either won or lost. War appeared to be a clear zero-sums game, particularly from the American viewpoint.

In Korea, the concept of limited war, in which the nature of targets and the extent of military operations were limited by policy makers, was difficult to accept by most military men. The controversy over General Douglas MacArthur's role in the Korean War was a reflection of not only concern about civilian-control of the military, but more specifically the attitude of the President that military operations had to be confined to specific political guidelines. It had been axiomatic that politicians were in command until the moment that war occurred. On the battlefield and in the conduct of the war, military men predominated. Many military men and scholars alike viewed this kind of delineated responsibility as historically legitimate - particularly with respect to the United States. The concept of limited war, with all of its political-military implications, was difficult to reconcile with this view. Following the Korean War, some scholars and military men attempted to reconstruct a military perspective incorporating a limited war dimension. However, most returned to the idea of the political-war delineation.

It was to be expected that one major perspective for the study of military professionalism in the immediate post-Korean War era perceived military efficiency in terms of apolitical military men whose primary focus was on developing military

skills for the proper and successful conduct of war. Underlying this was the return to the idea that politicians negotiated
and military men fought wars. Equally important, such a
posture for the military professional was relatively easy to
translate into education and training, and into a clear state of
civil-military relations. The military served society, and in
this service, the military was intellectually wedded to military
skills and military matters conceived in a narrow professional
sense.

Additionally, military professionalism, according to this
perspective, viewed the world in pessimistic terms. In light of
the late 1950s and early 1960s this appeared to be a logical
conclusion founded in historical evidence. The turmoils of
colonial struggles combined with the dramatic events in China
seemed to foresage decades of constant confrontation and
struggles in the international arena. This was reinforced by
the realization that other nations - i.e., the Soviet Union -
possessed nuclear weapons and that nuclear war was indeed a
possibility. Accordingly, military men could best perform their
professional duties by preparing for war and becoming expert
in military skills, while the politicians struggled to respond to
the fluid and unpredictable international order. Huntington's
thesis about the apolitical military and a strict interpretation of
professionalism appeared to be the most appropriate and
relevant perspective at this time.

Without a detailed recounting of the changes that took
place in the early 1960s, it is necessary to note that dramatic
events in the international environment stimulated shifts in
U.S. political-military perspectives. The collapse of the
colonial empires, the increasing capability of the Soviet Union
in nuclear weaponry, and the rise of Communist China provided an impetus for rethinking political-military matters.
Particularly important was the victory of the Chinese Communist Party over the Nationalists using unconventional
strategy and tactics. This gave increasing relevance (or so it
appeared) to revolutionary strategy against colonial or authoritarian systems and eroded the relevance of traditional professional views of the battlefield.

The concern of a number of military men regarding
contingencies in various parts of the world with possible unconventional tactics sparked a renewed interest in the reassessment of military professionalism. Huntington's construct
of military professionalism appeared to some to be not enough
in light of these changing international security issues. The
employment of force for less than battlefield victory and for
political and symbolic purposes became increasingly important
in terms of America's national interest. This thesis was best
expressed by Janowitz's idea of a "constabulary" force - a
force not in the traditional sense of a constabulary (a paramil-
itary police force), but one in which professionalism included

consideration of political-social dimensions and employment of force in non-battle configuration. Most important, Janowitz's thesis insisted that professional socialization include such a dimension.

The Janowitz thesis did not abandon the traditional perspective on military professionalism, but used this as the basis for developing a more flexible political-social professional perspective. Equally important, Janowitz recognized that the socio-economic character of the military profession had changed and was changing. For example, the concept of professionalism as a lifetime career was revised. The military now might be only one of several careers. Society had developed linkages with the military profession which provided a number of alternative sources for socialization. Moreover, the self-isolation of the military was eroding, partly as a reflection of societal changes and partly as a reflection of the changing demands of the international security environment.

Thus, during the early years of the 1960s, both the Huntington and Janowitz theses appeared relevant, or appeared to provide a useful framework for understanding professionalism - but for different reasons. One stressed the need for an apolitical military totally immersed in military training and skills in a traditional sense, and the other argued the need to go beyond this if the military was to remain effective.

The Vietnam experience brought dramatic challenges to professionalism (many of which still remain unanswered). In terms of the international environment, the Vietnam war appeared to show that professional socialization and professional competence in the traditional sense were not adequate to meet the demands of counter-revolutionary conflicts. Moreover, the U.S. experience in Vietnam seemed to indicate that the existing views on military intervention had become outdated. There have been volumes written on the U.S. experience in Vietnam, and more are in the works. Yet, much still needs to be done to develop some objectivity in the U.S. experience in Vietnam. The only point to be made here is that the profession went through a very traumatic soul-searching regarding its own capacity to deal with situations like Vietnam. The demands of counter-revolutionary war went beyond traditional perspectives, kill ratios, real estate, and battlefield victories appeared to be almost irrelevant to the outcome of the war. More important were political symbols, ideological orientation, and the psycho-political environment. Most of these were factors that had little relevance in conventional military terms.

The Huntington thesis appeared to be less relevant in such an environment, while Janowitz's perspectives appeared particularly valid as political-social issues dominated the international conflicts of the 1960s. This is not to denigrate Huntington's thesis. Indeed, even during the worst years of

the U.S. involvement, there remained a group of military men
as well as civilians who argued that the outcome in Vietnam
would have been different if policy makers had recognized that
the battlefield belongs to the military - if professionals had
been allowed to operate according to their own professional
expertise, the Viet Cong would have been handily defeated
early in the war.

Interestingly enough, both Huntington's assessment that
professionals had a Hobbesian view of the world and Janowitz's
view of the absolutist-pragmatic delineation appeared valid in
examining professionalism during the Vietnam era. Not only
did many professionals feel that Communism and the wars of
national liberation were the major challenges, but that such
struggles would continue in the foreseeable future. In
response to this challenge there were professionals who felt
that a strict application of military skills and the use of
weapons technology (absolutists) was the best response.
Another group of professionals (pragmatists) perceived the
need for a more flexible and adaptable employment of force to
respond to the political-social as well as military challenges.

The post-Vietnam era has brought with it another shift in
professional orientation. These shifts and those referred to
earlier did not develop overnight, nor were they necessarily
perceptible at the outset. By and large, such shifts were
incremental and in some instances imperceptible. Chastened by
the Vietnam experience and threatened by what they perceived
as a Soviet build-up of conventional and nuclear power,
military professionalism reverted to a European orientation
(i.e., the "no-more-Vietnam" syndrome). The battle in the
central plains of Europe became the crucial contest within
which professional training and education took place. Indeed,
it can be reasonably argued that a reaction against political-
social dimensions of professionalism occurred with many professionals arguing that the concern with such matters detracted
from the main purpose of the profession which was to develop
military skills to fight the enemy: in this case, military skills
and proficiency to fight the Soviets in Europe. This was and
is reflected in senior service schools, in the training of units,
and in the military budget.

The Huntington thesis again reasserted itself - in revised
form, to be sure. The professionally proficient military officer
was one who gave little heed to politics. He concentrated
almost exclusively on the development of military skills. The
revised perspective did acknowledge the need to appreciate the
political-social environment in the target area, but this was
only a background to the development of a military profession,
narrowly construed, and enmeshed in technical military
matters. Yet, the Janowitz thesis persisted. There remained
a continuing need for a political-social dimension of professionalism, particularly in light of the probable conflicts that would

characterize the post-Vietnam era. Equally important, most of the Western world was moving and, indeed, had moved to a different form of military recruiting: from selective service to volunteer service. This had an effect on the character of professionalism and the relationships between the officer corps and the enlisted structure. Moreover, this had an important influence on the capabilities of the military institution.

## THE DOMESTIC POLITICAL ENVIRONMENT

Both the Huntington and Janowitz theses are well suited to a democratic political system in one dimension and unsuited in another - but for differing reasons. The Huntington thesis stresses the apolitical nature of the military and persuasively argues that military men have no business whatsoever in politics. Huntington stresses the nature of controls over the military and the character of civil-military control. The military is controlled not only through constitutional arrangements, but also through the democratic value system as it interacts with the system in the military. Military socialization processes stress civilian control and the subordination of the military. According to Huntington, the subordination of political-social matters in the profession reinforces the subordination of the military to civilian leadership.

Janowitz's thesis also stresses the subordination of the military to civilian decision makers, not only as a result of the democratic political system, but also because of the professional value system. However, the argument for a political-social component to professionalism and the need for the military to seriously concern itself with such matters provides evidence to some critics that the military officer in Janowitz's perspective is more than a "military" professional - he is one that becomes involved in politics which may open the way for undue influence in the political system. However, the burden of Janowitz's thesis is that the political-social dimension is one that should be directed outward, towards the employment of force in external contingencies.

In terms of the unsuitability of parts of both theses to democratic systems, it can be argued that Huntington's professionalism and Janowitz's constabulary concept both contain the potential for erosion of civilian control. Huntington's stress on the apolitical professional has the potential for developing a military professionalism that is insensitive to democratic values and processes just as it can be insensitive to politics as a whole. To expect a military system to be insensitive to its own political-social system is not realistic, particularly in light of civilian socialization processes and democratic value systems. Similarly in Janowitz, professional involvement in political-social matters cannot be limited by regulations to the application of force. The inculcation of political ideas and political analysis opens the door to a political assessment of domestic society and the implicit involvement in a variety of informal political alliances. Without a strong intellectual base and explicit political dimension, such a posture can lead to political activities and views resting on oversimplified perceptions of democracy and politics. In both cases, the military profession can operate contrary to the values and ideals of the democratic system. Finally, Huntington's argument that professionals have a Hobbesian view of the world bodes ill for the military professional who views his own democratic society in Hobbesian terms.

Much has been written about the civil rights domestic turmoil of the 1960s compounded by the reaction to the U.S. involvement in Vietnam. One result of such political conflict was reflected in the denigration of the military profession's status. This negative view lingers on to a certain degree in the volunteer era. But more important, the volunteer concept provides another useful measure for examining the influence of Huntington and Janowitz. The Huntington thesis provides support for the volunteer concept since it is presumed that the manpower base would allow the military to isolate itself from the constant input of civilian political-social attitudes and subdue the political concerns and activity of military men. The volunteer military in such circumstances could be trained as a truly professional force, isolated from the eroding (and some would say corroding) influence of the political-social system. The problems of military effectiveness that first appeared during the Korean War and again emerged in dramatic form in the later parts of the Vietnam War could have been avoided by such a professional posture, according to the logical extension of this argument. In applying the Janowitz thesis, it could be argued that a better political-social understanding of the nature of the war and the role of the United States and the United Nations could have rectified much of the "why we are fighting" rhetoric as well as cemented and reinforced the legitimacy and credibility of the military's role in Korea and, more importantly, in Vietnam.

The greatest divergence of the two theses is in their applicability to the military profession during the Vietnam era. As suggested earlier, both views were used by groups of officers, not only to defend the role of the profession in Vietnam, but to establish guidelines for the military in the post-Vietnam era. In terms of the domestic political environment, the Huntington thesis gained strength as the U.S. involvement in the war became more questionable. Using his thesis, professionals could argue that the battlefield belongs to the military. What needs to be done to gain victory should be left in the hands of the professional. The nature of the weap-

onry and the strategy and tactics for success in any battlefield conflict must be in the hands of the professional - so the
argument goes. The failure of the military, if it can be called
a failure, was not in the military professional, but in the
political constraints and civilian interference in the proper
conduct of the war. One need but review some of the most
recent memoirs of the war published by high ranking officers
to understand the frustration, and indeed bitterness, with
which civilian interference has been viewed. This kind of
attitude was not limited to high ranking officers, however.
Many other professionals also felt that major institutions in the
political system did little to assist in the proper conduct of the
war. In sum, the Huntington thesis that military men should
remain apolitical and focus on their own purpose - success in
battle, both directly and indirectly - was seen as the answer
to failures in counter-revolutionary conflict.

Using Janowitz's thesis, military professionals could argue
that it was the lack of a real appreciation of the political-social
nature of the Vietnam war that was ultimately the basis for the
American military failure. The traditional and conventional
perspective could not cope with the highly political and social
nature of the revolution in Vietnam. This lead to an irrelevant strategy and equally irrelevant tactics. Both civilian and
military leaders can also be faulted in such a perspective for
not allowing the political-social aspect of the profession to be
seriously weighed in the conduct of the war. Equally important, the political-social dimension could have better
prepared the military to respond to the domestic turmoil and
social issues that spilled over into the military in the middle
and late 1960s. The drug scene, racism, dissidence, and
insubordination, to a degree previously unknown, caught many
military professionals by surprise. Yet, it is argued that
political awareness and appreciation of the political-social
changes taking place in society could have alerted military
professionals to the problems of maintaining discipline, morale,
and a fighting spirit in the military system.

In the post-Vietnam era, there remain adherents to the
Huntington thesis as well as those to the Janowitz thesis. In
its extreme form, the Huntington thesis is interpreted to mean
isolation from society so that the military can enjoy the
freedom to engage in the necessary training to succeed in
battle. If it is taken to its extreme, the Janowitz thesis is
interpreted to mean that the military professional must also be
a social scientist concerned about solving the military's
problems - problems which have been injected into the military
by society; i.e., illiteracy, race, drug abuse, dissidence, and
job dissatisfaction. In reviewing the literature, one can
identify a variety of themes articulated by scholars on these
matters - themes that owe their inception to the scholarship of
both Huntington and Janowitz.

MILITARY POSTURE


The philosophical distinctions between the Huntington and
Janowitz theses are most clearly seen in their impact on military posture.  The definition of military posture can include a
variety of considerations, from force structure to defense
budgetary considerations.  As it is used here, military posture
refers primarily to the professional view as to the most
probable use of the military institution, the substance of
education and training of the professional and his "world
view."
    The Hobbesian view of the world underlies the profes-
sional intellectual dimension, according to Huntington.
Whether military men actually identify themselves as Hobbesian
is not important.  Rather, it is the fact that military men
perceive the world as one in which states must operate in a
hostile environment and one in which military conflicts are
frequent.  For any state to survive, it must, therefore, have
a military force capable of protecting its political system.
    The "conservative" orientation complements the Hobbesian
view.  Professionals are characterized as men who see the
world populated by selfish men, who can only be controlled by
strong leaders.  Even then, the irrationalities of world politics
make disorders imminent.  Living in this type of world, military men accept "law and order" as a primary objective of any
political system and as something to be sought as inherently
"good."  With this kind of perspective, it is difficult for
military men to completely reconcile themselves to the dynamics, changes, and apparent instabilities that generally
characterize a liberal democratic system.
    Finally, military men see virtue in existing institutions -
a virtue that requires loyalty and commitment.  Thus, it is
difficult for most military men to accept criticism of American
political institutions.  This was evident during the Vietnam
era.  For example, military men felt that the mass media were
major culprits in presenting a distorted view of the Vietnam
War and of the military institution.  This professional view
remains, by and large, true today.
    The professional world, however, is fundamentally rooted
in a philosophical premise that accepts the apolitical nature of
the military institution.  According to Huntington, this is
necessary if the profession is to perform its military role
without the erosion from political influences.  Involvement in
politics shifts the energy of the profession from its main task
to the corrupting nature of politics.  The more professional
the military, the more it is isolated from politics.  Military
education and training, according to this argument, must
therefore focus on the special skills necessary to win battles
and wars.  The study of political-social phenomenon may be an

intellectual luxury and irrelevant to the main tasks of the profession.

Huntington argues that this kind of professional posture is best suited for a liberal democracy that prides itself on civilian control of the military. The variety of democratic controls, institutions, the value system involved, and the inculcation of military men with a commitment to the acquisition of military skills provides not only "objective" but "subjective" controls - those that derive from value systems and ethical considerations.

A major thread of current professionalism is characterized by this Huntington perspective. As discussed earlier, not only can this be used as an explanation of the Vietnam debacle, but it provides a reference point for the future professional training and socialization.

Less a philosophy than a professional orientation, Janowitz's constabulary concept not only views professionalism in certain political terms, but sees the military institution as a political instrument, as well as one in the traditional sense. The military should not be used as a partisan political tool, nor is it to be construed as primarily a "political" instrument, but military men must understand, according to this view, that battlefield victory is only one aspect of professionalism. Limited war with all its political-social characteristics must be part of the military professional baggage.

The constabulary perspective does not eliminate the traditional view that military professionalism is primarily based on military skills and competence performance. Rather, it adds a political-social dimension that is characteristic of Vietnam-type wars, reinforced by the military's role in such relatively nontraditional contingencies as arms control, conflict limitation, and international peacekeeping.

According to Janowitz, the world view of military men is not monolithic, but basically reflected in two perspectives: the "absolutists" and the "pragmaticists." Where the former views the world in "good" and "evil" terms, the latter accepts shades of gray, in which there are times when "good" and "evil" may not be discernible. For the absolutists, the employment of force to respond to world events parallels Huntington's apolitical professional. In its purest form, this means the application of all the means at the disposal of the military to achieve "victory." For the pragmaticists, however, the employment of force is a more complicated matter, with a number of political considerations. In a number of instances, according to the pragmaticists, military men must constrain their use of force, and may become involved in essentially nonmilitary contingencies.

The professional socialization process, including the components of military education, reflects the more complex dimension of the constabulary force. Military men need to do

more than learn purely military skills. Military schools,
particularly the senior schools, must study a number of political subjects, such as arms control, conflict limitation,
problems of political and social change, as well as the economics of national security. In the final analysis, the
professionalism of Janowitz requires a military competence as
well as a political-social sensitivity. This must, however, be
qualified by severely circumscribed political involvement and
activity by individual professionals.


## SUMMARY AND CONCLUSIONS


The examination of the Huntington and Janowitz theses must be
tempered by the recognition of their disciplinary perspectives.
Huntington's political science focus directs him to the operation
of the political system and the military's proper role in that
system. Janowitz is primarily concerned with the political-
social character of the profession and how this affects the
military institution. Both scholars draw conclusions from their
disciplinary roots relating to the needs of the military profession and the political system. Thus, it can be argued that the
nature of professionalism advanced by both scholars complement
each other in many respects. This is not to deny the basic
disagreement between Huntington's apolitical military and the
Janowitz constabulary force concept. Nevertheless, to articulate these disagreements without recognizing the complementary
nature, is to misinterpret the scholarship and contributions of
both men.
        Examining the philosophical premises of the scholar's
works does not necessarily reveal the details nor the extent of
the substantive analyses. But if one seeks to identify the
intellectual thrust and philosophical dimensions which establish
the context within which the scholars address the subject, then
a macro view is valid - one unencumbered by the incremental
details (not that these are unimportant). Interestingly
enough, the philosophical basis of the Huntington and Janowitz
works is reflected in the present debate in the U.S. Army
regarding the utility of Field Manual 100-5 and all that it
suggests regarding the battle in the Central Plains of Europe.
This debate is generally an operational manifestation of the
Huntington-Janowitz perspectives.
        In this respect, the decade of the 1980s may demand a
new type of military professionalism - one that combines
several aspects of the Huntington and Janowitz theses. It is
clear, for example, that battlefield skills and technology remain
important ingredients of military professionalism. It is also
apparent that the delineations between the military and society
are less clear than they were in the decades immediately after

World War II.  Finally, it may very well be that the synthesis of the traditional (as reflected in Huntington) with the political-social (as reflected by Janowitz) dimensions will lead to other models of civil-military relations and professionalism, aimed specifically at the lessons of Vietnam and the requirements of the next decade.

There have been other analyses and philosophical orientations which are useful in their own right, including the soldier-statesmen concept, the soldier-scholar, and the political soldier.  These approaches should also be examined in terms of their philosophical orientation and relevancy to the modern security environment.  Regardless of the criticisms that may be levelled at either the Huntington or Janowitz thesis, and the utility of other analyses, there is no question that both Huntington and Janowitz have made important contributions to the study of armed forces and society.  The insights provided by both scholars into the nature of military professionalism have motivated critical inquiry by a number of other scholars.

## NOTES

1.   Samuel Huntington, The Soldier and the State; The Theory and Politics of Civil-Military Relations.  New York: Vintage Books, 1964.  Morris Janowitz, The Professional Soldier: A Social and Political Portrait.  New York: The Free Press, 1971.

2.  Huntington has much to say throughout his book regarding the political impact on the profession and the military mind.  The selections quoted here illustrate his views.

A political officer corps, rent with faction, subordinated to ulterior ends, lacking prestige but sensitive to the appeals of popularity, would endanger the security of the state.  A strong, integrated, highly professional officer corps, on the other hand, immune to politics and respected for its military character, would be a steadying balance wheel in the conduct of policy. . . . In a liberal society the power of the military is the greatest threat to their professionalism.  Yet as long as American security is threatened, that power is not likely to diminish significantly.

Only an environment which is sympathetically conservative will permit American military leaders to combine the political power which society thrusts upon them with the military professionalism without which society cannot endure.  . . . [p. 464].

The military ethic emphasizes the permanence, irrationality, weakness, and evil in human nature. It stresses supremacy of society over the individual, and the importance of order, hierarchy, and division of function [p. 79].

3.   Janowitz refers to the absolutist-pragmatic approach, and the constabulary force concept at a variety of points throughout the book. The selections quoted here provide clear views of his definition and concept of these categories.

Each theory has its own philsophy of long-range political goals, a conception of politico-military strategy, an image of enemy intentions, and an estimate of the uncommitted nations. The absolute doctrine . . . emphasizes the permanency of warfare and continues to be concerned with victory . . . the pragmatic doctrine emphasizes the revolutionary character of atomic energy, and the discontinuity of the military past with the future. . . . The "absolutists" assume the end as given - total victory; the means must be adjusted in order to achieve it. The "pragmatists" are concerned not only with adapting military means to achieve desired political ends, but insist that the end must be conditioned by what military technology is capable of achieving . . . the distinction between "absolute" and "pragmatic" codes is roughly equivalent to that which obtains between conservative and liberal doctrine. . . . The meaning of these terms - absolute-pragmatic, or conservative-liberal - is clarified by reference to the issue of the inevitability of war, and the political objectives of military action [pp. 264-265].
The military establishment becomes a constabulary force when it is continuously prepared to act, committed to the minimum of force, and seeking viable international relations rather than victory because it has incorporated a protective military posture. The constabulary outlook is grounded in, and extends, pragmatic doctrine [p. 418].
Most fundamentally, the professional soldier is conservative . . . [p. 33].

# II

# Military Professionalism in a Changing Security Environment

# Part II
## An Introduction

This part examines the new demands on the profession as a result of the changed security environment. Problems of military capability and effectiveness in non-nuclear conflicts are examined in the first selection against the back-drop of nuclear war. These issues are closely linked to the traumatic experience of the military profession during the Vietnam war, which are examined in Chapter 5. In its aftermath, lingering doubts remain regarding the proper military professional posture and the capability to respond to a variety of military contingencies. The difficulties faced by the American military in attempting to intervene or engage in conflicts that are less than survival issues are examined in chapter 6. Additionally, there is a close look at the linkage between the military profession, the military institution, and the domestic political system. There is little that the military institution can do without some minimum level of support from society. Engaging in conflicts without such support will only erode the credibility of the institution and cast serious doubts on the capability of the military profession. In this respect, the greatest challenge may not be the European "Battle in the Central Plains," but the conflicts that are likely to occur on the periphery of Europe or in developing areas - those areas from which the Western states draw much of their energy supplies. The final selection addresses some of the major dilemmas faced in such an environment and prescribes a course or direction for the military profession in order to prepare for the security environment of the coming decade.

# 4 American Policy and Low Intensity Conflict: An Overview

Since the withdrawal from Vietnam, the United States has not developed a realistic political-military policy for the employment of force in non-nuclear contingencies. The failure to do so has important ramifications for international perceptions of our political will and military resolve, as well as our ability to respond to threats to U.S. interests. Even though recent events have reawakened interest in force employment, American military capability and political will to employ forces short of nuclear or major conventional conflict remain questionable and suspect.

Debate continues as to the reasons underlying this apparent failure of American policy: arguments range from the Vietnam syndrome and leadership weakness, to the futility of force employment. Regardless of the American position world events will not wait. Events in Iran and Afghanistan in 1979 and 1980 show the instability in the Third World and the character of Soviet political-military policy. Such events reinforce the view that the Third World environment will continue to pose threats to United States' interests. It seems unnecessary in such circumstances to advocate a coherent American policy response. Yet, the fact remains that present American political-military strategy is inadequate to respond to Third World security threats. This weakness is particularly evident in America's posture and policy with respect to low intensity conflicts - conflicts which are characteristic of the Third World.(1)

The problems facing American policy makers are compounded by disagreement over logistical and operational concepts. While there are a number of such issues, three are particularly relevant. First, there is little agreement on the meaning of low intensity conflict. The term can mean different things to different people depending on the organizational

59

perspective and anticipated level of involvement in the conflict.
For example, to the individual soldier, there may be little
sense in labelling any type of combat low intensity when survival on the battlefield is rarely low intensity. From the point
of view of the policy maker, low intensity could be meaningful
in terms of the level of combat expected, the limits placed on
force employment, and the restrictions on the scope and number of parties involved in the combat area. There is also the
possibility that protagonists may view the conflict differently,
creating serious asymmetry. One side may consider the conflict as a limited one, while the other may see it as a struggle
for survival and consider it a total war.

Second, there is little agreement as to the specifics of
policy to be adopted in responding to low intensity conflict.
There appears to be a consensus, however, that the United
States must be prepared to respond. But the force composition, the circumstances under which a force would be employed, and the areas into which such forces should be
introduced if necessary, remain major issues of disagreement.
It is generally thought that no force could be specifically
tailored beforehand for a particular contingency in a particular
country or situation; i.e., a military force structured specifically to respond to a low intensity conflict in Venezuela.
Rather, there is much to the argument advocating a force
posture with a flexibility to respond to low intensity conflict in
several areas in a variety of forms. Moreover, political
leaders need to develop and articulate clear purposes for the
use of military force - purposes, it might be added, that have
or can develop the necessary domestic support.

Third, there is disagreement regarding the quantity and
quality of the hardware available and logistical back-up for
response to non-nuclear contingencies. This is generally reflected in debates over the type of training needed, force
structures, and command and control procedures. Additionally, there is lack of agreement regarding American ability to
intervene rapidly and to escalate once troops have been committed. Such disagreements are probably due to more
fundamental problems regarding the specifics of policy and the
meaning of low intensity conflict; they are also important in
considering mobility and support after intervention.

Regardless of the disagreement and debate over such
issues, there appears to be a clear recognition that military
capability, national will, and political military policy need to be
integrated. Underlying this is the belief that American military intervention cannot be seriously undertaken without a
proportionate level of popular support. Equally important, the
concept of military professional must be broad enough to include political-social dimensions of conflict characteristic of the
Third World.

## DEFINITION AND CONCEPT

Aware of the difficulty in defining and conceptualizing the term, we nevertheless have formulated a working definition of low intensity conflict to use as the cornerstone for our analysis, noting that such a definition and conceptualization will undoubtedly be revised during the course of the analysis. Low intensity conflict as used here refers to the range of activities and operations on the lower end of the conflict spectrum involving the use of military or a variety of semi-military forces (both combat and non-combat) on the part of the intervening power to influence and compel the adversary to accept a particular political-military condition. Employment of force is a concept closely related but broader in scope and in policy option. The employment of force is not exclusively concerned with combat, but includes a variety of methods and strategies in which military force or its perceived use can influence the environment and actions of other states without necessarily resorting to battle. It encompasses the threat of force (without employment or combat), the employment of force (without combat), and the use of force in combat. Employment of force and low intensity conflict, as concepts, blend into one another. It is difficult to develop credibility for a policy for force employment without being prepared to commit forces to combat. A foreign state (or states) must be convinced that the state employing force is also prepared to use it in combat. Nevertheless, for the purpose of methodological clarity, distinctions are made between the two concepts. Additionally, it is necessary to identify characteristics of the environment in which low intensity conflict is likely to occur, as well as the character of the states in the Third World that compose the environment in which forces may be employed.

## The Third World environment

A number of scholars have recognized the fallacy of placing all of the Third World states in one category, since there exists a variety of distinctions that can be made between the developing states (i.e., oil producers and oil consumers). However, there are common characteristics that are particularly important in developing American political-military policy. The most obvious is that most developing areas are likely to remain unstable and have a high degree of revolutionary potential. There are many reasons for this, but four predominate: the diffusion of political power, lack of legitimate governing structures, the politicization into a modern context of historical ethnic and geographic animosities, and the introduction of technology. As one observer concludes:

The third world of one hundred less developed
countries (LDCs) has come to dominate the rhetoric
of the U.N. and other international agencies, but its
real power standing is remarkably weak. . . . The
under-developed world is riven with internecine
conflicts, domestic upheavals and a mounting burden
of surplus, unskilled people. Governed by military
juntas, one-party dictatorships or repressive oligar-
chies, they resent the "free trade imperialism" and
the neo-colonial exploitation that they associate with
either the former empires or the domineering dollars
of the West. . . . Most of the LDCs can not realistically hope to raise their opportunities for work or
to expand the bare necessities for survival (for their
bourgeoning populations). It will not be surprising
if they resort to regional wars, as in the horn of
Africa, simply to let off steam and to ease their
population pressures. They might yet prove that
the dire predictions of the Reverend Malthus were
flawed by optimism.(2)

Equally important, conventional armies of developing states may
not in the long run wield the coercive power nor have the
military capability to defend the state. The availability of
modern weaponry and the ethnic diversity within the various
developing states provide clusters of political-military groups
that can easily be arrayed against the existing government and
intervening forces. "People's war," in its broadest sense, is
the most likely conflict phenomenon in such an environment.
    The instability created by these developments provide
opportunities for solving problems through use of force by
indigenous groups or by the intervention of foreign states to
protect their own interests. The most critical result is that
existing governments and/or ruling elite are usually placed in
a fragile power position. Events in Iran and Afghanistan are
cases in point.
    Involvement in such an area presents a policy quagmire
for the West and the United States. But, while it may seem
prudent for the United States to avoid serious involvement in
such areas, energy needs and geopolitical considerations may
require it.

Low intensity conflict

    Conflicts that are most likely to occur in the Third World
areas are of the low intensity variety. They are limited geo-
graphically, in the number of participants, and in the nature
and scope of military operations. If "visible" intervention from
external sources should occur in such areas, nationalistic
passions are likely to be aroused with a high propensity for

the development of a "people's war." A "fluid" battle area not
bound by conventional considerations and enmeshed in the
political-social fabric of the political system is likely to create
difficulties for the intervening power, which may be insurmountable in terms of "conquest" or "victory." Moreover,
combat can include both rural and urban areas, and against
forces who possess sophisticated weapons. In these circumstances, the political-psychological dimensions of military
operations predominate over tactical considerations. Additionally, conventional means of ascertaining military progress
may be irrelevant as is the case with conventional military
training and doctrine. In broad terms, low intensity conflicts
are usually limited wars and/or wars of insurgency on a scale
less than Vietnam, but something more than isolated acts of
terrorism. As such, they demand a political-military response
rather than an exclusively police operation.

Employment of force

     This refers to the various uses of military force, short of
combat, to achieve a particular goal (coercive diplomacy). It
is used as a "signal" to the foreign country or countries of
the seriousness of the issue at hand from the point of view of
the state employing force, and the fact that national security
is at stake. Employment of force can include a variety of
measures ranging from a show of naval force, to increasing
military assistance, to the commitment of advisors.(3) Employment of force, however, must be buttressed by a policy of
resolve and may require the commitment of military units to
combat in low intensity conflict. Failure to follow through
beyond force employment (as that term is used here), when
circumstances require it, may signal the foreign state or states
of the lack of resolve, military inadequacy, or both, on the
part of the employing state. The erosion of credibility and
policy are sure to follow.


THE CONFLICT SPECTRUM


The relationship between various types of conflicts is shown
in figure 4.1. The figure also shows the perceived strategic
dimension and capability of the United States. The United
States has a reasonably adequate capability to conduct short
duration surgical operations and limited conventional wars in
the fashion of Korea. Additionally, the United States has a
reasonable capability and credibility to maintain a strategic
nuclear posture with respect to NATO and vis-a-vis the Soviet
Union. Increasingly, the United States is developing, along
with its NATO allies, a non-nuclear conventional capability in

| | Surgical Operations | Guerrilla I * | Guerrilla II ** | Guerrilla III *** | Vietnam Type | Limited Conv. War | General Conv. War | Nuclear War |
|---|---|---|---|---|---|---|---|---|
| Employment of force – non-combat | | | | | | | | |
| Intensity | Low | | | | | | | High |
| U.S. Credibility | Adequate | | | Low | | | | High |
| U.S. Military Capability | Adequate | | | Poor | | | Moderate | Best |

* Guerrilla I   – Weapons Assistance Teams – Police Training – Advisory Teams
** Guerrilla II  – Special Forces Teams – Cadre for Indigenous Forces (continuation of Guerrilla I)
*** Guerrilla III – Integration of U.S. Combat Units with Indigenous Forces (continuation of Guerrilla I and II)

All Guerrilla classifications include requisite economic assistance.

Fig. 4.1.  Conflict spectrum.

Europe.  However,  for  limited  wars  of  Guerrilla  types  II,  III
and  Vietnam  types,  the  United  States  at  the  present  time  not
only  lacks  the  credibility,  but  the  military  capability.   Thus,
along  the  spectrum  the  United  States  appears  to  have  an
adequate  capability  and  credibility  for  conflicts  on  the  extreme
ends  of  the  spectrum.   For  the  vast  middle  range  (consisting
primarily  of  low  intensity  conflicts  and  limited  wars),  however,
the  United  States  appears  to  have  limited  capability  and
minimal  credibility.   And  it  is  in  this  range  that  most  future
conflicts  are  likely  to  occur.

Assuming  the  validity  of  the  conflict  spectrum  and  the
political-military  capability  of  the  United  States,  three  issues
predominate.   What  should  be  the  political-military  policy  of
the  United  States  to  develop  a  credible  force  employment
capacity  and  response  to  low  intensity  conflict?   What  political
constraints  and  limitations  must  be  considered?   What  are  the
military  requirements  and  capabilities  necessary  to  carry  out
political-military  policy?   Let  us  briefly  examine  each  of  these
issues,  deferring  the  question  of  policy  until  the  last.

## POLITICAL CONSTRAINTS AND LIMITATIONS

Political  forces  and  pressures,  both  domestic  and  international,
play  a  crucial  role  in  the  capacity  of  the  United  States  to
employ  force  and  in  involvement  in  low  intensity  conflict.   Most
scholars  and  military  professionals  are  aware  of  the  contraints
imposed  by  the  domestic  environment.   These  were  clearly
manifested  during  the  American  involvement  in  Vietnam.
Congressional-executive  relationships,  the  state  of  domestic
politics,  the  attitudes  of  the  populace  regarding  threat  perceptions  and  force  employment,  and  the  "mind  set"  of  policy
makers  are  important  political  ingredients  in  determining  the
boundaries  of  political-military  policy.   For  example,  it  may  be
one  matter  to  commit  a  team  of  special  forces  to  a  particular
area  and  provide  military  and  economic  assistance.   It  is  another  matter  to  commit  a  battalion  size  combat  unit  in  the  same
area.   As  the  United  States  learned  (rather  hopefully  learned),
without  the  requisite  popular  support  and  consensus  of  important  political  actors,  force  employment  has  little  hope  of
achieving  intended  policy  goals.   In  this  respect,  there  are  a
number  of  observations  about  America's  Vietnam  experience
that  need  to  be  considered.

### Relevance of the Vietnam experience

There  is  a  considerable  body  of  opinion  in  both  military
and  civilian  quarters  that  places  little  value  on  the  United
States  experience  in  Vietnam  in  regard  to  the  conduct  of

future low intensity conflicts. While it is true that policy
makers should not be bound by the past, it is also true that
to forget the lessons of Vietnam is to invite similar results. If
one reviews the history of the United States military operations
against the Seminole Indians (1836-1843), in the Philippines
(1898-1901), and in Vietnam (1964-1972), one is struck by a
number of similarities regarding political-military problems,
military operations, and insurgency forces. Unfortunately,
there has been little historical analysis for purposes of developing doctrinal guidelines. Indeed, the military has a
singularly short institutional memory. It has had to relearn
lessons that should have been historically ingrained in the
institutional posture. To avoid mistakes of the past, therefore, there is a need to examine the doctrinal relevance and
irrelevance of Vietnam, both political and military, and assess
their applicability as policy and program guidelines to future
low intensity wars. Using such assessments, conceptual
frameworks can be designed and doctrinal feasibility examined
to provide guidelines and historical experience factors for
military and civilian decision makers.

This is not the appropriate place for a re-examination of
the U.S. involvement in Vietnam. The literature abounds with
such studies.(4) Several observations are relevant and appropriate for our purposes, however. First, the Vietnam War
developed into an asymmetrical relationship between the United
States and the Viet Cong/North Vietnamese. While we conducted a limited war, for the revolutionaries it was a total
war. Second, conventional military wisdom, training, and
professional education were apparently inadequate to meet the
challenges of the political-military dimensions characteristic of
revolutionary wars. Third, American domestic political attitudes were crucial in affecting the American military role in
Vietnam. Equally important, the crescendo of criticism from
domestic political groups had a decided affect on the policy
options available to the political leadership. All of these
factors reinforced the asymmetry of the relationships in Vietnam. Fourth, American military intervention in support of a
governing elite or political system that does not have some
minimum level of internal support is likely to erode any existing public support. This does not necessarily mean that
such intervention is doomed to failure. Rather, it means that
American intervention must be a balanced political-military one
and primarily concerned with the reinforcement and legitimizing
of the systems receiving some popular support. Fifth, the
American experience in Vietnam remains an important influence
in the world perspective of military and civilian leaders and,
as such, has a decided impact on political-military strategy.
The result is a very cautious approach that borders on a
"never again" attitude. Sixth, the Vietnam involvement
stimulated a military preoccupation with the "conventional"

environment of European wars. This is manifested in hardware and tactics as well as in professional military education and training. A further consequence is that perceptions of military capability and of the imperatives of political-military policy appear to have become closely wedded to a "conventional" mind set, where issues appear clearer and military capability and policy more rational.

Regardless of recent events, therefore, the American military intervention still weighs heavily in the minds of important political actors. Osgood notes:

> . . . the popular disaffection with the Vietnamese war does not indicate a reversion to pre-Korean attitudes towards limited war. Rather it indicates serious questioning of the premises about the utility of limited war as an instrument of American policy, the premises that originally moved the proponents of limited war strategy and that underlay the original confidence of the Kennedy Administration in America's power to cope with local Communist incursions of all kinds.(5)

Most important, as demonstrated in Vietnam, the employment of force for any length of time requires popular support. Without it, military intervention of any type will quickly lose its legitimacy.

As Ravenal points out:

> The . . . condition that will complicate the enforcement of international order is the lack of consensus in domestic support not when our system is free from external pressure, but precisely when it most needs steady support. Few societies – especially one such as the United States – will hold together in foreign exercises that are ill-defined or, conversely, dedicated to the maintenance of a balance of power. . . . The lack of public support might not prevent intervention, but it might critically inhibit its prosecution.(6)

## Superpower relationships

The security relationships between the U.S. and the U.S.S.R. are obvious elements in determining the nature of America's use of force and policy to respond to low intensity conflicts. It is common knowledge that the cornerstone of U.S.-Soviet security relationships is deterrence – mutually assured destruction capability. If the past is any guide, neither superpower intends to use nuclear weapons in conflicts not directly and immediately affecting its own survival. By and large, the use of nuclear weapons is conceivable only in the European context and possibly the Sino-Soviet confrontation along their common border. Comparable nuclear threats and military balance are absent in non-European areas. From a strategic point of view, the applicability of deterrence in the context of the Third World necessitates a military capability not exclusively rooted in nuclear weaponry.

The Soviet Union seems to have grapsed this fact and shaped its military capability to expand its non-nuclear flexibility without apparently surrendering any of its nuclear effectiveness. It is, for example, able to influence politics and events in Africa and the Middle East by a variety of strategies and methods. It has developed a political-military capability to exploit limited wars in various regions and support or deter insurgency wars as its policy dictates. It is difficult to predict the long-range benefits, if any, to the Soviet Union. In the short run, however, the Soviet Union has projected political resolve and strengthened its political-military credibility in areas outside the European context.

Since the denouement in Vietnam, the United States, in contrast to the Soviet Union, has displayed a decreasing capability and credibility to influence political-military matters outside the European area. Focusing primarily on Europe, the United States has strengthened its NATO commitment and is developing an increasingly effective non-nuclear capability for battle in the Central Plains. Few would argue the need for such a posture. Without a strong political-military base in Europe, political-military policy in other areas would be seriously jeopardized. Nonetheless, it appears that this preoccupation with the battles in Europe has caused the neglect of other areas – areas with a potential for serious security problems for the United States. Even with a reawakened interest in low intensity conflict because of the Iranian crisis of 1979 and 1980 and the Soviet incursions into Afghanistan in 1979 and 1980, the United States has not as yet demonstrated the political resolve nor the military posture to respond to threats outside the European context. While the development of an American "rapid deployment force" is proceeding, there remain outstanding issues of force composition and structure, the effectiveness of logistical back-up, and the combat effectiveness of such forces. Moreover, the United States has yet to demonstrate its ability to integrate political, military, and economic instruments into a coherent policy, effective in the Third World. This cannot be accomplished overnight or by one-time actions. The credibility of such a policy is a result of a pattern of consistent actions reflecting purposeful policy goals which are understood by other states.

In sum, the ability to deter is not exclusively based on nuclear capability. Successful deterrence policy requires a credible non-nuclear capability, among other things. It does not necessarily follow that non-nuclear forces must engage in conflict. An existing credible non-nuclear capability, combined with purposeful political strength, are likely to have important political overtones in any crisis or confrontation.

## Policy constraints

It is conceivable that once the United States intervenes, it will opt not to raise the intensity of the conflict beyond "low intensity." If so, the United States must be prepared to withdraw if the conflict goes beyond low intensity proportions; or, if the decision to remain is taken, then the character of the conflict may develop into a Vietnam or Korean type conflict, with a possibility of escalation and superpower confrontation. Serious attention must therefore be given to the political impact of force employment on the domestic political system.

The international ramifications of force employment are no less serious. Reaction of allies and potential aggressors must be included as part of the political calculations. Similarly, the political repercussions within the target area must be weighed in terms of intended outcome. It is difficult to isolate the target area. Intervention usually affects contiguous areas and regional balances of power, as well as nationalistic and racial sensitivities. No intervention can be undertaken without creating unforeseen political and social consequences which may be to the disadvantage of the intervening power. In such circumstances, multi-lateral employment of force may be the desired method, yet unilateral force employment may be the only alternative.

There are serious questions that must be answered before undertaking force employment. In less than clearly perceived crises and major wars, these questions limit the scope of force employment and narrow the range of policy options for the American policy elite. These questions include, but are not limited to the following: Under what conditions will Congress, the public, and other political actors support U.S. military intervention? Once intervention takes place, can the United States withdraw at an appropriate time without creating a sense of defeat or abandonment? What are the likely consequences of intervention? What are the consequences of withdrawal without accomplishing policy goals? Should intervention be attempted without clear domestic political support?

## MILITARY REQUIREMENTS AND CAPABILITIES

Military requirements and capabilities are dictated by the national interest as translated into political-military policy. In its ability to credibly employ force and engage in low intensity conflict, the American military appears inadequate. We have already identified a number of political reasons for this situation. There are also a number of military considerations, including the prevalence of a "conventional" military wisdom, perceived costs in resources, and the nature of military planning and organization.

Underlying American military philosophy is the assumption that military formations trained for conventional battle are adequate to engage in low intensity conflict. Moreover, this "generalist" attitude prevails throughout the military system. Simply stated, "common" service training for appropriate military units is considered adequate to respond to almost all contingencies. The fact of the matter is, however, that the highly political-social sensitive character of low intensity conflict and force employment require a dimension that is hardly touched upon in standard military training or professional education. Additionally, military planners find it difficult to reallocate funds and shift priorities. The costs of developing and maintaining adequate military posture for force employment outside the European context may be too costly, requiring reduction of the high technology and capital-intensive posture required for modern nuclear and major conventional wars.

As a result, military planning for force employment usually means reliance on ad hoc command structures devised from existing conventional formations and military forces composed of conventionally trained and equipped units. Similarly, well established procedures and operational guidelines govern, which are based on conventional considerations. Success in low intensity operations, however, usually requires intense efforts in all phases of political-military operations over a long period of time. Additionally, procedures and operational guidelines may require imagination and innovation - considerations that are usually absent from standard practice.

For example, Ranger battalions and Special Forces units in the Army may need to be restructured to develop a combined light infantry force capable of low intensity conflict. Such restructuring may require a Special Forces type organization with a capability generally associated with Ranger battalions. Additionally, doctrines need to be developed along with professional education aimed at developing a deep understanding of the political-social character of Third World areas and how these translate into the complex environment of low intensity conflicts.

The American military, to be sure, must prepare for a range of potential crises. The starting point for such preparation is a clear policy and military programs that are placed in a "real life" context. A number of scenarios should be developed based on the criteria and considerations discussed earlier. Such scenarios need not, nor can they, include every

conceivable   contingency.    Sufficient   scenarios   should   be
developed,   however,   to   cover   a   range   of   the   major   types   of
intervention;  i.e.,  less  than  Korean  type  limited  war,  various
types  of  insurgency  (Guerrilla  I,  II,  and  III),  and  Vietnam
type  operations  (see  figure  4.1).

Moreover,    forces-in-being    cannot    be    structured    to
respond  to  every  possible  low  intensity  contingency.    What  is
needed  is  an  examination  and  assessment  of  prototype  forces
(including  political  and  military  command  structure)  that  can
be   quickly   shaped   to   meet   the   most   likely   crises.    This
necessitates  flexibility  in  the  organization,  innovative  command
system,  highly  mobile  and  reactive  forces,  and  a  responsive
decision-making  structure.

Contingency  planning  must  also  be  based  on  something
more   than   "vault"   plans.    This   refers   to   the   tendency   of
military  planners  to  develop  plans  for  every  conceivable  contingency,  with  little  reference  to  the  issues  of  national  will,
political  considerations,  and  prevailing  military  posture.    These
plans  are  then  filed  in  "vaults"  to  be  used  when  an  appropriate  contingency  arises.    Such  plans  may  be  useful  for  clear
crises  -  i.e.,  a  NATO-Warsaw  pact  conflict  -  but  they  quickly
lose  their  validity  when  applied  to  force  employment  and  low
intensity   conflict   unless   they   are   constantly   revised   in   a
dynamic  way.    What  this  means  is  that  there  must  be  ongoing
military   training   and   education   programs   to   insure   that   appropriate  military  forces  develop  and  maintain  a  knowledge  of
the  Third  World,  and  understand  the  ambiguities  and  complexities  characteristic  of  military  intervention  in  a  Third  World
context.

For   example,   it   is   conceivable   that   a   realistic   scenario
considers  the  occupation  of  the  Panama  Canal  by  a  hostile
power  or  group  in  the  1980s.    To  be  sure,  a  conventional
U.S.  military  response  is  to  be  expected  -  but  without  serious
consideration  of  insurgency  warfare,  a  response  to  the  occupation  of  the  Panama  Canal  based  solely  on  conventional
operations  would,  in  the  long  run,  create  conditions  destruc-
tive  of  the  very  purpose  of  the  policy.    Major  considerations
in  such  a  scenario  should  include,  among  other  things,  the
type  and  number  of  U.S.  military  formations  required  for  the
recovery  of  the  Canal,  the  expected  nature  of  the  military
operations,  the  political-social  conditions  in  Panama,  identification  of  friendly  and  hostile  groups  within  the  target  area,  the
anticipated  reaction  of  Latin  American  states,  domestic  and
international  political  ramifications,  the  long-range  political
goal,  the  expected  costs  in  manpower  and  materiel,  and  the
effect   on   America's   military   posture   elsewhere.    Similar
questions  should  be  raised  in  each  scenario,  regardless  of  the
target  area.    The  important  point,  however,  is  that  military
requirements  and  capabilities  as  they  are  reflected  in  "forces-
in-being"  must  be  realistically  integrated  into  plans.

Military requirements are impossible to determine if they are not based on a consistent pattern of political-military policy that reflects clear national security interests. Attempting to develop military requirements in relationship to military capabilities, isolated from clearly defined policy goals, simply relegates military requirements to some perceived imminent crisis or financial criteria. In the first instance, military requirements become the prisoners of wide fluctuations reflecting threat perceptions of the moment. In the latter case, military requirements may have little relationship to military capabilities and political-military policy.

Brent Scowcroft's observations with respect to Soviet-American relationships is particularly appropriate in this context:

> We must therefore learn to curb our fast shifting reactions to the Soviet Union, both of fear and complacency. It is this oscillation between these two poles, this lack of consistency and conviction that can do the most harm. It prompts us to waste valued resources and to strain our alliance understandings. These oscillations increase the chance of miscalculation and they lead to crash programs whenever anxiety rises. To cut back military efforts in periods of calm and to swell them in times of crisis is a most inefficient way to operate a defense establishment.(7)

The reaction of the Carter administration in early 1980 to the Soviet intervention in Afghanistan is a case in point. Increased defense spending, as contrasted to the reduction of defense in the preceding three years, may well have been ". . . fast shifting reactions to the Soviet Union, both of fear and complacency."(8)

Assessments of military requirements in the context of force employment and issues of low intensity conflict, therefore, must begin with such questions as: What mix of nuclear and non-nuclear forces is necessary to achieve political-military goals? What training is necessary to prepare military units for non-nuclear contingencies? What logistical support is necessary to support military operations? What tactical doctrines are relevant? What should be the force structures and command and control arrangements? Under what conditions should the United States disengage following intervention and what does this mean in terms of military capability? What are the costs, political as well as in terms of resources, for developing a credible non-nuclear capability? What must be included in the education of the military professional to prepare the military institution to respond to a low intensity conflict?

## POLICY GUIDELINES

The translation of policy from the decision stage to implementation is a difficult task fraught with imponderables and miscalculations. But any policy must, at a minimum, integrate goals with programs and resources. American policy designed to respond to low intensity conflict and force employment must be based on the recognition of the special character of nonnuclear contingencies and their relation to the credibility of American deterrence and interests. The identification of American interests must be clear and articulated in understandable terms. Political-military strategy must be designed to protect those interests, with military posture and national will capable of supporting the strategy. Without a correlation of these elements, policy is doomed to failure. If these cannot be correlated, then the sights of policy must be lowered to realistically reflect capabilities and political resolve. Yet, if policy goals remain set, then military capability must be strengthened and national will sensitized to the level necessary to reach the goals.
As one commentator has written:

American power - economic, military and spiritual - must be shaped anew to protect free world interests. What is the meaning of war, what is our global strategy? We must recalibrate the mix of weapons and bases. We need to jar our allies to reconsider the purposes and forms of our alliances. We desperately need a new intelligence capacity. We need to recharge our technology and leap ahead of Soviet weaponry. We need an energy strategy for survival, not for re-election.
. . . We must certainly decide where and how we can wage the most effective "bloodless" battle to discourage terrorism and aggression. But we must, too, decide where and how we best can fight if blood must be shed.(9)

In the final analysis, the cornerstone of effective policy is the balancing of military posture, national will, and national interests. Successful policy is rarely the sole result of scientific application of this balance derived from mathematical assessments. It is generally the result of the meshing of the science of policy-making with the art of leadership. This requires wisdom based on political acumen, intellectual sensitivity, and a sense of history. What makes it more difficult is that the "meshing" of science and art is necessary at many levels of the policy process and from a number of those involved in the instrumentalities for implementing policy. There-

fore, military professionals, as well as civilian policy makers
and elected officials, need the wisdom to know when and how
to engage in "bloodless battles" and "where and how we best
can fight if blood must be shed."

## NOTES

1. The term non-nuclear contingencies or conflicts is
used in conjunction with low intensity conflict. They represent a scale of conflicts that are non-nuclear and not major
conventional wars and are on the lower end of the conflict
spectrum (see figure 4.1 on Conflict Spectrum).
2. Walter Goldstein, "Which is the West That is Likely to
Survive?", Walter Goldstein (Ed.), The Western Will to Survive
(Report of a Wingspread Conference, The Johnson Foundation,
June, 1977), p. 20.
3. For an extremely useful account of one aspect of
force employment, see Harry M. Blechman and Stephan S.
Kaplan, Force Without War: U.S. Armed Forces as a Political
Instrument. Washington, D.C.: Brookings Institution, 1978.
4. One of the most balanced accounts is Guenter Lewy,
America in Vietnam. New York: Oxford University Press,
1978.
5. Robert E. Osgood, "The Reappraisal of Limited War,"
in Eugene Rosi, American Defense and Detente; Readings in
National Security Policy. New York: Dodd, Mead and Co.,
1973, p. 466.
6. Earl C. Ravenal, "The Case for Strategic Disengagement," Foreign Affairs, April, 1973, p. 513.
7. Brent Scowcroft, "Western Security in the Coming
Years," in Goldstein, The Western Will, p. 14.
8. See note 7.
9. Hugh Sidey, "Carter Must Accept Today's Perilous
Truths," Chicago Sun-Times, January 6, 1980, p. 12.

# 5 Vietnam and the Professional Military

"I will be damned if I will permit the U.S. Army, its institutions, its doctrine and its tradition to be destroyed just to win this lousy war."(1) In a moment of candor and frustration, a senior American general thus expressed the real tragedy of the Vietnam involvement. The issue for the U.S. military in Vietnam was not whether the war was just or unjust, nor that they should serve there, but rather how well the job was done to defeat the enemy, and what impact the total experience would have on the military institution and the profession. At best, the issue is in doubt and the experience painful.

This chapter is an attempt to provide some insights into the nature of the professional reassessment occurring in the U.S. Army. Stemming primarily from the Vietnam experience, the issues involved have not yet been clearly articulated or specifically associated with distinct groups within the officer corps. Yet there are discernible signs indicating that the monistic military order may be struggling to reassert itself in a professional environment which has developed some internal criticism and skepticism.

Many military officers would prefer to label Vietnam an aberrant military experience. Because of the difficulties of the war, the highly political nature of our involvement, and the divisiveness it has caused in American society, they feel that it is not representative of the true role and efficiency of the military. Moreover, a number of political leaders as well as intellectuals believe it may be an isolated case of U.S. policy. On the other hand, various military officers particularly in the intermediate grades - the emerging elite - view Vietnam as the face of the future, a kind of war that the U.S. military must be prepared for from now on. For these officers, Vietnam represents a virtual watershed, not only in terms of victory or defeat, but in its impact on the profession and the military institutions.(2)

75

It would be foolish to blame the Vietnam involvement for all of the ills of our society or for those of the military. However, for the professional officer it undoubtedly has been a catalytic agent – the basis for self-examination and a re-assessment of professional norms. There is no doubt that the military will survive and that the profession will endure. What counts is the substance of professionalism that will emerge from the experience.

That the military has become highly introspective con-cerning the war is shown by recent articles in professional military journals arguing the virtues of the traditional military approach in countering insurgency war. In analyzing these articles, one can identify distinctions between the tradition-alists and modernists, and among modernists themselves, as to the proper response to this form of warfare. At professional schools, as well as the academies, there has been an am-biguous and ambivalent reaction to the U.S. role in Vietnam.

Given the highly publicized military operations in Vietnam, some professionals tend to be defensive, rationalizing the conduct of the war in apologetic tones. Others not only blame civilians for the involvement, but also charge that once the going got tough the military was abandoned by the same civilians who earlier had implored intervention. We have an interesting phenomenon in which civilians accuse the military and in turn are accused by the military of responsibility for the intervention and deepening commitment. Current charges and countercharges are only the prelude to serious recrimina-tions that eventually will bring into focus contending versions of the U.S. role in Vietnam.

From what do these problems stem? Faced with a major – and quite unprecedented – assignment in a war with little likelihood that conventional tactics and superior technology could bring about a victory, the U.S. military had to readjust its tactics, reassess its purpose and change its image. Com-pounding these difficulties was the lack of popular support of the war reflected in a variety of ways in the public attitude toward the military. The ambiguities of the conflict combined with its cost stimulated wide-ranging debate within the military concerning military policy and the limits of military power. Army officers from the rank of General on down were investi-gated and in some instances court-martialed for questionable roles in Vietnam operations. Uncertainty about the legality of commands and implementing orders brought into question a whole range of issues concerning not only morality but the strategy and tactics of the war. The consequences have been a general questioning of the modes of conventional leadership and discipline and a critical reassessment of the meaning of professionalism by military officers themselves.

## GUERRILLA WARFARE

It would seem unnecessary after our years of costly experience and the volumes published on the nature of guerrilla insurgency, especially the oft-quoted words of Mao Tse-tung, to review the concept of this type of war that has caused such repercussions within the United States and the American military profession. Yet, for all the analyses and assessments, prevailing opinions indicate a degree of ignorance concerning the fundamentals of revolutionary and counter-revolutionary guerrilla warfare.

One of the major difficulties is that no amount of intellectual analysis and study can translate principle into policy. It requires psychological and cultural empathy to tailor a counter-revolutionary tactic conceived by a Western, technological, democratic society to an environment reflecting a non-Caucasian, underdeveloped system and an Asian culture. Certainly, one has to look beyond traditional practices and Western organizational structures. In studying the impact of Vietnam on the U.S. professional, therefore, it would seem appropriate first to re-examine the nature of revolutionary warfare.

Although guerrilla warfare can be traced to the pre-Christian era, only in the most recent period of the twentieth century has it evolved into a systematic mode of action. In modern terms, it is not simply military action by irregular troops of militia but a form of warfare whose main purpose is to subvert or destroy the existing government so that the revolutionaries can impose their own government. Not only can this include all of the forms of warfare normally associated with the conventional battlefield; it also embraces those forms that we conveniently label "unconventional." Indeed, this type of warfare combines action in practically all fields of human endeavor - political, social, economic and psychological. Its strategy is to mobilize the masses, make them politically aware, and incite them to demand from the existing government the kinds of things, such as an improvement in the quality of life, that the government may not be able to produce. In essence the revolutionaries attempt to achieve political goals by mass organization combined with military action. The main target is the existing political and social system and the main participants are the people. Involvement of the "people" is one of the revolutionary's basic tasks. In this sense both revolutionaries and counter-revolutionaries must concentrate on organizing the peasants, who in Vietnam make up over 75 percent of the population.

The success of the revolution depends on the effectiveness of the political cadres and their influence with the masses. According to the primer of a leading revolutionary:

"Only on a basis of strong political organization could semi-armed organizations be set up firmly, guerrilla groups and guerrilla units organized which have close connection with the revolutionary masses, eventually to further their activities and development."(3)

Conditions for revolutionary warfare are found in political systems where the political organization and the government's administrative departments are incapable of dealing with problems at the local level; that is, where there are unresponsive rural societies, tensions, grievances, and in the main an uncompromising government. This well describes the situation in South Vietnam beginning with the Diem regime in 1958, through the military governments following Diem's assassination until the most recent period.

How do you counter a revolution? In simple terms, the proper counter-revolutionary measures are those connected with more effective and efficient government.

The most significant point to be noticed is that Communist influence can exist largely because of the absence of civil administration and government control in the areas concerned. This is basic in all Communist-dominated rural areas in all developing countries and is a crucial point in planning counter-measures against a Communist-led national liberation struggle to overthrow any government that is not Communist. No amount of military pressure can succeed unless it is carried out hand in hand with the introduction [of] government administration in the areas concerned.(4)

In other words, for counter-revolution to succeed in Vietnam the counter-revolutionary forces would have to get down to the village and hamlet level to create effective local government. In turn, the legitimacy of the South Vietnamese government would rest on the degree of its responsiveness to the village society. How could the U.S. military accomplish this? The obvious answer is that it could not. No amount of major U.S. military effort could create a successful counter-revolution without a relatively efficient and committed South Vietnamese government. The American contribution was chiefly in the miltary area, which most revolutionists would recognize as an auxiliary part of the revolutionary struggle. Additionally, the U.S. effort was conducted in conventional terms, using conventional responses and bringing about ambiguous results.

In 1965, when the first large-scale commitment of U.S. ground troops occurred, American units found themselves facing a Viet Cong on the verge of military victory and hence deployed in conventional, large-unit fashion. The Americans responded accordingly, and the casualties they suffered, although small in comparison with the enemy's, were significant enough to cause dismay in the United States and a certain degree of uneasiness in professional ranks. Furthermore, enemy casualties coupled with the destruction of enemy units did not necessarily lead to progress in prosecuting the war. There are professionals who would argue that the search-and-destroy and attrition tactics followed by the United States were counter-productive to the cause of counter-insurgency; adhering to conventional perceptions, they were completely divorced from the psychological and political realities of guerrilla warfare.

A number of new tactics evolved, including helicopter troop movements and the massive use of air strikes and artillery. This not only limited U.S. casualties but provided a counter-revolutionary weapon that was difficult for the enemy to cope with. If enemy units could be located and pinpointed, they could be attacked successfully. However, in more populated areas, or where there was difficulty in locating and confining enemy units, the massive use of firepower destroyed huts, animals, and ricelands, as well as Vietnamese who happened to be in the way. Eventually, the use of advanced technology and massive firepower led to increasing criticism of battlefield tactics that failed to distinguish between peasants and the Viet Cong. Many critics began to wonder how such tactics could create sympathy for the counter-revolution, and questions were also raised in the professional ranks.

After the 1968 Tet offensive proved that military victory was improbable for either side, the U.S. military concerned itself more with the political and social aspects of the revolutionary war. Attempts were made to modernize the South Vietnamese army and give it a broader combat role - in what became the Vietnamization policy. By the time the North Vietnamese launched their offensive in 1972, which was predominantly a conventional invasion of the South, most American ground units had departed Vietnam, and for better or worse the Vietnamese experience had left its mark on the profession.


## AMERICAN COUNTER-INSURGENCY


The apparent inability of the U.S. military to bring the Vietnam war to an early conclusion, despite its vaunted technological skills and relatively limitless resources, is at the root of the latest antimilitary sentiments in the United States. On the other hand, few Americans recognize that not only were highly technical skills not always well adapted to the task at hand but resources were indeed limited insofar as permission to apply them to the enemy was concerned. Military logic rarely operates on the assumption that the weapons and resources available will be deliberately restricted with respect to the battlefield. Undoubtedly a quick victory - or one within a two-to-three-year period - would not have raised such issues concerning military effectiveness. It is forgotten that a number of the techniques used in Vietnam were also used in Korea with little public outcry; for example, mass B-29 bombing raids, napalm, and free-fire zones in which anything moving became a legitimate target.

The large-scale use of manpower and the rapid turnover of combat troops brought into the military institutions large groups of young men who had been exposed to the emerging youth culture and its antimilitary sentiments. It was inevitable that these sentiments and lifestyles would find their way into combat units in Vietnam. Moreover, this occurred, beginning in 1968, coincident with the political dramatics at home, which saw President Lyndon Johnson declining to run for a second term, the Eugene McCarthy phenomenon, the assassination of Robert Kennedy, and the chaos erupting at the Democratic National Convention in Chicago.

In such circumstances, it became difficult for the professionals to justify the war in the eyes of their men and to create the combat spirit and legitimacy needed to maintain organizational cohesion. While various sectors of American society, as well as a number of elected national officials and members of the academic community, were condemning the war and the military for the perpetuation of what they considered to be the United States' imperialist aggression in Vietnam, the profession was committed to seeing the war through against all odds.

In the professional view it appeared that the society had committed the nation to war while at the same time condemning the military for implementing a policy initiated by elected civilian leaders. What is more important, this feeling gave rise to professional suspicion concerning the working of the political system and generated doubt about the military objectives associated with the war. Antiwar activities led to dissent even at the combat unit level. In a number of instances, officers at the small unit level were faced with recalcitrance and subordinates' outright opposition to carrying out combat missions. Occasionally, combat leaders found themselves attempting to develop a consensus among their subordinates before undertaking a mission. Some junior officers, not far removed in age and experience from their men, sympathized with the troops and created difficulties in implementing orders. Sometimes passive acquiescence to orders reduced combat missions to "lip service" exercises. It was not unknown, for example, for combat patrols into contested or enemy-held territory to move a few yards from friendly positions, remain all night in relative safety, and return the following morning reporting no enemy contact. Traditional professionals shook their heads and wondered what had happened to the U.S. Army.

Following the large-scale commitment of U.S. ground troops to Vietnam in 1965, many professional military men felt that the military solution to the war could be found within a relatively short period of time. For the professional officer, it also meant that he had to "get his ticket punched," not only with a tour in Vietnam, but hopefully with command duty. For the infantryman, working for his combat infantryman's badge, also, service in Vietnam was a highly desirable assignment. After all, as Army men were inclined to say, "It's the only war we've got." As a result from 1965 to 1970 the military sought ticket-punching service in Vietnam as a prerequisite for success in their later careers. It was during this time that Army professionals became notorious for their scramble for command duty. A command position filled for six months or even less was readily evacuated to allow another professional to obtain his command time. Although the short tours of duty in Vietnam as a whole and the much shorter tours for commanders created difficulties in combat and impaired efficiency and morale, the procedure served the purpose of allowing a great number of professionals to acquire combat command experience.

## THE PROFESSIONAL MILITARY GAP

Besides assignment to U.S. combat units, professionals served as advisers to South Vietnamese army units or regional and provincial militia forces. Generally, these assignments were considered less important than service with U.S. units - at least for career purposes. The name of the game was to secure command duty or serve in your specialty in the U.S. command structure. Only belatedly was service with South Vietnamese forces recognized as an important element in the total counter-revolutionary role. But it still remained of secondary importance in career consideration. The ideal for career purposes was to have two tours of duty in Vietnam or an extended tour of up to 18 months. In this way, the officer could not only serve with U.S. troops but could acquire experience with Vietnamese units as well.

Many professionals who served with the Vietnamese found their jobs frustrating. Recognizing that their function called for something more than small unit tactics and conventional military relationships, they became immersed in the Vietnamese social fabric and the complex social and political interrelationships of the South Vietnamese military system. In such positions, many discovered that they were ill prepared to deal with an alien culture. Professional competence and technical skills proved inadequate to cope with the myriad problems associated with an Asian military structure bound up in governing as well as conducting counter-revolutionary war. Trying to assist, or simply to move, an enigmatic ally proved frustrating. The Oriental qualities of indirectness, patience, and political shrewdness, to note but a few, were incompatible with the American culture and the professional military attitude of "getting on with it." The experience convinced many professionals of the need for a highly political and social approach to counter-revolution. As a result, some felt that the U.S. effort had been misdirected, while others felt that engaging in counter-revolutionary efforts was futile given the cultural complexities of the Vietnamese personality.

Staff duty, epitomized by the Military Assistance Command Vietnam in Saigon, was generally pleasant for senior officers. But for intermediate-grade officers who were younger, more aggressive, and perhaps more sensitive to the ambiguous nature of the war, Saigon represented many of the ills of the U.S. Army's involvement in Vietnam. A significant gap opened up between perceptions of the war in Saigon and those in the field, and officers who served in both arenas were inevitably struck by the unreal view of the war from Saigon. Furthermore, the lifestyle of the U.S. military in Saigon greatly differed from that in the field: Vietnamese mistresses, nightclubs, garden parties, and the helter-skelter life of urban Saigon plainly did not fit in with the realities at Firebase Charlie or Lai Khe.

While the optimists at higher echelons proclaimed the "light at the end of the tunnel," frustrated professionals serving in the field, particularly with the Vietnamese, knew better. Their attempts at correcting distortions regarding the progress of the conflict generally met with official indifference, and in some cases admonition. To them, Saigon represented an unresponsive bureaucracy divorced from the realities of the war.

Moreover, Special Forces units, operating primarily with the Vietnamese, hill people, or mercenaries in covert counter-revolutionary efforts, comprised a nontraditional military structure and this created resentment among many regular military men. Because of this attitude, Special Forces officers were convinced that accusations in 1969 against five of their number concerning their role in killing a suspected double agent were part of a determined effort within the traditional Army to discredit the Green Berets. For the professional officer to be continually associated with the Special Forces and their activities came close to sounding the death knell to his career. The Green Berets and the purposes for which they were organized stood apart from and at variance with the formal Army structure, and they were thought of as unorthodox - their units an outlet for mavericks and rebels.

Even though the Special Force may be one of the most effective organizations in a counter-revolutionary campaign, such professional struggles were common on the battlefields of Vietnam.

## THE AFTERMATH

Officers' views on the war have obviously been influenced by their personal experience. Many who served in military assistance capacities or as advisers to the Vietnamese feel that the main effort should have been in these areas. In the long run, they may be right. Those who served with U.S. units, on the other hand, believe a greater U.S. combat effort would have solved the problem. In any case, the different experiences and outlooks have evoked varied reactions to the U.S. role in Vietnam. Within the U.S. Army, a "great debate" resulting from professional assessments and analysis regarding the Vietnam experience finds some arguing that the military was successful since its prime purpose was to apply military power against the enemy's military power. In contrast, there are those who argue that the use of military power divorced from the realities of the environment creates a distortion in the relative success of the total war effort. Still others would argue that counter-insurgency wars are to be shunned and the focus placed on what the U.S. military is best at - the conduct of highly technical and sophisticated combat. The traditional orientation seems to favor a return to the Europe-type ground war for which American forces are so splendidly equipped and prepared.

An ethical or moral content for the profession has also developed out of the Vietnam war, stemming particularly from the My Lai massacre and the case of Lieutenant Calley. For many, it is difficult to reconcile the wanton killing of civilians with the precepts of professional competence and ethics. To be sure, some military men consider My Lai an aberration, atypical of U.S. Army operations, while others claim that it is a virtue of the profession that more My Lai's did not occur. Nevertheless, there is a nagging suspicion that My Lai uncovered serious professional inadequacies, given the fact that it involved a number of professionals, including General officers. This incident has done much to stimulate a general reassessment of the profession, not only in terms of its corporateness, but primarily as regards individual attitudes and behavior. It may be years before the results are manifested in the profession and the military institution.

Most military men, feeling that they are ultimately servants of the state, view their Vietnamese involvement without bitterness, as part of their professional commitment.

However, few desire to become involved in a war such as Vietnam to gain combat experience or so that the profession may undergo testing under fire. Critics to the contrary, professional military men have needs and desires and a sense of right and wrong just as other human beings do. They do not subscribe to the idea of killing simply for the sake of killing. To be sure, there are those who relish combat duty, but rarely do modern professionals seek to lead the nation into war. As a matter of fact, a number of years prior to the United States' active involvement in Vietnam, some of the highest ranking officers in the U.S. Army were counseling against it. General Matthew B. Ridgway, Chief of Staff in 1954 and 1955, wrote the following prophetic words in 1956:

> As I have pointed out earlier in this narrative, when the day comes for me to face my Maker and account for my actions, the thing I would be most humbly proud of was the fact that I fought against, and perhaps contributed to preventing the carrying out of, some hare-brained tactical schemes which would have cost the lives of thousands of men. To that list of tragic accidents that fortunately never happened I would add the Indo-China intervention. . . .
> We could have fought in Indo-China. We could have won, if we had been willing to pay the tremendous cost in men and money that such intervention would have required - a cost that in my opinion would have eventually been as great as, or greater than, that we paid in Korea. In Korea, we had learned that air and naval power alone cannot win a war and the inadequate ground forces cannot win one either. It was incredible to me that we had forgotten that bitter lesson so soon - that we were on the verge of making the same tragic error. . . .
> If we did go into Indo-China, we would have to win. We would have to go in with a military force adequate in all branches, and that meant a very strong ground force - an Army that could not only stand the normal attrition of battle, but could absorb heavy casualties from the jungle heat, and the rots and fevers which afflict the white man in the tropics. We could not afford to accept anything short of decisive military victory.(5)

All that General Ridgway warned against in 1956 had taken place by 1972. Aside from the tragedies wrought by lives lost, divisiveness in society, and frustration's effect on the American psyche, the greatest casualty of Vietnam in the long run may prove to be the military profession.

## CONCLUSIONS

What will ultimately emerge from this painful experience for the military is difficult to foresee.  Providing a unique environment and a different kind of war, Vietnam has tested the profession and the military institution to such a point that the professionals themselves became openly critical of the system.

A number of officers were dismayed because they felt that the traditional approach to war was in this case inappropriate. Concern for body count and real estate simply did not get to the heart of the matter in combating revolutionary war.  The use of air power and traditional modes of leadership likewise failed to make a decisive impact.  Most of the larger unit (brigade and division) leaders had received their initial combat training and command duty in World War II or Korea.  In essence, therefore, the tactics of World War II as modified by the Korean experience were applied to Vietnam.  Only the most farsighted officer could in the early years of the war sense the ineffectiveness of this policy or identify the basic dilemma inhering in the conventional military commitment.  It is only in recent years that a number of professionals, frustrated and disillusioned by the U.S. military role in Vietnam, have spoken out.  Although by no means in the majority, there are still enough of them to suggest a possible alternative view of the war while stimulating debate within the professional ranks and casting some suspicion on prevailing norms.

As suggested earlier, the professional officer is probably not as concerned with the social morality of the war itself as with the military institution's response to the demands of the war - and especially with professional competence to deal with the nontraditional environment of revolutionary war.  This concern has engendered debate among traditionalists, transitionalists, and modernists within the professional ranks.(6) The traditionalists generally feel that more application of power in accordance with accepted Western concepts of the principles of war would have won.  Transitionalists believe proper application of power with some new techniques and approaches could have given a significant advantage to the U.S. forces and might even have been enough to win.  Modernists are apt to argue that revolutionary war in an alien culture cannot be "won" by the conventional employment of troops whose cultures rests on a modern, Western value system.  These are not to be taken as neat categories, but they do give some indication of the nature of the debate.

The profession, of course, can defend itself while rationalizing its role in Vietnam by simply stressing that "We did our job."  This not only avoids the major issue but suggests the dominance of the traditional view.  It also invites increasing criticism from civilian intellectuals and political leaders

who could justifiably raise the specter of a robot-like institution and naive military leaders.  For their part, a number of
modernist officers as well as some transitionalists would question the "professionalism" in this kind of response.  They see
the danger in perpetuating a profession that increasingly rests
on past glories and prevailing institutional inertia while losing
its ability to develop innovative and imaginative concepts for
the future.  The impact on the profession could be disastrous,
leading to institutional decay and professional incompetence.
Society, attuned to the new demands of the postindustrial era,
could move rapidly ahead, leaving an obsolete military in its
wake.

Hence, the debate over Vietnam in reality reflects a
larger concern with the nature of professionalism in the post-
Vietnam era, the premise being that the ambiguities of the
Vietnam experience and the ambivalence it has created in the
professional ethic (within a context of societal disenchantment
with the military) calls for a resuscitation of professionalism.
It is not suggested that the profession undergo institutional
revolution or ethical rebirth.  Rather, there is a need to
create greater institutional sensitivity and responsiveness
consonant with professional reality and honesty.  To do this,
there must be a concerted effort to stimulate independent
thought and foster an intellectual atmosphere in which an
individual can inquire without being accused of professional
treason.  Moreover, these professional initiatives must be
accompanied by new institutional "rules of the game" which
foster adaptability and dynamism.

Whether this can be accomplished will depend on how
quickly the younger modernist officers and those sharing their
views reach the rank of General, and how quickly they can
infuse the institution and the profession with a greater flexibility and a broader outlook.  This assumes, of course, that
today's modernist officers will retain their "modern" views.
The institution has a built-in socialization process which favors
orthodoxy, and the danger is that the institution will capture
such officers before they can capture the institution.


NOTES


1.  Quoted in Ward Just, Military Men.  New York:
Alfred Knopf, 1970, p. 185.
2.  In a survey of over 400 military officers attending the
various war colleges in 1973, it was found that almost 70
percent felt that counter-insurgency was the type of war most
likely to be fought by the United States in the next decade.
The survey was conducted by Bruce Russett, Yale University.

3.   General   Vo   Nguyen   Giap,   People's War,   People's
Army.   New York:   Praeger, 1962, pp. 77-78.
    4.   C. C. Too, "Some Salient Features in the Experience
of Defeating Communism in Malaya, with Particular Regard to
the Method of New Villages."   Paper presented at the International Seminar on Communism in Asia, Onyang, Korea, June
19-25, 1966, p. 3.
    5.   Matthew  B.  Ridgway,  Soldier:  Memoirs of Matthew
B. Ridgway.   New York:   Harper & Row, 1956, p. 277-278.
    6.   See  Sam  C. Sarkesian,  "Political  Soldiers:   Per-
spectives on Professionalism in the U.S. Military," in Midwest
Journal of Political Science, May 1972, pp. 239-258.   Generally, the traditionalists are officers who gained most of their
combat experience in World War II.   Dominated by academy
graduates, they are now usually of senior rank.   The transitionalists' experience derives from the Korean War and shortly
thereafter.   Although many of these are today Lieutenant
Colonels or Colonels (with some Generals), they were not so
imbued with the professional ethic that they were oblivious to
the ambiguities of limited war.   The modernist category identifies those officers who are closest to the youth culture and
the Vietnam era and perhaps have the greatest empathy with
civilian society and its problems.   Most of the modernists are
in the company grade or junior fieldgrade category with
academy graduates in the minority.   Obviously, however, these
categorizations are relative.   The younger officer with Vietnam
experience today will be the traditionalist of tomorrow.   See
chapter 8.

# 6 Revolution and the Limits of Military Power: The Haunting Specter of Vietnam

Over 500 years before the time of Christ, Sun Tzu wrote that war was a vital matter to the State and that it should be appraised in terms of five fundamental factors. The first of these factors, he noted, was moral influence. "By moral influence I mean that which causes the people to be in harmony with their leaders, so that they will accompany them in life and unto death without fear of mortal peril."(1)

About 2,200 years later, the British Army struggled over the issue of moral influence. During the American War of Independence, in 1775, "There was a considerable feeling amongst army officers that they were being called on to suppress rebellion in a just cause. . . . Lord Amherst, the Commander-in-Chief, refused to take command in the field of America. . . ."(2) In repudiating his orders to take his regiment to America, the Earl of Effingham, in 1775, stated in the House of Lords, "When the duties of a soldier and a citizen become inconsistent, I shall always think myself obliged to sink the character of the soldier in that of the citizen, till such time as those duties shall again, by the malice of our real enemies, become united."

We are still pondering the dilemma of moral influence and military effectiveness 2,500 years after Sun Tzu. Scholars, officials, military men, and students still argue the contradictions of the U.S. role in Vietnam. Within the professional military ranks there remains restiveness about Vietnam, most recently manifested by the publication of two volumes of the Peers report about the My Lai massacres.(3)

In the many issues associated with the U.S. involvement, some of the most important have to do with moral influence and ethics both in society and the military. These arise in most wars, but it can be argued that in no modern war prior to Vietnam has the moral issue been crucial in determining the outcome. Indeed, one can reasonably argue that wars in the future, aside from a nuclear holocaust, may very well evolve around the questions of nationalism and revolution in terms of developing versus developed nations. Thus, a key question evolving from the U.S. Vietnam experience is whether a democratic society such as the United States can successfully engage in counter-revolutionary wars outside of its own borders. It seems that much of the answer lies in a moral and ethical perspective rather than questions of tactical or strategic military concerns.

The purpose of this chapter is to examine the question of democratic society and counter-revolutionary war within the context of Sun Tzu's "moral influence." We will inquire into the relationships between the military institution and society, the value systems, and the imperatives of revolution and counter-revolution in the context of a developing society. On the premise that a revolutionary war is to a greater degree "political" than conventional conflicts and is more likely to be a conflict characteristic of societies in the throes of industrialization and political change, the issues involved rest on political-psychological factors rather than military posture. Furthermore, lest we become conditioned to perceive revolutionary conflict only in terms of policy alternatives, strategic and tactical rationalizations, and technological criteria, we need to develop an appreciation of the human dimension. This is the crucial variable of what can or cannot be done in revolutionary war. On another level, the human dimension raises the question of the degree of adaptability of individuals from a modern industrial democratic society to the political-psychological environment of revolution in a non-industrial peasant society based on distinctly different value systems.

The fundamental issue is whether a democratic society, in possession of modern weapons and generally adequate sources of supply, can successfully engage in counter-revolutionary warfare in support of an existing regime in a developing society. These issues are much broader in scope than policy, strategy, and technology; they involve questions of values, legitimacy, and perceptions. Linked as they are to the political psychological issues of revolutionary warfare and values of democracy, these questions directly affect the cohesiveness and purpose of the military institution and its involvement in counter-revolutionary warfare.

## MILITARY LEGITIMACY

Professional cohesion and institutional purpose are the cornerstones of military legitimacy. These are linked in explicit and, at times, subtle ways. Presuming that there is a high degree

of interpenetration between the military and society (as there
is likely to be in modern democratic societies), the military is
sensitive and responsive to the values and perceptions of
society.  More specifically, military purpose must be congruent
to social values while at the same time corresponding to professional military expectations and attitudes.  The greater the
degree of this congruence, the greater the degree of military
cohesion, the more likely that cohesion will reinforce and
increase the convergence between military purpose and social
values.  Thus, society bestows legitimacy on the military
through its perceptions of the military's purpose and its
ideological cohesion.

Society's perceptions of the military rest partly on traditional relationships between armed forces and society, and to a
great degree on professional conduct, attitudes, and institutional effectiveness in dealing with combat as well as with
social and political issues of military society.  In this context,
not only does the concept of "winning" become part of the
legitimacy, but how it is "won" also becomes important.

Military legitimacy alone does not necessarily lead to
successful application of military power, however; military
posture is an essential factor.  There must be a supportive
balance between these two major factors.  It is difficult to be
precise concerning the degree of legitimacy and the kind of
military posture required in any given period or combat situation.  The post-Vietnam era demands one particular intermix,
while the Korean War demanded another.  One can reasonably
argue that Vietnam involvement never achieved an effective
intermix.  More of this later.  Nevertheless, military power, to
be effective, must not only have a military institution capable
of engaging in combat, but must also have the material and
political support of, as well as psychological linkage with,
society.  In simple terms, the military can be only as effective
as society will allow; and conversely, if society supports the
military's involvement in conflict, the military must have the
proper posture to effectively apply military power.  This is
the basic premise behind the concept of "management of
violence in the service of the state."  It is the state that
identifies the enemy, society that provides the political-
psychological succor to carry out necessary policies, and the
military which implements the will of the state.  Each of these
elements are interrelated and must reinforce each other if
successful military policy is to be followed.

To assess the relative balance between military legitimacy
and military posture, one must develop indicators of the
substance of each of these factors.  Where military legitimacy
rests primarily upon image, values, prestige, and purpose,
military posture rests on organization, training, technology,
and leadership.  In other words, military legitimacy is
primarily a psychological dimension or subjective.  Military

posture, on the other hand, is primarily empirically oriented, with emphasis on quantitative and qualitative data; i.e., objective.

To insure an effective degree of military power, therefore, there must be symmetry between subjective and objective factors. We use the term symmetry here rather than balance, because symmetry suggests congruence and support between elements, whereas balance implies equal portions. As we will discuss later, it is conceivable that military legitimacy and military posture need not be balanced to achieve effective military power. Rather, they need to be congruent and supportive of each other.

These relationships can be expressed as follows:

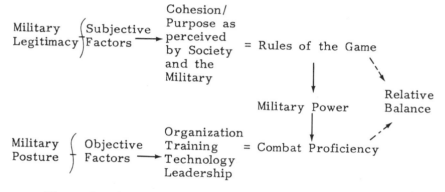

There is always the danger of asymmetry - where subjective factors, for example, may become increasingly dominant while objective factors become less able to achieve minimum influence on application of military power. This situation can lead to the politicization of the military and a high degree of civilization, eroding the professional basis of the military institution. Similarly, it is possible for objective factors to become dominant, subduing the influence of subjective factors to such a degree that the military perspective dominates the political institutions - a garrison state condition.

In a democratic society, asymmetry is most likely to develop as a result of contradictions between subjective and objective factors. Thus, the perceptions of society regarding military purpose and behavior may not be in accord with professional military perceptions, and, indeed, absolutely opposed to them. The military in a democratic society cannot remain in this kind of asymmetric relationship with society without destroying its institutional purpose and cohesion. Given the relationships between society and the military in a democratic system, political and social forces will generate pressures for the restoration of symmetry - even at the expense of the military institution.

The contradictions between subjective and objective factors can occur for a variety of reasons: domestic violence, new political perspectives, changing civil-military relations. A major precipitating factor is the military's involvement in external conflict, particularly where the conflict is of a limited nature. All of these situations are interrelated, but each has its own particular thrust and environmental factors. For example, the U.S. involvement in Vietnam was probably the cause of a number of violent domestic acts, which in turn contributed to a new political perspective on politics, developed criticism of the military's role in Vietnam, and ultimately led to a new civil-military relationship.

This chapter will be limited to the study of contradictions developing between subjective and objective factors as a result of the involvement of a third power in an external conflict - revolutionary guerrilla warfare.

In sum, military legitimacy is a function of military cohesion and purpose, which in turn must be in accord with the "rules of the game" as perceived by society. These subjective factors must be harmoniously intermixed with objective factors if symmetry is to be achieved. This is more likely to occur in conventional conflicts where conventional wisdom and unambiguous issues predominate and are not unsettling to traditional civil-military relations within a modern democratic society. Involvement in revolutionary wars distorts the intermix, creating asymmetry. Why this occurs will be discussed in detail later. Suffice it to say here, the nature of revolutionary war does not conform to conventional wisdom, is ambiguous, and places upon the military institution a role which is not congruent to traditional civil-military relationships in a modern democratic system.

## SOLDIERS, SOCIETY, AND VALUES

In a modern democracy, as in virtually all political systems, the military reflects society and must achieve some degree of convergence between societal and military values and expectations if the military is to maintain legitimacy. Democratic society, moreover, presumes that there is a high moral quality to its value system. In this regard, one of the more important elements affecting society's perceptions of the military (and thus military legitimacy) is the correlation between individual behavior and the norms of society. On a more mundane level, the individual actions of a soldier on the battlefield must meet some minimum societal norms while also conforming to certain professional expectations. Thus, the military effectiveness of the individual soldier rests in no small measure on the correspondence of his battlefield behavior with the moral quality of the social values of his society.

Battlefield conduct therefore becomes a visible indicator of institutional purpose, professional conduct, and ideological cohesion. In turn, these visible indicators directly affect the legitimacy with which the military institution is viewed by society. Indeed, such visible indicators are also at the root of the professional's assessment of his own profession. This is not a relationship that can be easily identified or examined. However, it can be reasonably assumed that the behavior of American troops at My Lai, for example, deviated considerably from values of American society and from professional military expectations, thus decreasing military legitimacy in the eyes of society and creating doubts among military men themselves about professional conduct.

In the case of conventional wars such as World War II and, to a great extent, Korea, the behavior patterns and combat responses of the individual are likely to be predictable, coherent and generally within the "rules of the game" of society and in accordance with military expectations. Even in nuclear wars, it may be presumed that there will be a high degree of symmetry and congruence between military institution and society in which the role of the soldier and the enemy can be perceived in "good guy" and "bad guy" terms. Furthermore, the objective factors would more than likely have a clear and direct relationship to the nature of the war and a relevant indicator of its outcome. In other words, in wars where the distinctions between "bad guys" and "good guys" are not ambiguous and the purposes of the military institution are articulated in terms compatible with societal expectations, there is likely to be a high degree of military legitimacy, thus reinforcing military posture.

On the other hand, in revolutionary guerrilla wars, where the soldier must operate closely within the political-social context of another society whose values and perceptions are quite different from his own, and where the outcome of the struggle is viewed in terms of sympathy and loyalty of the indigenous people, the relative clarity of purpose diminishes while the dimensions of the battlefield become submerged in society. Traditional combat responses become inadequate and institutional proficiency suffers. The result easily leads to individual frustration, loss of confidence in the institution, and the general deterioration of cohesion and purpose.

This political-psychological character of revolutionary guerrilla war is the precipitating factor leading directly to asymmetry. Responses to this type of warfare require professional flexibility, institutional adaptation, political astuteness and understanding on the part of civilian and military leaders. In essence, such a response requires a restructuring of traditional civil-military relationships - not an easy adjustment for any society, nor one that is necessarily desired.

The basic issue in Vietnam is this: Can a free
society fight a limited war? That is a strategic
war, a war without hate, a war without massive
popular involvement. To put it differently, the war
in Vietnam is being fought for an abstraction:
American national interest in a nontotalitarian Asian
future. And it is being fought by a new set of
rules which began to emerge during the Korean
War but were forgotten in the subsequent years.
It is very difficult to tell a young soldier, "Go
out there and fight, perhaps die, for a good bargaining position." It is almost impossible to explain
to Congressmen that Vietnam is a crucial testing
ground - on one side for a brilliantly mounted "war
of Liberation," on the other, for our capability to
cope with (and in the future better) such liberators.
What sense, moreover, can the average American
make of our offer to a non-aggressive Hanoi? What,
in short, has happened to the concept of "the
enemy"?(4)

It is this characteristic of revolutionary war that, in the
final analysis, is the most deleterious to the capacity of a
democratic industrial power to influence the course and direction of the struggle. Also, it is this consideration, deriving
from the political-psychological nature of revolutionary war,
that creates tension and conflict with a democratic society,
influences the military institution, and detrimentally affects the
capacity of both the individual soldier and the military institution to perform successfully within the revolutionary war
environment.

A basic dilemma exists in the proposition that an individual from a democratic industrial society can be trained to
acquire the highly complex skills and survival instinct required
for combat, while at the same time instilled with the political-
social knowledge, experience, and commitment to conduct
himself in a professionally competent and socially humane
fashion on the battlefields of revolutionary guerrilla war.
Although similar problems may exist for all forms of combat, it
is the premise here that the struggle associated with revolutionary guerrilla warfare compounds and magnifies the problem
while simultaneously adding new dimensions, requiring not only
a reexamination of the role of the combat soldier, but also a
reassessment of the effectiveness of the military institution in
terms of professional purpose and ideological cohesion.

A revolutionary war is never confined within the
bounds of military action. Because its purpose is to
destroy an existing society and its institutions and
to replace them with a completely new state struc-

ture, any revolutionary war is a unity of which the constituent parts, in varying importance are military, political, economic, social and psychological. For this reason it is endowed with a dynamic quality and a dimension in depth that orthodox wars, whatever their scale, lack. This is particularly true of revolutionary guerrilla war, which is not susceptible to the type of superficial military treatment frequently advocated by antediluvian doctrinaires.(5)

The essential hypothesis rests on the assumption that it is not necessarily the technology of the conflict which places restraints upon military power, but the effect of the environment upon the conduct and efficiency of the individual soldier and the military institution. In exploring the validity of the hypothesis, a number of salient issues must be studied, beginning with the very concept of revolutionary guerrilla warfare.

Admittedly, the hypothesis suggested here becomes invalid if a society and its military institution pursue the goal of "complete victory" regardless of the consequences. This would presume that the industrial democracy engaged in a revolutionary war within a developing society would consider implementing total mobilization at home and use of all of its military arsenal to try to achieve total victory. In essence, this situation presupposes that societal commitment and military purpose would be in accord and held with a sufficient degree of cohesiveness to view the revolutionary war as an overt and direct threat to the nation. However, the probability of a total war involving an industrial democracy within a revolutionary guerrilla war environment is improbable given the context of international politics. The more likely situation is one which would be analogous with the U.S. involvement in Vietnam. Although no attempt will be made to develop "models" concerning democratic industrial society and revolutionary war, it is important to note that whether an industrial society is authoritarian or democratic, it is faced with similar problems of societal expectations, professional commitment, and ideological cohesion, in less than total wars. Both the U.S. involvement in Vietnam and the Soviet role in Hungary and Czechoslovakia are cases in point. Although the latter two are hardly representative of the relationships between industrial and developing societies, they do point out problems similar to the issues discussed in this paper.

## REVOLUTION AND COUNTER-REVOLUTION

As most are aware, Mao Tse-tung's analysis of the nature of revolutionary war has served as a model, more or less, for revolutionary wars in Asia and, in some respects, throughout the world. The three-stage theory of revolutionary guerrilla warfare, combined with societal penetration and finally the consolidation stage, is fundamental to Maoist theory. The essential focus is on political mobilization of the people combined with armed units, which are first and foremost political action cadres.

When revolutionary and counter-revolutionary strategy is translated into more mundane terms on the village level, it creates an environment in which weapons technology and conventional tactics become generally inadequate, while the political-psychological aspects of the struggle become dominant. Attempts at distinguishing friend from foe are many times unsuccessful. Additionally, success at this level normally goes to that side with the greatest political astuteness and ideological identity with the peasantry. In this respect, major concern for both revolutionary and counter-revolutionary forces are the attitudes, sympathies, and activities of the peasants.

Revolutionary cadre organize cells at the village level in an effort to expand the political structure and to persuade villagers to support revolutionary activity. The techniques used in infiltration into and establishing a revolutionary village are highly refined and implemented by trained cadre. The following discussion concerning the sequence of activities by which a village is infiltrated and mobilized is illustrative of these techniques.

One or two members of the revolutionary cadre may appear in a village and seek out the village chief, telling him of the great things they have seen being done for the people in far off places. Before this audience goes very far, the cadre have volunteered their services to help the villagers with their daily chores and the harvest. During the evenings, the villagers are entertained with folk songs and stories, at which time the revolutionary cadre tell of the good life and justice they have witnessed in other lands. Eventually the villagers and the cadre discuss social and economic life in the village, identifying grievances, aspirations, and social relationships. Through their empathy and rapport, the cadre soon become assimilated into village life. In the meantime, the revolutionaries have acquired a comprehensive picture of the social patterns and way of life of the villagers, thereby identifying strengths and weaknesses. It is this knowledge that provides the basis for furthering the revolutionary organization.

During the course of the cadre's discussions and evening
entertainment, very little is said of communism, democracy,
and forms of government. Rather, the stress is on a "good
life" stemming from ownership of land and productive harvests.
The villagers are able to compare the good life to the inequi-
ties and injustice of the present life, real or imagined, as the
cadre carefully point out the basic contrasts. The problems
and grievances are easily transferred to and identified with
the established government. What compounds and gives
credence to this picture is the fact that government representatives probably have not established any meaningful
administrative or grievance structure in the village. It may
well have been months since the last visit of a government
representative. More than likely, the last visit by government
officials took the form of military patrols. Consequently, the
government becomes identified as "they" contrasted to the "we"
of the village. Thus begins the process by which the revolutionary cadre hope to isolate the government from the people.
        As the revolutionary organization expands, it establishes
a school, perhaps a dispensary, and a regular system of wel-
fare and taxation. The villagers, perhaps for the first time,
enjoy a regular system of government which appears just and
incorrupt. In this manner, sympathy and allegiance develops
for the revolution. The villagers, in turn, provide their sons
and daughters for the revolutionary cause.
        Each villager is persuaded, pressured, or terrorized into
some activity designed to commit him to the revolution. As the
extent of this support grows, so does the number of villagers
mobilized for the revolution. When the process is successful,
entire villages become people's villages arrayed against the
government. The villages are formed into revolutionary
districts, and districts into provinces. Simultaneously, a
revolutionary administrative structure develops. This tech-
nique is fundamental to the process of mobilizing the people
and establishing the roots of the revolutionary organizations.(6)
        Counter-revolutionary forces conducting operations
against such villages are not only faced with village militia and
revolutionary military units, but must cope with the problem of
rooting out the revolutionary political organization which, in
most cases, is submerged within the village structure. Additionally, successful operations depend upon reliable intelligence services and cooperation of the villagers, yet the
villagers are either apathetic to the government cause or
clearly sympathetic to the revolution.
        The peasant and village become the main target areas.
However, these rarely provide clearly distinguishable targets
for the application of superior firepower or conventional military techniques. Using the village as a base, the revolutionary military force is able to strike at government troops,

capture materiel, disrupt lines of communications, and engage in a number of military activities at a time and place of its own choosing, thereby almost assuring surprise and temporary superiority.

The political nature of the war means that the revolutionaries are not overly concerned with real estate or kill ratios, but with the political and psychological impact of their actions on the people. This in turn makes the war multi-dimensional, in which military action is but one aspect of the total picture. For counter-revolutionary forces, this may on many occasions require considerable restraint from conducting operations against a known or suspected enemy for fear of alienating part of the populace. It may mean watching comrades killed or wounded for no apparent military reason and with few feasible counter-measures.

For the soldier, revolutionary war magnifies his concern and anxiety for survival and creates questions of military purpose. There is no rear area. The soldier is either on a defensive perimeter or on operations of one type or another. The only place where rest and relaxation may be enjoyed in relative safety is outside the country. Days and sometimes weeks may pass with very little combat. Military operations may take on the air of a peacetime training exercise until the moment when the revolutionary military force conducts a surprise attack, catching a unit in ambush. This is followed by increased vigilance until the days and weeks begin to wear on with no combat. This constant cycle of violent combat normally condensed into a short period of time, combined with relatively long stretches of endless patrolling and waiting, is psychologically demanding.

For the U.S. soldier in Vietnam, such problems were an inherent part of the revolutionary atmosphere. As succinctly stated by one journalist:

> The American in Vietnam. Caught in a war without fixed battle lines, without stirring slogans or Hitler-type villains, without real estate objectives, without conventional tactics or even conventional weapons, he must share the daily fighting with a smiling ally who at times is as difficult to understand as the enemy, for he too is an Oriental cut from the same enigmatic mold. There is an Old West quality about the war in ingenuity and daring. But there is an Old East quality about it too, that is exasperating and wears down even the most dedicated. . . .(7)

Since the key to success is in the villages, the problem for the counter-revolutionary forces is how to combat the influence of the revolution on the villagers. For the soldier, it may require performing a variety of duties of a non-combat nature, including such things as guarding peasants while they harvest the crop, conducting road blocks and searches, and coordinating operations with local police, civilian officials, and indigenous troops. It may also require building roads and teaching school. The purpose of all of this is to "win the hearts and minds of the people." To put it in other terms, the purpose is to take the revolution out of the hands of the revolutionaries. For U.S. troops in Vietnam, this was a trying experience.

> In what other war was the American soldier asked to be a killer, for that is what his profession entails, but also a diplomat, missionary, and social worker? For an eighteen year old, this is a tall order, far more complex than the demands of the Peace Corps. He is asked to kill one day and put the pieces back together the next.(8)

The fact remains, however, that war is still a matter of combat survival. Should the soldier shoot the person in black pajamas running out of the village hut? If he does and finds later that the person was no more than an old, frightened peasant, what moral criteria should prevail? If the soldier does not shoot, only to be killed by this enemy in black pajamas, moral criteria become irrelevant. How is the soldier expected to react to villagers if he sees friends killed or wounded as a result of village sympathy for the revolutionary cause? How should he react if villagers knowingly allow troops to walk into mine fields and booby traps? Revolutionary military forces cannot be found, but isn't the village the real enemy? As the revolutionary military forces become more elusive and the war continues, the soldier is placed in an increasingly frustrating predicament, in which the need for performance and survival is hindered by the obscurity of the target and the attitude of the peasants.

> The search for the enemy has frequently been in vain and has therefore frustrated and demoralized the searching troops, as has the impossibility of distinguishing between combatant insurgent and the hostile or indifferent civilian population.(9)

The number of conflicting pressures are created which are liable to affect judgment and precipitate reactions which in conventional combat operations are more manageable, more predictable, and more subdued in their impact. These anxieties and frustrations may well find targets which do not have a clear and direct association with the revolutionary forces.(10) As a result, the soldier is inclined to view most villagers as the "enemy." Actions against villagers thus

become an accepted means of engaging the enemy and providing tangible results. The consequences of such judgment
and actions in a revolutionary war environment can do much to
alienate the populace and undermine the counter-revolutionary
effort. The extent of the problem, however, is not limited
solely to the environment. The nature of the military profession and the training measures are not conducive to developing
the understanding required for revolutionary war, nor are
they conducive to establishing a realistic criteria related to the
type of judgment necessary in an obscure and rapidly
changing combat situation.(11)

The protracted nature of the war and the apparent inability to bring it to a successful conclusion are readily transferred into a negative domestic view of the war within the
democratic society. Public opinion, as recognized by the
revolutionaries, plays an important role in the conduct of the
war.

In the case of the third power, it can become a force
militating against continued involvement while depreciating the
efforts of the individual soldier on the battlefield. Indeed,
such a situation can easily turn into a vicious cycle in which
continued military operations which disrupt the peasant environment and gain little in the way of tangible results
stimulate the domestic environment at home to increasingly
question military purpose. The ultimate result of these interactions is to undermine the military image and its professional
purpose, institutionally as well as individually.

Furthermore, part of the military ethic derives from the
need for some measurable criteria of its accomplishments.
When this is absent, it becomes difficult to correlate purpose
and cohesion. There is nothing so frustrating and demoralizing to the soldier than to engage in operations or activities
that have little meaning in terms of being a "soldier," or in
combat, in terms of achieving "victory."


## TRAINING AND THE NATURE OF THE MILITARY


One of the major problems faced by the military is the conduct
of realistic training in preparation for combat. It is difficult
to create combat situations in training, since the soldier is
aware that the exercise is not intended to hurt him. For
conventional wars, the problem is difficult enough. For
revolutionary war and unconventional tactics, new elements are
added which makes the training problem almost insoluable.
The fact that the revolutionary battlefield may include a con-
glomeration of revolutionary military forces, civilians, officials,
police, and indistinct lines delineating enemy from friend and
combatant from non-combatant, makes it highly problematical

that realistic simulation can be achieved, not only in the physical, but also in the psychological sense. Superimposed on this environment is the requirement for learning combat skills and instinctive response. Not only must the soldier be trained in combat skills, but he must also be trained in understanding the nature of revolutionary war and the social and political context in which he must operate. Given the nature of the cultural gap between industrial and developing societies, this becomes, at best, a rather dubious undertaking.

The observations of a soldier in Vietnam clearly indicate the dilemma between training and combat environment:

> When I got here, some of the villages were wiped out, but quite a lot were still there. . . . Then every time I went out there were a few less, and now the whole place is wiped out as far as you can see. The G.I.'s are supposed to win the people's confidence, but they weren't taught any of that stuff. I went through that training, and I learned how to shoot, but no one ever told me a thing about having to love people who look different from us and who've got an ideological orientation that's about a hundred and eighty degrees different from us. We don't understand what they're thinking. When we got here, we landed on a different planet. In Germany and Japan, I guess there was a thread of contact, but even when a Vietnamese guy speaks perfect English I don't know what the hell he's talking about.(12)

Compounding the training problem is that problem associated with maintaining a humane view of war and instilling the need for "proper" moral conduct on the battlefield. On one hand, in counter-revolutionary wars the soldier must be taught the instinctiveness of survival and combat; on the other, he must be taught to be a "righteous" killer; and this, in an environment which generally lacks the signposts of conventional combat. One manifestation of this problem of training and morality is reflected in the precedence established by the Nuremberg trials. The tribunal established the precedent that all soldiers, regardless of rank and capacity, will be held liable for the moral quality of their actions. In other words, unlawful orders will not be carried out.(13) Military operations in a revolutionary war, with its ambiguities and obscurities, may well involve the exercise of judgment at the small unit level, and in many cases by individual soldiers, which could mean the difference between survival or death, morality or immorality. The subtle distinctions in interpretation and implementation of orders could spell the difference in many cases. Yet, the fact remains that the Nuremberg precedent requires that the soldier distinguish between the legality and illegality of orders, the humanity and inhumanity of his action.

On one level, the soldier needs to be trained for all of the complexities of revolutionary war, to include combat skills and instinctive response, and unquestioning implementation of orders; at another level, he is supposed to be trained in exercising moral judgment as to the method of implementation as well as interpretation of an order to insure its moral worth; and at still another level, he is to be trained in the criteria by which he can legitimately disregard orders as being unlawful. To add to this confusing and contradictory set of requirements, combat survival and effectiveness may rest heavily on how quickly and effectively orders can be carried out. Yet, the nature of counter-revolutionary warfare is likely to create situations in which the legality of orders and moral basis for military actions are at best ambiguous.

The military institution rests on the presumption that orders of superiors will be obeyed. "Duty, Honor, Country" form the core of the professional ethic, reinforcing institutional legitimacy and providing an almost sacrosanct aura to orders "from above." Many would argue that without such a professional ethic and institutional fabric, the military establishment would lose its cohesion and purpose. One can imagine the reaction of the military professional to a situation in which individual judgment and discretion were substituted for command decisions and the hierarchy of command relationships. The training considerations and the nature of the military organization do not, in any sense of the imagination, prepare the soldier to exercise judgment based on moral criteria in a revolutionary war environment replete with moral issues.

The problems associated with the nature of counter-revolutionary warfare, combined with moral considerations and training problems, create a situation in which military necessity and survival are diametrically opposed to considerations of humane conduct. Where combatants and non-combatants are inextricably intermingled on the battlefield, and where the combat training of the soldier is matched against the ideological commitment and skill of the revolutionary operating in his own environment, there is very little room for clear criteria of moral conduct; nor does there exist a clear distinction between necessity and humanity. All of the training experience and instincts of the soldier predispose him toward military proficiency and survival, with survival the underlying motivation for all his actions. In such a situation, the technological advantage is with the industrial power, but the political-psychological advantage - and that of time - rests with the revolutionaries.

What are the consequences of these moral, operational, and training considerations on the total capacity of the military institution? What constraints are imposed by the nature of the revolutionary guerrilla war environment and the limitations of the character of the professional military ethic stemming from an industrial society? What are the strategic limitations upon policy?

The consequences of this situation go beyond the legalities and moralities associated with the Nuremberg precedent or the laws of land warfare. Much more important is the impact that questionable behavior has on the societal attitudes concerning the conduct of its soldiers on the battlefield. Furthermore, the norms of professional conduct become tarnished in the eyes of society, as well as in the eyes of a number of military men, if conduct on the battlefield becomes increasingly perceived as immoral and contrary to the professional image and social values. Finally, the environment in which the revolutionary struggle takes place is affected. The seemingly indiscriminate drive for tangible results (body counts in Vietnam) by soldiers of an alien society is not lost on the peasantry. Regardless of the good intentions, the kind of combat and involvement necessary to root out the revolutionary political system invariably involves the peasants and the social system. The stage is thus set for a classic case of asymmetry, where the military posture regardless of combat proficiency is detrimentally affected by the continuing perceptions of society that the military conduct is not in accord with social values. (We are speaking, of course, of the democratic society and its involvement in an external conflict.) These considerations have some important strategic and policy dimensions.

## STRATEGIC AND POLICY DIMENSIONS

If the revolutionary war cannot be resolved prior to Phase Two - Stalemate (Mao's terminology), then it can be surmised that the revolutionary ideology and organization have become an inextricable part of the social system. Consequently, questions of morality, combat effectiveness, and efficacy of military power become exposed to the demoralizing and disintegrating effects of a long-term war that must be fought by non-indigenous forces within the very heart of the political-social system of an alien society. The military institution of a third power would find it virtually impossible to operate as a political-social agent substituting for indigenous institutions and ideology. Yet, this becomes the key to successful counter-revolution. The dilemma increases when revolutionary war enters Phase Two.

Morality and just war become key issues as the third power finds itself embroiled in a conflict between two com-

peting political systems.  In fact, the third-power involvement
may become an increasing liability to the indigenous counter-
revolutionary forces as the military question becomes closely
identified with political-psychological operations and thrusts
directly into the political-social environment of the village.
The possibility increases that soldiers will become drawn into
military operations, which by the very nature of Phase Two
revolutionary guerrilla warfare requires a more visible and
questionable involvement, intermingling and indiscriminating
military and non-military environments.  The image of the
soldier and ultimately the military institution in such a situation can readily be translated into that of the "invading
foreigner" regardless of the peasantry's sympathies.  The
consequences of this relationship, combined with its detrimental
affect on military operations, can do much to create domestic
skepticism and frustration within the democratic system.
Furthermore, it is likely that feedback into the military institution will precipitate a vicious cycle, in which frustration
and criticism may foster more aggressive military operations
exacerbating the political-psychological aspect of the war,
further widening the gap between the peasantry and the third
power forces while increasing asymmetry.

    Military institutions of industrial democratic societies stem
from a political-social and economic milieu that provides little
individual empathy for developing societies or any real understanding of revolutionary war.  The technological orientation of
advanced societies is inherently embedded in a scientific outlook and, it might be added, a scientific view of the conduct
of wars.  The professionalism of the military is similarly
measured in terms of technological competence, sophistication
of weaponry, and scientific management.  The consequences of
this orientation suggest that technological wars are professionally coherent and symmetrical.  On the other hand, involvement in a revolutionary war (which is, in the main,
unconventional and a relatively low level technological engagement) creates asymmetry.  It is relatively easier, for example,
for the U.S. military to think in terms of armored division,
airborne assault, amphibious operations, and nuclear war, than
it is to plan, train, and engage in revolutionary warfare.

    The soldier from an industrial environment when placed in
a revolutionary war environment has great difficulty in per-
ceiving the nature of the struggle, much less the purpose of
his presence.  Traditional professional criteria provide little in
the way of guidance.  There may be much truth in the idea
that good revolutionaries come from revolutionary-prepared
people.  Similarly, to understand counter-revolution, one must
understand revolution.  The soldier from a non-revolutionary
industrial society is not likely to be the type of individual who
can be ideologically motivated to engage in counter-revolutionary warfare outside his own country.  It is insufficient to

merely perform a professional role in a type of warfare that is limited in its receptivity to applications of industrial proficiency. Ideological commitment provides the emotional stimulus and belief in salvation that provide a political-psychological superiority to the revolutionary forces. Consequently, both the individual soldier and institutional effectiveness suffer.

The difficulty in achieving a clear and quick decision in a revolutionary war exacerbates the asymmetry between military legitimacy and military posture. The search for tangible criteria for measuring effectiveness and progress becomes more elusive as the revolutionary war continues. Yet, the need for tangible results is an inherent part of the military orientation, both individual and institutional. It can be reasonably surmised that the inconclusiveness of many U.S. military operations in Vietnam was in no small measure responsible for individual frustrations, decline in confidence, and limited effectiveness of the military institution. In such circumstances, the individual soldier is likely to react to these frustrations and ambiguities in a manner not necessarily compatible with traditional professional conduct. At the same time, the military institution tends to be bound by tactics and technology which have decreasing influence on shaping the outcome of the revolutionary war. In this respect, the individual soldier becomes increasingly disoriented while the military institution becomes increasingly incapable of maintaining its effectiveness and sense of purpose. In more intellectual terms, the impact of the non-indigenous military is limited by the constraints of the political social milieu of the developing society and the imperatives of revolutionary warfare.

With the real restraints resting on political-psychological factors, there are limits beyond which the involvement of industrial democracy in revolutionary war can become counterproductive to both the counter-revolutionary effort and to the interests of the outside power. Not only does the revolutionary war become less susceptible to applications of power, but the standards of professional conduct and institutional capacity of the military are reduced to a point at which continuing involvement in a revolutionary war "de-legitimizes" the role of the combat soldier, as well as that of the institution. To carry this one step further, the revolutionary forces may well become increasingly legitimate as the visibility of the non-indigenous military forces increases and their involvement becomes protracted, while the democratic society, impatient for results and suffering from a moral consciousness, increasingly questions its government's role and the role of the military. In essence, the increasing asymmetry correlates inversely to the use of military power.

This presents limited alternatives to the policy maker. The most favorable strategy under these circumstances is a "low visibility" involvement in support of existing regimes and

a "no visibility" involvement in counter-revolutionary warfare.
(See Figure 4.1, Conflict Spectrum).  The purpose would be
assistance in the development of relatively stable and efficient
governments in order to usurp the causes of revolution.
Once, however, the revolutionary war commences and moves
well into Phase One (strategic defensive), the success or
failure of the counter-revolutionary effort is dependent to a
great degree on the indigenous government, not the commitment of third power troops.
      The point is succinctly made by a noted expert on revolu-
tionary guerrilla warfare.  Commenting on Vietnam, he writes:

> The point to be stressed is that the war has always
> remained basically an insurgency, boosted by in-
> filtration and aided, to a certain but limited extent,
> by both invasion and raids. . . . People's Revolu-
> tionary War is therefore, by nature a civil war of a
> very sophisticated type and using highly refined
> techniques to seize power and take over a country.
> The significant feature of it, which needs to be
> recognized, is its immunity to the applications of
> power.(14)

      Another policy alternative is to apply massive military
power at the outset and in a relatively short span of time to
attempt a quick "victory."  The very conditions of revolutionary war militate against this type of policy - indeed, there are
few alternatives except a protracted engagement.  Even in
conditions in which there are major elements of the population
in favor of the third power - such as in Malaya - the third
power involvement is likely to be protracted.  (The emergency
in Malaya officially lasted 12 years.)
      A protracted involvement may be possible as long as the
conflict remains manageable and isolated from major power
plays; i.e., Malaya, 1948-1960.  Moreover, a purely professional military involvement (a limited number of regular military
forces) may make it possible to limit the impact of the involvement on the third power domestic society.  In such circumstances, however, there must still be at least some degree
of symmetry.  This option presumes that the third power
perceives the revolution as a threat or a potential threat to its
security.  Finally, we could easily argue that a democratic
society should never again become involved in a counter-
revolutionary war in a developing society, because there is
little likelihood of success.  This presumes that any society
faced with revolutionary guerrilla warfare is ipso facto il-
legitimate and not worthy of assistance.  Given the fact that
most developing societies develop an environment that is
susceptible to revolutionary guerrilla warfare, this option could
easily lead to the disregard and abandonment of existing gov-

ernments which **may** be legitimate and which may be attempting to overcome problems of development and change.

## CONCLUSIONS

Revolutionary war rests on the fact that a politically organized group within a particular territory has embarked on a course of action with the objective of changing the established government. The revolutionary program requires the participation of a number of the civilian populace, as well as generation of sympathy for the revolutionary cause. Unconventional warfare is a basic means to achieve the objective. The success of unconventional warfare rests on the fact that it is independent of large armies and the paraphernalia of conventional combat while resting its support on political organization and the peasant. Additionally, revolution may well be a manifestation of the indigenous government's initial political and administrative ineffectiveness and unresponsiveness.

The counter-revolutionary strategy must be based on militarily defeating the revolutionary military arm while simultaneously creating an efficient government and adopting and implementing programs designed to regain and retain the allegiance of the peasants. For a third (intervening) power, this requires a judicious and limited use of military force tempered by the realization that the nature of the war is primarily political and psychological. More important, it necessitates a reasonably effective indigenous counter-revolutionary effort.

The frustrations and anxieties of conventional combat are present in unconventional combat situations. However, the problems are magnified and less manageable since the meaning of "enemy" is obscure, and military operations, in most cases, are ambiguous in their results. Compounding these factors is the nature of counter-revolutionary military operations; i.e., small unit operations, endless hours of seemingly useless patrols, and an elusive enemy, submerged in the village structure and almost indistinguishable from the peasants. The soldier's desire to achieve identifiable results, attain a degree of self-satisfaction, combined with the need for combat effectiveness and survival, may cause aggression against those who are identified or associated, directly or indirectly, with the revolution. This normally means that the villager becomes the most expedient and visible target.

Interpretations of moral criteria and human conduct which are infrequently mentioned in training, and only remotely understood as compared to the necessity of combat skills, tend to narrow; hence, the line between morality and military necessity becomes obscure. Even in times of war, there is a need to maintain a measure of humanity if brutality toward the enemy and within the soldier is to be minimized. However, as this chapter has attempted to demonstrate, the line between humanity and brutality is a "razor's edge" in revolutionary wars where combatants and non-combatants may be constantly changing roles and where a whole range of unconventional operations and conspiratorial activities are "acceptable" means to achieve the objective.

Although there are a number of other factors relevant to the study of revolutionary warfare, the focus of this chapter has been primarily on the political-psychological factor. It is this factor that is the essence of revolutionary war. And, it needs to be added, it is this factor that creates the ambiguities and frustrations in the individual soldier. As long as the soldier must perform his role from within the perceptions of traditional professionalism, the involvement in a revolutionary war will in the long run tend to erode military legitimacy and dehumanize battlefield conduct with negative impact on cohesion, purpose, and commitment.

At best, a policy of military assistance and support can be followed, but must fall short of troop commitment beyond the first stage of revolutionary war unless there are positive signs that the indigenous government has established the necessary degree of legitimacy and commitment to counter the revolution.

In the final analysis, the lack of appreciation and understanding of the nature of revolutionary war has been at the root of unsystematic and inadequate guidelines concerning realistic application of military force. Adding to this situation is the fact that in revolutionary wars, the soldier is placed in a position in which there is a great degree of discretion and a wide range of situations in which he must exercise judgment. This places much of the responsibility of distinguishing between military necessity and humane conduct on the judgment of the individual soldier. Societal values and training, the military "ethic," and combat skills and effectiveness place varying degrees of and contradictory pressures on the soldier. When he is faced with exercising judgment on the battlefield in which people are an inherent and most significant part, the soldier is likely to instinctively fall back on military training rather than on complex mental analysis as to the correctness of his conduct. A clear case of inhumane conduct is one matter, but the exercise of bad judgment and questionable reaction in a psychologically frustrating and morally ambiguous situation wrought with a kill-or-get-killed equation, is another.

The problem of atrocities and inhumane conduct crop up in every war. In no other type of war, however, is it likely to be so quickly transformed into political and psychological dimensions. Every military action in a revolutionary war sets in motion a number of non-military forces that become the real criteria for success or failure. In no other type of war is it likely that individual actions on the battlefield will be compounded and shaped to the point where they will cast doubt upon the intentions and effectiveness of the government and the counter-revolutionary effort. Yet, the soldier does not come fully equipped to ascertain the significance of these factors. Regardless of the intonations of winning the hearts and minds of the people, the soldier is primarily motivated by survival and killing the enemy. For most professionals, military success still rests on kill ratios, weapons captured and destroyed, and successful tactical operations.

These are the conditions that precipitate a divergence between subjective and objective factors within a democratic society. Society seeks moral purpose and humane behavior in achieving these purposes. In those cases where there is an identifiable enemy threatening the security of democratic society, it is relatively easy to perceive an underdog role while cloaking actions and behavior against the enemy in moralistic terms. But when the enemy is unrecognizable and the peasant is the underdog, it is difficult to perceive the struggle in terms of the defense of the country against a powerful enemy. The behavior of soldiers in countering the revolution can easily be perceived as contradictory to democratic values. The military purpose suffers as society increasingly questions its role. Eventually, the cohesiveness of the military is affected which accelerates the de-legitimization of the military's involvement.

Having raised issues concerning the ambiguities inherent in revolutionary war and the problems they pose to the individual soldier and the military institution, and their impact on society, it is readily admitted that possible solutions are at best a reflection of the problems; that is to say, the solutions themselves are in the main ambiguous. The most conventional answer would be to stress better training, leadership, motivation, management, and tactics. Yet the answer may not lie in "better" everything, but in recognizing the limits of a third power role in revolutionary war situations. It seems highly unlikely that third powers can commit troops within a revolutionary environment in support of counter-revolutionary systems with any hope for a neat "surgical" operation. On the contrary, it is more likely that such a commitment will increase the politicization of the conflict while exposing the third power military to internal stresses and strains which will increasingly erode professionalism while decreasing the legitimacy of the military institution.

Finally, when viewed from the policy level, it becomes clear that there are political-psychological limits to military power in revolutionary war by a democratic political system. These limits, when translated into strategic terms, militate against a policy of committing troops into an ambiguous, multi-dimensional environment, associated with revolutionary war. For any hope of a successful military policy, there must be symmetry between military legitimacy and military posture. Inherent in any revolutionary situation is asymmetry between the military posture of a third power and its military legitimacy. Any society that prides itself on democratic values will find it extremely difficult, if not impossible, to create symmetry in such a situation.

## NOTES

1. Sun Tzu, The Art of War, translated by Samuel B. Griffith. New York: Oxford University Press, 1971, pp. 63-64.
2. Katherine Chorley. Armies and the Art of Revolution. Boston: Beacon Press, 1973, pp. 17-18. Quotes in this paragraph are from Chorley.
3. See William R. Peers. The My Lai Massacre and Its Cover-Up: Beyond the Reach of Law? New York: The Free Press, 1976.
4. John P. Roche, "Can a Free Society Fight a Limited War?" in The New Leader, Oct. 21, 1968. pp. 6-11.
5. Mao Tse-tung on Guerrilla Warfare, translated and with an introduction by B.G. Samuel, B. Griffith, USMC (ret.). New York: Frederick a Praeger, p. 7.
6. The general scheme of these techniques is based on Franklin Mark Osanka, "Social Dynamics of Revolutionary Guerrilla Warfare," in Roger W. Little (Ed.), A Survey of Military Institutions. The Inter-University Seminar on Armed Forces and Society, Chicago, 1969.
7. Hugh Mulligan. No Place to Die: The Agony of Vietnam. New York: William Morrow and Co., Inc., 1967, p. 318.
8. Ibid.
9. Hans Morgenthau, "What Price Victory?" in The New Republic, February 20, 1971, p. 22.
10. There are some theories explaining the effect of frustrations on human behavior. Although psychological analysis is not the real concern of this chapter, it is interesting to note that frustrations often manifest themselves in aggressive behavior. This aggressive behavior may take several forms, one of which is displacement of aggression; i.e., the venting of frustration in the form of aggression not directly against the object but against another target. In many cases, aggression is repressed until a certain point is reached, at which time it is released all at once on a specific, perhaps innocent target. In such cases, it is conceivable that aggression far outweighs the nature of the offense. This may also take unpredictable form.

11. For the U.S. soldier in Vietnam, the dilemma posed here was made more difficult by the domestic atmosphere in the United States. The schisms in U.S. society precipitated by the Vietnam war and reflected in demonstrations, debates, and dissent influenced the soldier's overall view of the war and his role in it. It was another element which created additional pressures influencing perceptions of performance and morality.

In no other war have respected voices in the community, people in authority, people of eminence - senators, representatives, clergymen, professors, even some military men - questioned the morality as well as wisdom of our intervention and raised grave doubts about our motives. The pacifists and conscientious objectors we have always had with us, but never before have the halls of Congress and the hearing rooms of the Senate Foreign Relations committee echoed for our involvement, while half a world away 400,000 American troops already are committed to fighting and dying. (Mulligan, p. 317)

12. Jonathan Schell, The Military Half. New York: Alfred A. Knopf, 1968, p. 42.

13. Department of the Army, Law of Land Warfare, FM 27-10 (Washington D.C. Government Printing Office, July 1956), p. 3, states, "The law of war is binding not only upon states as such but also upon individuals and, in particular, the members of their armed forces."

14. Sir Robert Thompson, No Exit From Vietnam. New York: David McKay Co., Inc., 1968, p. 45. Underlining added for emphasis.

# 7 Professional Dilemmas, Adaptations, and Military Intervention

Since the end of World War II, while conventional military forces remain essential ingredients in strategic deterrence, the utility of such forces for purposes of intervention has declined. At the same time, there has been a general persistence in political confrontations and an expansion of diplomatic maneuverability. Within the context of general interstate tension, this has created a vastly different environment for the resolution of conflicts. Domestically, the legacy of Vietnam remains a crucial conditioning factor in U.S. military posture, while the issues raised by a volunteer military system compound the problems of adjustment to the changed environment. As a result, the U.S. military profession is faced with a series of difficult dilemmas. Dilemmas which have a direct bearing on the character of professionalism and the ability of the military to successfully engage in foreign operations.

The purpose of this chapter is to examine professional dilemmas stemming from the new dimensions of military purpose - those specifically related to military intervention. In examining these issues we will explore the relationships between international constraints, domestic values, and military purpose. Attention will also be given to institutional and professional dimensions associated with the advent of the volunteer military. In this context, important questions are also raised

---

*I wish to thank Charles C. Moskos, Jr., for his valuable assistance. Selections from his paper, "Trends in Military Social Organization," prepared for delivery at the conference on "The Consequences of Military Intervention," The University of Chicago, June 17-19, 1976, were included in this chapter.

regarding concepts of war, institutional orientation, and professional ethics.

There are six premises basic to this study. First, the presumption is that military intervention means the commitment of U.S. military forces to a foreign operation. Second, the least likely limited war is direct confrontation between the United States and the Soviet Union or the United States and China. If it does occur, it is likely to involve the deployment of tactical nuclear weapons. Third, deployment of tactical nuclear weapons is likely to escalate the confrontation and may be viewed by the enemy as a strategic factor crossing the threshold into general war. Fourth, the focus of professional issues is primarily, but not exclusively, concerned with professionalism within the ground forces. Given the nature of sea and air warfare, professional dilemmas are more likely to be strongly associated with ground troop commitment. Fifth, limited wars are most likely to occur in non-developed regions; i.e., the Third World.(1)  Finally, strategies of limited war remain elusive. The experience of Vietnam did not necessarily establish a policy of "no more Vietnams." Indeed, the acceptance of this perspective would hamper the development of a flexible and prudent approach to the prospects of limited war.(2)

Although limited wars are conditioned by their own special characteristics, realistically they cannot be separated from considerations of overall military capability and nuclear deterrence. Limited war and nuclear deterrence are part of an integrated military continuum. The ability to deter means the ability to maintain an effective limited war readiness in all arms, and to maintain such readiness in the absence of actual hostilities. Thus, the U.S. military is faced with problems of combat readiness in a series of contingencies ranging from general nuclear war to indirect confrontation. Equally important, the strength and weaknesses in any major contingency has an impact on other capabilities.

There are, nevertheless, special features of limited war that distinguish it from other categories of warfare. The fundamental character is that of restraint. "What distinguishes limited war from total war? The answer is that limited war involves an important kind and degree of restraint - deliberate restraint. . . . The restraint must also be massive . . . the restraint necessary to keep wars limited is primarily a restraint on means, not ends."(3)

The ends do have an important conditioning function, however. If complete annihilation of the enemy is a goal, for example, it is unlikely that other restraints will have any real meaning.(4)  Thus, political goals must be realistic in terms of the ultimate outcome of limited war - that is, military strategy must be effectively linked to the political purpose. More importantly, political purpose must be identified and articulated so as to insure legitimate military purpose. This question will be addressed in more detail later.

Wars can also be limited by restraint on the use of force, to include the type of weapons deployed. The presumption is that weapons of a strategic nature - those that have a high propensity for escalating the conflict - and those weapons that are indiscriminate in their targets will either not be used or be very carefully restrained in their application.

In such circumstances, the nation with a major strategic capability may well find that it is severely limited in its ability to bring to bear its military power. Brodie for example, observes that:

> Among the military lessons we have learned is that restraint in the application of force - in order to keep that application compatible with its purpose - may make the force applied ineffective for its purpose. Thus to grant sanctuary and to withhold tactical nuclear weapons may be utterly correct policy, but such restraints have to be recognized as being costly, possibly very costly, in military effectiveness. For the future, this is bound to mean, and should mean, not fewer limitations upon the use of force, but rather fewer occasions for applying force under circumstances requiring such restraints.(5)

The nature of the force applied and the type of weapons deployed is also contingent upon the character of the limited war. Until the last decade, this has generally been associated with a Korean type conflict. Essentially, this rested on the premise that the war would be reminiscent of a "World War II" type setting, with its identifiable front line, conventionally organized enemy, and employing generally conventional military tactics within specified geographical boundaries. Since the late 1950s, however, the changed nature of the international system has significantly influenced the character of limited wars. It is more likely that limited wars will now include a mix of conventional as well as unconventional ingredients.(6) For example, it is unlikely that an intervening power will be able to gain a foothold and maintain itself in foreign countries without first defeating a conventional force, but more important, successfully defeating a hostile population conducting a "people's war." Indeed, one can reasonably argue that the defeat of the enemy's conventional forces may be the less difficult part of the operation.

Limited wars are also characterized by the use of surrogate forces or wars by proxy.(7) Beginning in Greece (1947), the United States adopted a policy using advisory teams to assist and in many respects supervise the indigenous forces in combating opposing forces. As we learned in South Vietnam, however, the use of surrogate forces can lead directly to the use of combat troops to support and eventually supplant indigenous forces.

Finally, military intervention (employing ground troops) must ultimately face the problem of disengagement. South Vietnam provides an example of the chaos and trauma associated with disengagement during an impending defeat. South Korea, on the other hand, is an example of the quicksand quality of intervention - even after 20 years, U.S. troops are still deemed necessary to prevent recurrence of a Korean type war. Indeed, disengagement may trigger political as well as military events that may well erode the very purpose of the intervention in the first place.

These characteristics raise four salient features for U.S. policy. First, there is an inherent asymmetry; that is, under a number of circumstances it is conceivable that the limited war involvement of the United States may be met by total war by the enemy. Second, limited war is highly political in character. In light of the nationalistic sentiments, the delicate balance of terror between superpowers, the general antagonism against any action that hints of imperialism, and the general North-South tensions in the world, U.S. military intervention may create political pressures and responses beyond the boundaries of conventional military capability. Third, military intervention may have limited utility and be politically counterproductive. Moreover, to succeed, the application of force may require subtle and low visibility operations rather than military intervention in conventional terms. Fourth, in any case, the rules of the game of limited war must be clearly articulated and generally accepted by the protagonists. In light of the first three features, it appears highly unlikely that rules regarding limited war that are directly connected with political and nationalistic issues will be accepted if they limit the ability to achieve political goals. This may well destroy the very purpose of the intervention in the first place. It is within these general policy considerations that professional military dilemmas are addressed.

## CHANGING MILITARY ORGANIZATION

The issues of military purpose and professional dilemmas are also manifested in the context of changing conceptions of military organization. There is a need therefore to examine the proposition that the American military is moving from a predominantly institutional format resting on professionalism to one resembling that of an occupation. This changing conception also presumes that the concept of a "calling" inherent in professionalism is considerably reduced with economic considerations and status becoming paramount. While it is not necessary to predict such a shift, it is necessary to be aware of this potential trend and its implications.

Terms like occupation, profession, or institutional format suffer from imprecision both in popular and scholarly discussion. Nevertheless, they each contain core connotations which serve to distinguish them from one another. For our purposes, these distinctions can be described as follows:

An occupation is legitimated in terms of the marketplace; i.e., what are prevailing monetary rewards for equivalent skills. In a modern industrial society, employees usually enjoy some voice in the determination of appropriate salary and work conditions. Such rights are counterbalanced by responsibilities to meet contractual obligations. The occupational model implies first priority inherent in self-interest rather than in the task itself or in the employing organization. A common form of advancement of group interest is the trade union.

A profession is legitimated in terms of specialized expertise; i.e., a purpose transcending individual self-interest in favor of a presumed higher good. A calling usually enjoys high esteem in the larger community because it is associated with notions of self-sacrifice and complete dedication to one's role. A calling does not command monetary reward comparable to what one might expect in the general economy. But this is often compensated for by an array of social benefits which simultaneously signals the institution's intent to take care of its own, and which sets the institution apart from the general society.

An institution is usually identified as an organization whose purpose is public service and whose members do not necessarily organize into self-interest groups. If grievances occur or redress is sought, it usually takes the form of one-on-one recourse to superiors within the organization or simply placing the matter into proper channels, trusting the paternalism of the institution.

Of course, the above specified models of an occupation, profession, or calling/institution are as much caricatures as they are descriptions of reality. In the case of the armed forces, moreover, the situation is complicated in that the military has elements of all three models. But the clearly dominant trend in contemporary military social organization is the decline of the institutional format and the corresponding ascendancy of the occupational model.

Whether the occupational model will become the organizational mode for the professionals - i.e., the officers corps - is problematical. In the current professional environment, there is resistance to the idea of professionalism defined in terms of economics. Indeed, there is evidence to suggest that many in the profession seek a professional purity based on time-honored concepts of Duty, Honor, Country.

Although antecedents predated the appearance of the all-volunteer force in early 1973, it was the end of the draft which served as the major thrust to move the military away from an institutional format. In contrast to the all-volunteer force, the selective service system was premised on the notion of citizenship obligation - with concomitant low salaries for draftees - and the ideal of a broadly representative enlisted force (though this ideal was not always realized in practice). In point of fact, it was the occupational model which clearly underpinned the philosophic rationale of the 1970 Report of the President's Commission on an All-Volunteer Armed Force (Gates Commission Report).(8) Instead of a military system anchored in the normative values of a calling - captured in words like Duty, Honor, Country - the Gates Commission explicitly argued that primary reliance to recruit an armed force be based on monetary incentives determined by marketplace standards. Perhaps the ultimate in monetary inducements has been reached in the "bonus" used to recruit young men into the combat arms since the end of the draft.

While the termination of the selective service system is the most dramatic change in the contemporary military system, other indicators of the trend away from the institutional format toward the occupational model can also be noted: (1) the significant salary increase given the armed forces since 1971 in an effort to make military salaries competitive with civilian rates; (2) proposals to make civilian-military pay "comparable" - e.g., doing away with the allotment system by which service remuneration is partly determined by the service member's marital and family status; (3) proposals to eliminate or reduce a host of military benefits - e.g., subsidies to commisaries and exchanges, the G.I. Bill, health care for dependents, the pension system; (4) the separation of work and residence locales accompanying the growing proportion of enlisted men residing off the military base; (5) the increasing aversion of many military wives at officer and noncom levels to take part in customary social functions; and (6) the increased discussion and debate about the legality and relevance of trade unions for active duty military personnel. The sum of these trends is to highlight the strain toward the occupational model in the emergent military organization.

## INSTITUTIONAL CHARACTER AND CONSTRAINTS

While the changing organizational mode may have a long-range impact on military purpose and professionalism, the military institution, as it is structured now, creates immediate professional dilemmas. The nature of the volunteer force, problems of combat readiness, and demands of institutional loyalty impose operational definitions upon the environment limiting the professional's ability to develop flexible and realistic responses to limited war.

The volunteer military places manpower and budgetary constraints on the ability of the U.S. military to undertake external operations.(9) Put simply, volunteer forces have limited manpower.(10) To conduct sustained operations in any given limited war situation requires a reservoir of replacements and the ability to expand force levels. This may mean involvement of National Guard, Reserves, or both, as well as the possibility of reinstituting the selective service system. In light of the attitudes of American people and the nature and character of limited war, it is unlikely that such policies will gain the support of Congress or the American people. On the other hand, the nature of volunteer forces may isolate the military from society to an extent where even if they were committed to external operations, they would receive little support from the American people.

Budgetary restraints prohibit significant expansion of the military establishment during peace to meet sustained limited war contingencies. While the defense budget may increase to meet the perceived Soviet advances in nuclear missilery and military capability, it is unlikely that much financial support will be provided for additional manpower and limited war capabilities that are not directed at the Soviet Union or major war contingencies.

Many professionals lack faith in the capability of the volunteer forces and see as a result a general weakening of the American military purpose.(11) Indeed, there seems to be a latent fear that the American forces would find it difficult to conduct limited wars, not only in terms of quantity but in quality of forces. Moreover, professional concern with such matters are reflected in institutional preoccupation with raising the general quality of the military for the purposes of pre-training for combat. Thus, general education, remedial training, recruiting incentives, and administrative techniques may become institutional programs and goals at the expense of serious combat training.

Aside from constraints imposed by the volunteer system, there are those associated with combat readiness. This is a term used to signify the degree to which the military forces are capable of conducting successful military operations. In light of the international environment, combat elements of the military must remain in a state of perpetual readiness. This is perhaps one of the most perplexing training problems facing the military. It is clear that maintaining a high level of combat readiness during times of relative peace is a difficult matter. It is even more difficult when it is not clear who is the enemy. Moreover, maintaining combat readiness over long periods of time presumes a general consensus that there is indeed a threat. In light of the current environment and the inclination of American society to oppose foreign adventures, it is not clear how the institution will be able to maintain a consistent combat readiness.

Force structure is generally based on conventional concepts associated with general war. The concept of "forces-in-being" that is the basis for U.S. force structures presumes a capability to conduct wars with current manpower levels. Moreover, this approach rests on the premise that the most likely future wars will be fought and ended quickly with little or no time for mobilization. Thus, the "forces-in-being" gives only secondary consideration to cadre or mobilization posture and to force structures for conducting limited war operations.

In light of these considerations, the U.S. military appears to be developing a narrow operational perspective - the use of nuclear weapons in support of ground operations. That is, there is a high propensity for the main military effort to be directed towards European style combat, resting on a presumption that tactical nuclear weapons would be available to support ground operations. Yet, the new dimensions of military purpose demand a multi-dimensional military posture in a variety of combat environments.

Finally the institution, in any case, demands loyalty. Since the military institution and the profession rests on time-honored concepts, "Duty, Honor, Country," and on the demand for institutional loyalty and obedience, there is little room for resistance against institution demands. This is also true in terms of orders from above. The demand for prompt and unquestioning response is so engrained in the professional ethos that it is inconceivable that many officers would question either institutional policies or orders from superiors. Under such conditions, critical inquiry from within the profession is reduced to almost meaningless rhetoric while institutional orientation precludes flexibility and adaptability.

The dilemmas with respect to institutional considerations seem clear: institutional demands and requirements do not foster a military purpose responsive to the new environment, nor do they respond to the broader demands of professionalism. Equally important, there does not appear to be a political perspective that is realistically tied to the capabilities of the military institution. Given the close relationship between deterrence capability and a range of contingencies from general nuclear war to indirect confrontation, the U.S. military appears to be hard pressed to successfully engage in limited war operations.

## PROFESSIONAL AND INSTITUTIONAL ADAPTABILITY

In the post-Vietnam period, the most difficult task of adaptability has faced the ground forces and related units under pressure to maintain an effective force for military intervention. Two interesting trends can be discerned: one is an effort to create elite ground forces; and the second, paradoxically, has been the contracting out of military functions to civilian personnel and civilian agencies. Both are manifestations of the trend toward the occupational model.

Proponents of elite units have typically been accorded a mixed reception in American military circles.(12) Because elite units could be regarded as an institution within an institution, specialized fighting units often found themselves at the margin or even at odds with the regular command structure. But if the armed forces continue to move toward an occupational model, the status of elite units in military social organization will be fundamentally different from past experience. In reaction to the occupational model, that is, certain numbers of servicemen - largely through self-selection - will gravitate toward units where the traditional qualities of the military are maintained and valued.

Preliminary evidence indicative of the new circumstances of elite units is found in a study of four combat battalions conducted in the spring of 1975.(13) These battalions, all stationed in the southeastern part of the United States, covered the gamut of combat units. There were, in ascending order of "eliteness," an infantry battalion, a tank or armored battalion, an airborne infantry battalion, and a ranger battalion. A representative sample - between 85 and 90 lower ranking soldiers (pay grades E-3 and E-4) from each battalion - were surveyed with regard to social background characteristics and attitudinal items measuring military commitment.

Looking at the social background of the battalions, there was wide variation in their racial composition. The proportion of blacks was 53.3 percent in the infantry, 51.7 percent in the armored, 22.0 percent in the airborne, and 9.3 percent in the rangers. Correspondingly, the white ratios were the inverse of the black figures. For the same pay grades, the Army-wide figure was 23.7 percent black in 1975. Certainly the southeastern regional basis of the recruitment pool contributed to the disproportionate number of blacks in the armored and infantry battalions, but this only puts into sharper contrast the fact of the nearly all-white composition of the ranger battalion.

Parallel comparsions can be made with regard to educational levels. The proportion of soldiers who had at least some college was 10.9 percent in the infantry, 11.8 percent in the armored, 17.2 percent in the airborne, and 30.2 percent in the rangers. It is important to note, however, that even when race was held constant, the educational differences between the units persisted, although they were somewhat less pronounced. Contrary to much conventional wisdom, the most elite combat units in the all-volunteer Army are largely made up of middle-class white youth. At the same time, the non-elite units which make up the large bulk of the ground combat arms are overproportionately representative of lower educated and minority groups, though not nearly to the extent of the armored and infantry battalions described here.

Turning to the attitudinal data, the soldiers were queried as to their willingness to serve in hypothetical combat situations. Miniature scenarios were presented for six hypothetical situations: (1) an invasion of the United States by a foreign enemy; (2) fighting revolutionaries in America; (3) defense of a U.S. ally in Western Europe - say, Germany; (4) defense of a U.S. ally in the Far East - say, Korea; (5) defense of a U.S. friend in the Middle East - say, Israel; and (6) an overseas civil war in which the government asks for American help. Of course, it is extremely risky to extrapolate from attitudes toward hypothetical situations to predictions of actual behavior in a real combat circumstance. Nevertheless, these items do offer themselves as primitive indicators of level of military commitment.

Table 7.1. Percentage of Troops Who Would Volunteer or Willingly Follow Orders to Go into Combat in Hypothetical Situations, by Type of Unit

| Combat Situation | Rangers | Airborne | Armored | Infantry |
|---|---|---|---|---|
| U.S.A. invaded by foreign enemy | 97.8 | 93.4 | 88.5 | 81.4 |
| Fight revolutionaries in America | 96.4 | 77.6 | 71.1 | 59.2 |
| Defend Western European ally - Germany | 92.9 | 77.8 | 75.8 | 59.4 |
| Defend Far Eastern ally - Korea | 92.9 | 75.5 | 75.6 | 60.4 |
| Defend Middle Eastern friend - Israel | 90.5 | 76.4 | 73.6 | 58.3 |
| Overseas civil war in which government asks for American help | 84.5 | 72.2 | 64.3 | 52.8 |
| (Modal number of cases) | (86) | (90) | (87) | (90) |

Given in table 7.1 are the percentages of soldiers who
stated they would either volunteer or willingly follow orders to
serve in each of the hypothetical combat situations. Two
patterns of response appear in these data. First, willingness
to serve is highest - as one would anticipate - in defense of
the United States from foreign invasion. Not so expected,
however, is the finding that combat willingness varies hardly
at all regardless of which U.S. ally may be invaded. Second,
and most important for our purposes, the more elite units -
especially the rangers - consistently indicated a greater
willingness to go into combat, while the non-elite units -
especially the infantry battalion - just as consistently indicated
the greatest reluctance to go into combat.

Additional data dealt directly with the salience of the
institutional versus occupational model of military social organization. For purposes of contrast, we focus our attention on
the two polar units - the ranger battalion and the infantry
battalion. A series of items probed for reasons why the
soldier joined the service. Among the infantrymen, 61.1
percent compared to 28.2 percent of the rangers, stated they
had difficulty in finding a decent civilian job; 50.6 percent of
the infantrymen, compared to 37.7 percent of the rangers,
said the combat enlistment bonus was an important factor; and
59.4 percent of the infantry battalion, compared to 83.5
percent of the ranger battalion, reported serving the country
was an important consideration. Finally, only 34.4 percent of
the infantrymen, compared to 58.1 percent of the rangers,
agreed with the statement that the "Army should try to
maintain traditions which make it different from civilian life."

To sum up, the evidence indicates that soldiers who were
most compatible with the institutional format of the military
were also the soldiers most likely to indicate willingness to
serve in combat. Conversely, for those soldiers most in
accord with the occupational model, the level of military
commitment is markedly lower. Yet, because of the ascendant
occupational model, a small number of young men - overproportionately white and middleclass - are being self-selected
into the most traditional of combat groups - the elite units of
the all-volunteer Army. In terms of military social organization, we are witnessing a differentiation - both in social
composition and military commitment - <u>within</u> the ground combat
arms and not just <u>between</u> the combat arms and the technical
support branches.(14)

Another consequence of the ascendent occupational model
departs entirely from formal military social organization. This
is the use of civilians to perform tasks which by any conventional measure would be seen as military in content.(15) The
private armies of the Central Intelligence Agency have long
been an object of concern with the regular military command.
But what is anomalous in the emerging order is that, rather

than assigning its own military personnel, the U.S. government increasingly gives contracts directly to civilian firms - with salary levels much higher than comparable military rates - to perform difficult military jobs. The very structure of the military system, that is, no longer encompasses the range of military functions.

It is hard to overstate the degree to which the operational side of the military system is now reliant on civilian technicians. The large warships of the U.S. Navy are combat-ineffective without the technical skills of the contract civilians who permanently serve aboard those ships. Major Army ordinance centers, including those in the combat theater, require the skills of contract civilians to perform necessary repairs and assembly. Missile warning systems in Greenland are in effect civilian-manned military installations run by firms who are responsible to the U.S. Air Force. In Southeast Asia and Saudi Arabia, private companies such as Air America and Vinnel Corporation are given U.S. government contracts to recruit civilians who carry out military activities. Bell Helicopter and Grumman established a quasi-military base in Isfahan, Iran, staffed by former American military personnel who trained Iranian pilots. The American monitoring force in the Sinai is contracted out to private industry with the government retaining only policy control.

External political considerations certainly impinge upon the decisions to use civilian contracts for military tasks. But if task efficiency is the issue, a more nagging implication also suggests itself: Namely, military personnel cannot or will not perform arduous long-term duty with the efficacy of contract civilians. The trend toward the employment of contract civilians to carry out military tasks could well be the final culmination of the industrialization of the military purpose.

While these matters are primarily focused on the enlisted structure, they do have an impact on professionalism. If the occupational model and contract civilian roles were to become the accepted norm, beliefs conducive to organizational and societal respect - the whole notion of military legitimacy - become untenable. If military legitimacy erodes, then the very basis of military professionalism erodes. Indeed, the uniqueness of military purpose which has been the basis of professional expertise and authority in society will become highly suspect. Moreover, the ability of the military to respond to a range of policy alternatives and contingencies will certainly be significantly diminished.

## MILITARY PURPOSE AND SOCIETY

The contradictions between military purpose and values of society create one of the most complex dilemmas, since it involves questions of values, attitudes, and linkages between the military and political system. Additionally, questions regarding legitimacy, civil-military relations, institutional norms, and individual behavior patterns are inherent parts of the issues. Thus, military professionalism and military purpose cannot realistically be studied outside the context of the values and attitudes of society. Military legitimacy is bestowed by society. Consequently, the ability of the military to conduct limited wars is not solely a function of combat effectiveness, but is a combination of this factor and legitimacy - specifically the legitimacy of purpose.

Professional ethics and institutional purpose are the cornerstones of military legitimacy. These are linked in explicit and at times subtle ways. Presuming that there is a high degree of interpenetration between the military and society (as is likely to be in modern democratic soieties), the military is sensitive and responsive to the values and perceptions of society. More specifically, military purpose must be congruent with social values while at the same time correspond to professional military perspectives. In sum, society bestows legitimacy on the military through its acceptance of the military's purpose and the perception that social norms are closely linked to professional ethics and behavior.

Military legitimacy alone does not necessarily lead to successful application of military power; however, military posture is an essential factor. (As used here, legitimacy is not a question of the legitimacy of the profession in the wider context of the political system. Rather, it is a question of professional esteem, prestige, and credibility - a legitimacy of purpose and professional ethics.) There must be a supportive balance between these two major factors. It is difficult to be precise concerning the degree of legitimacy and the kind of military posture required in any given period or combat situation. The post-Vietnam era demands one particular intermix, while the Korean war demanded another. One can reasonably argue that Vietnam involvement never achieved an effective intermix. Military power to be effective, must not only have a military institution capable of engaging in combat, but it must also have the material and political support of, as well as psychological linkage with, society. In simple terms, the military can be only as effective as society will allow. Conversely, if society supports the military's involvement in conflict, the military must have the proper posture to effectively apply military power. This is the basic premise behind the concept of "management of violence in the service of the state." It is the state that identifies the enemy, and society that provides the political-psychological succor to carry out necessary policies, while the military implements the will of the state. Each of these elements are inter-related and must reinforce each other if successful military policy is to be followed.

Where military legitimacy rests primarily upon image, values, prestige, and purpose, military posture rests on organization, training, technology, and leadership. In other words, military legitimacy is primarily a psychological dimension or subjective. Military posture, on the other hand, is primarily organizational with emphasis on quantitative standards; i.e., objective.

To insure an effective degree of military power, therefore, there must be symmetry between military legitimacy (subjective) and military posture (objective). There is always the danger of asymmetry - where subjective factors, for example, may become increasingly dominant while objective factors become less able to achieve minimum influence on application of military power. This situation can lead to the politicization of the military and a high degree of civilianization, eroding the professional basis of the military institution. Similarly, it is possible for objective factors to become dominant, subduing the influence of subjective factors to such a degree that the military perspective dominates the political institutions - a garrison state condition.

In a democratic society, asymmetry is most likely to develop as a result of contradictions between subjective and objective factors. Thus, the perceptions of society regarding military purpose and behavior may not be in accord with professional military perceptions, and, indeed, may be absolutely opposed to them. The military in a democratic society cannot remain in this kind of asymmetric relationship with society without destroying its institutional purpose and cohesion. Given the relationships between society and the military in a democratic system, political and social forces will generate pressures for the restoration of symmetry - even at the expense of the military institution. This is particularly relevant in the conduct of limited wars.

Equally important, policies followed by the government committing ground troops and other military forces to limited war situations create tension between professional purpose, ethics, and society. Professional propensities to use military force to its maximum to achieve quick and decisive victory are mitigated by the tendency of society to demand proper behavior in the conduct of war and clearly articulated military purposes within a context of acceptable political goals.

Moreover, while many military men see "military intervention as potentially necessary," the attitude of society questions the need for such action.(16)

. . . the popular disaffection with the Vietnamese
war does not indicate a reversion to pre-Korean
attitudes toward limited war. Rather it indicates
serious questioning of the premises about the utility
of limited war as an instrument of American policy,
the premises that originally moved the proponents of
limited-war strategy and that underlay the original
confidence of the Kennedy Administration in America's power to cope with local Communist incursions
of all kinds.(17)

In such circumstances, the military establishment and the
profession become particularly susceptible to divisiveness and
lack of credibility created by the contradictory demands
between society and military purpose.

Democratic ideology dictates high standards of morality
and ethical behavior. Thus, assessments of military behavior
and the credibility of the military institution are, in some
measure, a reflection of society's perception of the conduct of
individual military men. This conduct must meet some minimal
societal norms, even on the battlefield. The military effectiveness of the professional therefore, rests in part on the
correspondence of professional behavior with the moral quality
of the social values in society.

As we discussed earlier in this volume, military purpose
and moral quality are crucial in determining the legitimacy of
military purpose. However, there is a difference in perspectives between the military and society. While the professional
views his mission through an operational lens, the civilian
views it through a political lens. More specifically, purposes
of the political system are the boundaries within which the
military must operate. Military purposes must, therefore, be
congruent to the general will of society if the military is to
maintain its legitimacy. Yet, there is some contradiction
between these concepts and professional perceptions.

The problem is equally complex in contingencies involving
the use of tactical nuclear weapons. The threshold between
tactical nuclear war and general war is thin - even if such
distinctions were to be accepted. To accept the deployment of
tactical nuclear weapons, society must perceive the crisis as
clear and threatening to the national security. Equally important, decision makers will be placed in a quandary in
trying to distinguish between actions that require a tactical
nuclear response and those in the general war category. The
reluctance to use nuclear weapons in less than general wars
remains imbedded in the institutional decision-making process.
Yet, there remain rational arguments regarding the substitu-
tion of nuclear weapons for military manpower. How this can
be accomplished while maintaining restraint and remain within
limited political goals remains a mystery and indeed a dilemma.

As Knorr observes, ". . . the uncertainty about whether escalation can be avoided looms very large. And this uncertainty itself is therefore apt to deter these (nuclear) powers from lightly initiating even the most limited application of military force against each other."(18)

The issues and relationships between military purpose and society are best summed up by a noted military historian who writes:

> To use - and restrain - its immense social, economic and political influence wisely and effectively, the Army obviously must hold itself in close rapport with the people. To secure military success in so complex and difficult a war as the one in Vietnam, it must also depend upon its rapport with the people. Unless the people decide that the war in Vietnam is in truth their war, the Army must finally fall.(19)

## ETHICAL DILEMMAS

The dilemmas arising out of relationships and requirements between professionalism, society, and the institution are in the broader sense questions of professional ethics. The fundamental ethical problem facing the military profession is how to accommodate itself to its growing volunteer character while reinforcing its links to society, yet maintain its uniqueness as a profession and be able to respond to the new environment. In the words of a soldier-scholar:

> Solutions to the dilemma facing the military profession fall somewhere between two unacceptable extremes: returning to traditional professionalism, involving withdrawal from society; or discarding traditional values and severely impairing cohesiveness and discipline. Obviously the two should be reconciled, but the prescription of preserving essential military values while maintaining a close relationship with civilian society is inordinately difficult.(20)

Answers to these questions will not be found in more elaborate technology, increased military discipline, isolation, or aloofness from society, but in understanding the role the military plays in society and appreciating the "politics" of democratic systems. This requires a commitment to the idea that the military professional is part of the American political system and civilian value structure. The military must understand the political "rules of the game" - not only of their own institution but those prevailing in the broader political system.

Using this approach, professional ethics takes on a wider meaning and is particularly sensitive to individual attitudes and behavior. More specifically, ethical questions become linked with the purpose and utility of military force; the degree of political influence of the military within the political system or nature of civil-military relations; the extent to which individual military officers can become involved in the "politics" of the political system; and the conflict between individual conscience and institutional demands.

Questions, for example, about the utility and purpose of military force require basic rethinking of professional purposes. Should military force serve society in other ways aside from preparation for and waging war? There are a number of advocates of the peaceful use of military force, which include involvement in civic-action, educational programs, social-welfare roles. Indeed, some would argue that waging war is not sufficient to sustain professional purpose. A system of ethics, they would argue, cannot be based solely on a concept of "management of violence."

Concern over civil-military relations focuses on such problems as the influence of military men over political decisions. Equally important is the question of national priorities. Should military men include in their military calculus a concern over domestic priorities? Or should there be a purely military perspective based on the assumption that other branches of government provide executive and legislative monitoring? To what degree should the military reinforce civilian value systems?

In this context questions are raised regarding the professional as opposed to the political nature of military service. While some argue that professionalism is enhanced by a non-political military, others argue that only through political knowledge can professionals properly fulfill their responsibilities. Indeed, some scholars argue for the notion of political soldiers who are at home in a political environment – particularly that associated with limited war.

We must understand that nowadays the armed forces of a nation are instruments of external politics and must be trained for such activities. In this sense, I say yes to political activity by our military commanders; they must be highly trained in external politics, otherwise they will carry their political naivete into highly sophisticated political arenas, seeing communists under every bush, and, worse still, supporting political losers purely because they seem affluent and respectable on the surface. Military commanders must be trained in armed diplomacy, a training that must start in their early years. Most important, they must be trained in

political and social science which is as important as
technological education in the armed services.(21)

Legitimate dissent is an essential part of the political
dimension of professionalism required for the conduct of
modern limited war, among other things.  Additionally, legitimate dissent allows a close linkage between the junior and
subordinate levels of the military establishment and the senior
levels - something that was lacking in the conduct of the
Vietnam War.  Indeed, this inadequacy had much to do with
the difference between the realities of the war in the field and
that perceived in Saigon.  In limited wars, with the military
instrument directly involved in a "Vietnam" type environment,
responsiveness and appreciation of the senior officers regarding the attitudes of small unit commanders is a necessity.
The political and social intertwining is most apparent at the
lower-unit operational levels and must be translated into
operational considerations at all levels.  In the long run,
legitimate dissent will provide a new dimension to the professional ethos that will make it more responsive to the necessities
of policies requiring military intervention.  It will provide the
impetus to clearly articulate the military position; it will allow
a variety of views to be assessed broadening the generally
monolithic view of the professional's perspective on military
purpose.(22)

The relationship between individual behavior and institutional norms has been examined earlier in this volume.  As
we learned, a number of military professionals saw in the
aftermath of Vietnam a fundamental gap between the requirements of the institution and the search for professional satisfaction and inner enjoyment of being a military man.  Using
traditional professional norms as a criteria, many individual
professionals found the profession as a whole seriously lacking.(23)  If such conditions remain the rule, rather than the
exception, what can be done to solve the problem (if indeed,
there are solutions)?

The concern for career success and the apparent gap
between the ideals of the profession and the behavior of a
number of professionals also raises serious moral and ethical
questions and suspicions about the quality of higher ranking
military officers.  Moreover, the continuing tendency to push
for career success and comply with institutional demands,
regardless of the moral and ethical implications, is likely to
produce a number of professionals working at the highest
levels of the military hierarchy, whose institutional commitment
and loyalty dominate all other considerations.

What ethical standards are likely to prevail if those who
consider career success the dominant norm become the professional elite?  Professional dilemmas associated with limited
war, therefore, raise a number of broader issues regarding

military purpose, civil-military relations, and the boundaries of professionalism in general. Yet, existing interpretations of professional ethics are likely to obscure the fundamental meaning and study of issues raised here, while perpetuating what McWilliams labels "bureaucratic tendencies":

> All the bureaucratic tendencies visible in the Army are characteristic of all organized power in America. But the Army accentuates and exaggerates bureaucracy because it is a bureaucracy without competitors; conformity, careerism, cultivation of the right attitudes and the safe style become almost necessary obsessions, difficult for any but a very few to resist.(24)

Thus, the traditional perspectives regarding the use of military force, institutional loyalty, and mission orientation reinforced by situational ethics rationalize narrow professional perspectives as the key to institutional and individual success.

This characteristic of the profession is summed up by Gray who writes:

> Not all certain whether they will later be considered by their own people as heroes or as scoundrels, great numbers find it simpler to ignore the moral problems by thinking of them as little as possible. Better to let the conscience sleep, to do as the others are doing and as one is told to do and the future will bring what it will. Who knows what the future will bring anyway? Most soldiers in wartime feel caught in the present so completely that they surrender their wills to their superiors and exist in the comforting anonymity of the crowd.(25)

## CONCLUSIONS

It would, of course, be in the traditional mode to respond to the dilemmas addressed here by recommending that the military requires better training, leadership, motivation, management, and tactics. Yet, the answer may not lie in "better" everything, but in recognizing the limits of the intervention. It seems unlikely that the United States will be able to intervene in limited war situations with hopes for a neat "surgical" operation. On the contrary, it is more likely that military intervention will increase the politicization of the conflict and stimulate a nationalistic reaction, while exposing the United States to internal tensions and conflict. Increasingly, this will erode "professionalism" while decreasing the legitimacy of the military institution at home.

The dilemma is clear. Military intervention raises serious problems of military purpose. Not only is there major linkages between society and military purpose, but also between professionalism, society, and military purpose. Without relatively clear goals and unambiguous roles and purpose for the military in modern limited war, it is unlikely that military professionalism will be able to maintain an ethical and purposeful posture so necessary for maintaining its linkage with and legitimacy of society. Equally important, the political-psychological dimensions of modern limited war may quickly involve the intervening power in the political-social systems of an alien culture. The professional ethos and traditional perspective do not provide the professional dimensions for sustained operations in such an environment. Thus, a dilemma is created not only with respect to pursuing the policy with respect to modern limited war but also with respect to its actual conduct.

When viewed from the policy level, it is clear that there are political-psychological limits to the application of military power. These limits, when translated into strategic terms, militate against a policy committing troops into an ambiguous, milti-dimensional environment, associated with modern limited war. For any hope of a successful military policy, there must be symmetry between military legitimacy and military purpose.

In light of these considerations, the military profession is faced with three options. First, it can adopt a traditional professionalism posture; second, it can assume a civil service role; and third, it can develop a new rationale for the profession. The first option is the most comfortable position and has been the presumed basis for civil-military relationships for some time. But this option tends to relegate the professional military man to a robot-like role in which is is presumed to be an unconditional servant of the state. It is based on the premise that military men have distinct and purely military roles limited to the battlefield. Moreover, it places military professionals in a position which requires the uncritical acceptance of policies, programs, and political-military strategy, vacating intellectual analysis to civilians and political leaders. This option is one that is least valid to the complexities of modern military life.

The second option presumes that the military profession is a public service with little uniqueness and subordinates its internal environment to that associated with the procedures and intricacies of the federal bureaucracy. The greatest danger in such a posture is that self-interest and concern for the material benefits linked with an occupation may dominate the motivation of individual officers. Equally important such a civil service role would probably civilianize the military to such a point that it would erode the basis for professional uniqueness and make the profession and institution vulnerable to political manipulation from within as well as from without.

In the long run, this would create dangers not only for the profession but for the political system.

The third option is based on the development of a new rationale in which military men are seen as more than unconditional servants or paid employees of the state. This would require that the military develop political understanding and expertise, a sense of realistic and enlightened self-interest, and professional perspectives transcending boundaries that we have traditionally associated with duty, honor, and country. The profession must accept a political dimension - not partisan politics. It must be capable of dealing with environments that are not purely military and recognize the professional military man's right to engage in politics within a domestic system, as long as he adheres to the rules of the game. In this third option, the profession would see itself as a political interest group trying to reach the civilian leadership and the public to explain its case and develop a consensus for its objectives. To implement this option requires a military leadership and profession which has a specific but limited political posture.

We are not suggesting that military professionals should make political decisions regarding the goals of the political system, whether in peace or war. But surely they must be equipped to look beyond immediate exigencies and develop the intellectual tools and insights to appreciate the interdependence between war and politics. Such a perspective is not acquired in professional military schools - at least not in the present curriculum. In order to present the "military" point of view in a judicious and well-articulated manner, military professionals must understand the total concern of the political system. They must go beyond the simple loyalty of "managers of violence in the service of the state." Moreover, war itself raises questions of morality which require more than a "military" solution.

The third option is clearly the most challenging and useful; yet it, too, has its dangers. Not only must the profession accept a political dimension to its ethical values, but it must always remember that it remains a servant of the state and is not an autonomous decision-making body. To take on this critical political dimension is only a short step away from assuming a self-righteous stance as the ultimate arbiter of society's political disputes. This third option provides a wider range of activity, mainly consultative, for the professional officer. Indeed, it requires an active, responsible self-interest and a non-partisan involvement in the policy process and politics in general. The American political system is partially based on the assumption that groups and interest must have access to policy makers; articulation and aggregation of interests on a wide scale, unencumbered by government restrictions, are basic premises of democratic society. Even the military ought to be given the opportunity to argue its case within the accepted "rules of the game."

From the individual point of view, this third option requires that the profession recognize the limits to military institutional demands and individual subservience even in combat situations. The institutionalization of healthy skep-ticism, reasonable inquiry, and legitimate dissent would do much to reinforce the worth of the "individual" while providing a momentum to innovation, imagination, and self-examination. Obviously, this option requires substantive changes in profes-sional ethics, and a broader view of military professionalism.

## NOTES

1. Robert E. Osgood, "The Reappraisal of Limited War" in Eugene J. Rosi, American Defense and Detente; Readings in National Security Policy. New York: Dodd, Mead and Co., 1973, pp. 468-469. The author concludes:

. . . These doubts seem likely to lead to a marked differentiation of interests in the application of containment - a downgrading of interests in the Third World and a greater distinction between these interests, and those pertaining to the security of the advanced democratic countries. . . . What they seem to preclude, at least for a while, is any re-newed effort to strengthen military deterrence and resistance in the Third World by actively developing and projecting United States' capacity to fight local wars.

2. Osgood, p. 470. The author notes:

What we are almost certain not to witness is the perfection of limited-war conceptions and practice in accordance with some predictable, rational calculus and reliable, universal rules of the game. The conditions and modalities of international conflict are too varied, dynamic, and subjective for limited war to be that determinate.

See also Herbert K. Tillema, Appear to Force: American Mili-tary Intervention in the Era of Containment. New York: Thomas Y. Crowell, 1973. According to Tillema, the United States has been involved in four overt military interventions since World War II: Korea, 1950; Lebanon, 1958; Vietnam, 1961; and the Dominican Republic, 1965. These are considered overt military interventions because of the commitment of ground troops. Thus, in 30 years since the end of World War II, the United States has been involved in four limited war situations requiring U.S. ground troops. Although in two instances, Dominican Republic and Lebanon, casualties were few and numbers of troops small, the total casualties of the four interventions are over 80,000 killed and thousands more wounded and disabled. Tillema discusses these interventions and what he perceives as the basis for U.S. policy. Equally interesting is his discussion of why the U.S. did not intervene more frequently, given the nature of the international environment over the past 30 years.

    3.  Bernard Brodie, War and Politics. New York: Macmillan Publishing Co., Inc., 1973, pp. 127-128.

    4.  Osgood, p. 471. According to the author:

> A limited war is generally conceived to be a war fought for ends far short of the complete subordination of one state's will to anothers' and by means involving far less than the total military resources of the belligerente, leaving the civilian life and the armed forces of the belligerente largely intact and leading to a bargaining termination . . . the term local war is not often reserved for the great number of local conventional wars in which neither of the super-powers is directly or indirectly involved. The difficulty of defining limited war arises partly because the relevant limits are matters of degree and partly because they are a matter of perspective, since a war that is limited on one side might be virtually total from the standpoint of the other, on whose territory the war is fought. Furthermore, a limited war may be carefully restricted in some respects (e.g., geographically) and much less in others (e.g., in weapons, targets, or political objectives).

    5.  Brodie, p. 358.

    6.  The Chinese Communist victory in 1949 provided a modern demonstration effect for the remainder of the world regarding the effectiveness of a "people's war." Regardless of the number of failures, the disagreement over tactics, and the sacrifices required, "people's war" became a symbol and a model not only for use against colonial powers, but against established regimes and their supporters.

    7.  Klaus Knorr, On the Uses of Military Power in the Nuclear Age. Princeton: Princeton University Press, 1966, p. 108.

    8.  President's Commission on an All-Volunteer Force, Report. Washington, D.C.: G.P.O., 1970.

    9.  Zeb B. Bradford and Frederic J. Brown, The United States Army in Transition. Beverly Hills, Cal., Sage Publications, 1973, pp. 38-42.

10. For example, at the height of the Vietnam War, there were approximately 500,000 U.S. military men in Vietnam. To prosecute the war and still maintain some semblance of a world-wide military posture, there were over 1.3 million men drafted into the Army over the period 1965-1969. Additionally, there were close to 1 million enlistments and re-enlistments. Thus, for the Army alone, over 2 million men were either inducted or enlisted over a five-year period. For the same period of time, over 5 million personnel were either drafted or enlisted in all of the services.

11. Frank Margiotta, "A Military Elite in Transition: Air Force Leaders in the 1980's," Armed Forces and Society, Volume 2, No. 2, Winter, 1976.

12. Roger A. Beaumont, Military Elites. Indianapolis, Bobbs Merrill, 1974, p. 171-184. Sam C. Sarkesian, The Professional Army Officer in a Changing Society. Chicago: Nelson-Hall Co., 1975, pp. 93-102.

13. Charles W. Brown and Charles C. Moskos, Jr., "The Volunteer Soldier - Will He Fight?" in Military Review, 1976.

14. Charles C. Moskos, Jr., "The Emergent Military; Civil, Traditional, or Plural?" Pacific Sociological Review, April, 1973, Volume 16, No. 2, pp. 255-279; David R. Segal, et al., "Consequence Isomorphism and Interdependence at the Civil-Military Interface," Journal of Political and Military Sociology, 2, Fall 1974, pp. 161-171; Bradford and Brown, pp. 189-202; William L. Hauser, America's Army in Crisis. Baltimore: The Johns Hopkins University Press, 1973, pp. 207-218; Sarkesian, pp. 93-102.

15. The original argument that the military was being segmented into a civilianized technical component and a traditional combat element is found in Moskos (1973). Extensions of the "plural military" thesis are found in Bradford and Brown (1973), Hauser (1973), Segal (1974).

16. Jerald G. Bachman, and John D. Blair, Soldiers, Sailors and Civilians; The 'Military Mind' and the All-Volunteer Force. Ann Arbor, Mich.: Survey Research Center, November, 1975, p. 62.

17. Osgood, p. 466.

18. Knorr, pp. 99-100.

19. Russell F. Weigley, History of the United States Army. New York: The Macmillan Co., 1967, p. 556.

20. Robert G. Gard, Jr., "The Military and American Society," Foreign Affairs, July, 1971, Volume 49, No. 4, p. 707.

21. Michael Elliot-Bateman, "The Form of People's War" in Michael Elliot-Bateman (Ed.) The Fourth Dimension of Warfare, Volume I. New York: Praeger, 1970, p. 147.

22. On the need for dissent see, William P. Mack (USN-Ret), "The Need for Dissent," The Army Times Magazine, January 17, 1976.

23. See U.S. Army War College, Study on Military Professionalism. Carlisle Barracks, Pennsylvania: USAWC, June 30, 1970, pp. 28-29.

24. Wilson C. McWilliams, Military Honor after Mylai. New York: The Council on Religion and International Affairs, 1972, p. 28.

25. Glenn J. Gray, The Warriors. New York: Harper, 1967, p. 183.

# III

# Politics, Professionalism, and the Political System

# Part III
## An Introduction

Part 3 examines the political-social environment within which the military must operate and the impact this has on professionalism. The first selection focuses specifically on the Vietnam involvement, noting that many of the problems within the military are linked with domestic turmoil and attitudes on the war. These are reflected in different attitudes within the officer corps. Both in the conduct of the war and in functioning within a liberal democratic environment, military professionals must respond to and operate within political-social boundaries of democratic ideology. Given the political-social nature of the Vietnam War and the ambiguities of the environment, combined with the conventional posture of the American military, the military professional found himself unable to adapt to the necessities of counter-revolutionary conflict. This was compounded by the opposition to the war in American society and the spill-over of these attitudes into the military system. The political-social challenges evolving out of the Vietnam War and the role of the military in a democratic society place the military professional in a political environment. In this context, the military institution is, among other things a political institution, and, accordingly, the profession has a political dimension. The second selection examines military professionalism in the context of the American political system and the characteristics of the international security environment. To respond effectively, military professionals must be educated in the meaning of democracy and the proper role of the military in a liberal society. Since it is the value system of democracy that is the basis for the strategic and military policy of America, the military professional must also understand and appreciate the interaction between all of these elements and military operations. While there are a number of educational channels that can prepare the professional in this respect, it is liberal education at the university level or its equivalent that serves best. In any case, the military profession is enmeshed in a political-social environment both in terms of the domestic system and in the conduct of military operations. Thus, a new professional posture is necessary. One that can intelligently assess political-military priorities, advocate reasonable courses of action, and recognize and assess the consequences of such action.

# 8 Political Soldiers: Perspectives on Professionalism in the United States Military

Almost two decades have passed since the American withdrawal from Vietnam. During that period of time a number of events have taken place which have had a profound impact on American military posture. These include, among other things, the establishment of a volunteer military system in America; the rise to prominence of oil producing states; the extension of Soviet military power; inter-state confrontations of lesser powers; and American domestic political-social forces. Such events not only changed the international security position and military posture of the United States, but they created an environment which raises a number of questions regarding the adequacy of American military professionalism. This did not occur overnight. Early signs had appeared during the latter years of the Vietnam War.

The purpose of this chapter is to explore the nature of American military professionalism and the character of the military institution as they emerged from the final years of the Vietnam War, to identify the apparent trends of that time, and to compare these to what emerged in the 1980s. The underlying theme of this study is that there is a political dimension to the military profession and the institution, and that it has been persistent and expanding since the end of World War II. Equally important, this political dimension has been particularly significant over the past two decades. Yet, it is argued here that the military profession and the institution have not responded adequately to this political dimension.

POLITICS AND THE PROFESSION


Immediately following the Civil War, the conviction of the Army
officer corps concerning political involvement rested on the
premise that professionalism and politics did not mix.

> The concept of an impartial, nonpartisan, objective
> career service, loyally serving whatever adminis-
> tration or party was in power became the ideal of
> the military profession. The military were proud of
> the extent to which they had realized this ideal, and
> compared themselves favorably with the more back-
> ward and still largely politics-ridden civil service.(1)

Until World War II, the U.S. military appeared to follow
this non-political orientation. As a self-contained, relatively
isolated social system, the military viewed its mission as unique
and, consequently, perceived its existence as divergent from
and generally non-participatory in the political processes. The
post-World War II period and the onset of a vastly changed
international environment combined with the new technological
age ushered in by nuclear weapons, precipitated significant
changes in the military establishment. "Military requirements
thus became a fundamental ingredient of foreign policy, and
military men and institutions acquired authority and influences
far surpassing that ever previously possessed by military professionals on the American scene."(2)   The preoccupation with
national security and a proper defense posture stimulated the
growth of a vast defense establishment and concomitant political power and involvement in the political process.
Although a reaction developed against this military dominance in the late 1960s, the forces generated by the experience of the past two decades not only changed the political
and social environment in which the military operated, but also
transformed the military establishment "from a relatively
self-contained organization (. . . primitive) to a complex and
civilian interrelated agency (. . . a competitive organization).(3)

> Interpenetration of the civil and military sectors has
> deeply modified the insularity of the military pro-
> fession.  The new skill requirements, the growing
> importance of academic rather than strictly military
> education, modifications of the military rank hier-
> archy mirroring changes in civilian society, and a
> diversification of military careers are all elements in
> this process.  One can speak of these developments
> in their entirety as a "civilianization" of the military;
> yet the militarization of society proves an equally apt

image, describing dependence of the military on the total national resources as a base of mobilization.(4)

While these changes occurred over the past two decades, the Vietnam period ushered in a relatively new era with respect to the military establishment, both in its domestic and political dimensions. Among other things, these factors served to expand and sharpen the political character of the military profession.

The military was aware of the changing environment brought on by Vietnam, but it was unable to establish an effective institutional response to the problems that emerged. A number of military men struggled to reconcile traditional military techniques and wisdom with the new environment. Some new institutional procedures developed. But in the main, there was little agreement as to the most effective way to maintain institutional efficiency and still respond to the changed domestic and international environments.

These issues seriously raised over a decade ago remain relevant today, albeit in a less strident form. For example, the American military preoccupation with Europe raises serious questions regarding its capability to respond to low intensity conflicts. The American military's concern for traditional battlefield skills also raises questions about its ability to understand and appreciate the battlefield of the 1980s, particularly in non-European areas.

In assessing the military profession as it emerged from the Vietnam experience and the problems it faced in the post-Vietnam period, one can see the importance of a political perspective. This becomes clearer upon studying three major factors that strongly influence the character of the military profession. These are: professional cohesiveness; strategic political-military considerations; and the American domestic political-social context.

Before we examine these issues in detail, there is a need to clarify the concept of politics and its link to the military profession. It is generally presumed that everyone knows the meaning of politics. This is not the case, however. Politics can mean a great many different things to different people. It may be useful therefore, to suggest a concept of politics that is directly linked to the military profession and to the various themes underlying this volume.

Politics as a concept includes three elements; condition, relationship, and process. Thus, politics presumes disagreement over values, interests, or desires. It also suggests some type of hierarchical positioning of individuals and between individuals and the system. Finally, politics presumes that disagreements are resolved and relationships determined by the application of power through a systematized and legitimate procedure.

As Harold Lasswell has stated, "The study of politics is the study of influence and the influential."(5)  In the same vein, George Catlin, an English political theorist, states that politics is the "study of the act of control, or as the act of human or social control."(6)  V.O. Key notes, "Politics as power consists fundamentally of relationships of super-ordination and subordination, of dominance and submission, of the governors and the governed."(7)  Key goes on to state, "To comprehend politics one must look not only at the man who draws power from a keg, so to speak, but at the relation between him and those his actions may affect.  In this re-lationship lies the essence of politics."

The dilemma for the military profession is how to adapt to the politics associated with the political system it is to serve, how to develop the proper posture to insure effective func-tioning of the military system, and how to develop the in-tellectual insights and capability to deal with the modern security environment in which politics and the military are inextricable.

## DIFFERENTIATION AND CHANGE WITHIN THE OFFICERS CORPS

The varied, sometimes contradictory, pressures on the military from external and internal sources during the Vietnam period left their impact on the orientation of officers.  Values and perceptions, in the main, stem from the cultural base from which the officer develops his initial life experiences.  This is furthered by his educational patterns and institutional exper-iences, all of which must be tempered by the values instilled by the military institution itself.  During the latter stages of the Vietnam War, the military institution and the profession came under serious criticism and its conventional wisdom was challenged.  One result was that within the military profession, there appeared several groups of officers whose ideological orientation differed in terms of their perceptions of the War, stimulating serious internal debate and making the institution more susceptible to external pressures.  Equally important, an understanding of the various perspectives within the pro-fession, how these evolved, and their consequences reflect the relative cohesiveness and intellectual state of the military profession.

Officers coalesced around three particular ideological orientations.  These were the traditionalists, the transition-alists, and the modernists.  Obviously, there were no clear delineations and overlaps occurred.  Nevertheless, there were sufficient distinctions to identify three categories.(8)  These were characterized during the Vietnam period as follows.

The traditionalists were generally those senior officers in the services consisting of the World War II-Korean Group; that is, these officers were, in the main, Academy graduates who came into service immediately before, during, or immediately after World War II. A number saw action in World War II; many saw action in Korea. The orientation of this group was still towards the conventional wisdom with its emphasis on the heroic role, traditional techniques, and unquestioned legitimacy attached to the military role. This group was perhaps most separated from the youth culture of the 1960s and unappreciative of the changing nature and motivations of the young enlisted man or young officer.(9)

The second group - i.e., the transitionalists - generally comprised those officers who came into service during the Korean War or immediately thereafter. They carried with them some of the experiences of the Korean War characterized by conventional orientation and tempered by experiences of the military during its rise to dominance in budgetary considerations and involvement in political-military operations; i.e., the Cuban missile crisis, American involvement in the Dominican Republic, and the initial years of the Vietnam War. These officers were in the Lieutenant Colonel/Colonel category with their service education wedded to traditional orientation while their experiences stemmed from an "unconventional" environment. There was a greater degree of flexibility in their intellectual approach - attributable, perhaps, to the scope of graduate school experience and closer association with civilian academic circles intermingled with professional experience. Additionally, traditional orientation was not so entrenched that the uncertainties of the post-Korean era and the evolution of the political-military environment in domestic politics had not influenced values and perceptions. This group of officers were those primarily associated with the emerging elite.

The third group of officers - i.e., the modernists - represented primarily the Vietnam era officers. These were a product of a period characterized by domestic dissent, youth culture, antimilitary sentiments, campus disturbances, and political involvement of the youth. These officers generally came into service in the 1960s and as a body were faced with the prospects of service in Vietnam as part of their first tour of duty. A majority of the junior officers (Captains and Lieutenants) were non-Academy graduates and thus reflected in a more visible manner the social dynamics of civilian society. This is not to suggest that the Academy graduates were isolated from this orientation. In fact, Academy education and teaching techniques provide a flexibility which is attuned, in many respects, to the social dynamics in U.S. society.(10)

In themselves, perhaps, these factors did not cause undue influence on the traditional military orientation. But in

conjunction with the political dynamics stemming from the
Vietnam era, they provided an additional impetus and reinforced the politicization of the military, and specifically in this
instance, perpetuated and heightened the internal debate and
competition.

The experiences in Vietnam served as a catalyst for
changes within the officer corps. The greatest impact was on
the "modernist" group of officers. Not only was the Vietnam
War a disillusioning experience, but in many respects a frustrating one. The nature of the war, with all of its revolutionary characteristics, not only seemed to defy application of
technological war, but also provided few signposts for measuring success or failure. Although important successes were
scored against the revolutionary military forces, real success
rested within the political-social environment of the village
structure. The inability to affect this structure negated much
of the conventional wisdom and effect of modern weaponry.
Regardless of the lip service given to the principles of Mao
and revolutionary warfare, the U.S. military manifested little
appreciation of these principles in actual operations. The
brief training periods prior to being committed to the Vietnam
War provided little motivation or battlefield knowledge to
conduct an effective counter-revolutionary operation:

> The American in Vietnam. Caught in a war without
> fixed battle lines, without stirring slogans or Hitler-
> type villains, without real estate objectives, without
> conventional tactics or even conventional weapons,
> he must share the daily fighting with a smiling ally
> who at times is as difficult to understand as the
> enemy, for he too is an Oriental cut from the same
> enigmatic mold. There is an Old West quality about
> the war in Vietnam that is exciting and demands the
> most of a soldier in ingenuity and daring. But
> there is an Old East quality about it too, that is
> exasperating and wears down even the most dedi-
> cated. . . .(11)

Since the key to success was in the villages, the problem
was how to combat the influence of the guerrillas on the
villagers. For the soldier it required performing a variety of
duties of a non-bombat nature, including such things as
guarding peasants while they harvested the crop, conducting
road blocks and searches, coordinating operations with local
police and civilian officials, and, in the case of U.S. troops,
coordinating with indigenous government troops. It also
required involvement in all forms of civic activities, from
building schools and repairing roads to teaching school. The
purpose in all of this was to "win the hearts and minds of the
people." To put it in other terms, it was to take the revolution out of the hands of the revolutionaries.

The experience in Vietnam clearly indicated that the external power - i.e., the U.S. in Vietnam - had limited impact on the political aspects of the counter-revolutionary campaign. The agents for mobilization of the masses as a counter to the guerrilas must be indigenous to the culture of the peasants. For political counter mobilization to be effective, there must be a relatively effective political system with policies that will motivate the "kinds" of political agents and actions required to follow up military actions and create and maintain loyalty to the existing government. While battle after battle were fought and won by American troops in Vietnam, these became almost meaningless, because no effective political followup policy was implemented. And this had to come from the South Vietnamese themselves.

Thus, in Vietnam the war did not show any visible move towards solution, regardless of the application of U.S. military power. For the dedicated and experienced professional, this may have been rationalized in terms of the complexities of revolutionary wars and political-social factors, but for the "modernists" sensitive to the U.S domestic environment and the changing orientation of domestic politics, the war smacked of inefficiency, ineffectiveness, and immorality. Whether we speak of the dedicated and experienced professional or the "modernist," the experience provided a relatively new ingredient to the military establishment: uneasiness regarding efficacy of strategy and tactics; generation of political forces within; exposure to external political-social forces; and a diminution of the rigid hierarchical structure within the rank system. All of these factors pointed in the direction of political dimensions rarely known within the military establishment.

Perhaps some of the frustrations and dissatisfaction amongst the military with the nature of the U.S. involvement can be traced to these political aspects of the war. Brought up with the traditional approach and conventional wisdom to unconventional warfare, many officers were faced with the problem of giving some meaning to military operations, while trying to adapt conventional thought and tactics to a political-social battleground; that is, limited in its susceptibility to external influence. Many of the emerging elite of that time served tours in Vietnam and experienced the frustrations associated with the counter-revolutionary effort. Officers who served with the Vietnamese or with Pacification and Revolutionary Development efforts perhaps experienced these frustrations in a much more pervasive manner. In any case, most officers became aware of the political and social character of these kinds of wars. Perhaps more importantly, political-social action inadvertently became part of the concept of professionalism.(12)

The military profession of the 1980s exhibits similar ideological differentiations, although the delineations are more obscure and some of the characteristics have changed. The traditionalist is now the officer who probably saw service in Vietnam and generally accepts the notion that American military involvement in the Third World is to be avoided. Indeed, these officers seem oriented towards a European type battle-field. Equally important, such officers are generally convinced that the military must concentrate primarily, if not solely, on battlefield skills. The transitionalists are officers who are ambivalent regarding military intervention in Third World areas and are convinced of the need for nuclear strength and a strong European orientation. Yet, there is concern that professionalism needs to include an understanding of political-social processes and the nature of international politics. The modernists are those officers who are convinced that Third World contingencies may be more serious and pressing for the American military than battles in the Central Plains of Europe. Moreover, they recognize that battlefield skills alone are not sufficient for successful use of force in non-European areas; that political-social knowledge and political expertise are essential. Interestingly enough, it appears that age differ-ences as a characteristic of the three groups is now relatively unimportant, albeit, younger officers tend to identify more with transitionalists and modernists. However, the ideological differentation within the officers corps has diminished con-siderably since the end of the Vietnam War. The traditionalist view predominates, with only a few voices representing other orientations.

The fading of the Vietnam experience combined with the Soviet military actions in 1979 and 1980 have in no small measure, reinforced the European orientation (and fear of superpower confrontation in military terms) of the American military profession. Moreover, it has reduced the concern for political-social action and has shifted orientation towards a more conventional and traditional posture. But such a posture ill-prepares the profession to respond to domestic political and social expectations or to the range of strategic contigencies facing it in the 1980s.

## STRATEGIC DIMENSIONS

Limited war takes place in the context of nuclear issues. It is reasonable to assume that the probabilities of nuclear war will remain remote while attempts will continue to improve weapons technology and maintain a credible deterrent. Similarly, the probabilities that the United States will become involved in a limited conventional war will also remain remote. While the

U.S. military will attempt to retain a capacity to conduct these
types of wars, policy options in this direction will be tempered
by the distinct possibility that such actions will escalate into
nuclear warfare. Consequently, the possibilities of limited
conventional wars will be limited by the highly restrictive
conditions placed on such involvement. The U.S. reaction to
the Vietnam War also imposed stringent conditions and limitations upon such commitments in the future. There is a distinct possibility therefore that the U.S. military will be faced
with the task of attempting to accomplish its mission without
the option of committing ground troops.

Following the Vietnam War, many saw the decrease in the
possibility of general war in Europe. Thus, American forces
in NATO fell into a peacetime garrison syndrome with its
frustrations, dissatisfaction, and semi-soldiering. Even with
respect to the Middle East, where the possibility existed (and
still exists) that American forces would be deployed, the
political nature of the commitment remained uppermost, rather
than the specifics of military force. In both areas therefore,
the primary considerations were perceptions of American credibility and military posture, and the political impact of American
presence. Even with the events in Afghanistan and the Middle
East in 1979 and 1980, these considerations remain relevant.

Arms limitation and arms control have emerged as important facets of the international political-military picture.
Aside from the purely technical considerations, a number of
political factors are relevant. Issues to be considered in this
respect include the limits of minimum armaments coincident with
public acceptability, national security perspectives, domestic
and international political dynamics, negotiable issues, techniques of implementation, channels of cross-national contacts,
participation in and the role of international organizations.
The military participation in the planning, negotiating, and
executing will demand political as well as technical skills and
an understanding of the political implications associated with
arms limitations and arms control.

Although, it is likely that use of U.S. military in a
ground combat role will be severely restricted, barring a
dramatic change in world events or domestic attitudes, the
need for American assistance in revolutionary or counter
revolutionary situations will increase. The efficacy of revolutionary wars has been well demonstrated in the past two
decades. There is no reason to believe that such conditions
will subside in the coming decade. On the contrary, a brief
survey of the conditions in Africa and Southeast Asia, for
example, suggests that revolutionary conditions still exist and
in some instances are increasing in a number of developing
states. Barring a complete isolationist policy, the United
States must be prepared for involvement in one form or another in these areas. This does not necessarily mean military

intervention, but can include a variety of non-military means (see Chapter 4). Moreover, if military intervention should occur, it does not necessarily mean on a scale that occurred in Vietnam. In any case, the lessons of Vietnam should be instructive, if they are heeded.

Nevertheless, many of the strategic aspects of American political-military policy remain in a state of transition. The United States still has not settled on a clear articulation of national interests in various areas, nor has it determined the configuration of its military forces. After Vietnam, attempts were made to establish some guidance with respect to military policy. As the following Department of the Army memorandum shows, these were based on certain premises that are only partly true in the current environment.

> A major change is thought to be in the making as the result of the unpopularity of Vietnam. The limited war concept will likely not receive public or popular support in the future. The United States, as primarily represented by its military establish-ment, will likely not be the "policeman" of the world. Increasingly, therefore, the emphasis is being placed on determining what the military (Army) can do in assisting other countries to help themselves. Cur-rently popular are the ideas of nation-building and institution-building. One result of this movement has been the establishment of the Directorate of International and Civil Affairs within ODCSOPS. This directorate as now organized is approximately one year old. Its major areas of concern are with such things as unconventional warfare, counter-insurgency, and analysis of underground and revolutionary movements. . . . A final modification mentioned was an increasing emphasis on and number of positions which call for management rather than strictly leadership skills.(13)

What has occured is a shift of American military per-spectives to a European orientation and a technological battle-field. While there is validity in developing such a capability, there are dangers in preoccupation with it to the detriment of capabilities in non-conventional warfare. Equally important, the concern with the technological aspects of large battles and modern weaponry has significantly diminished the concern for the political-social and humanistic aspects of the battlefield. Even in the perceived major battles between major powers, the political-social dimension remains important.

The redefinition of the military institutional role and in-dividual orientation, therefore, must take into account a whole range of political-military activities associated with revolutionary wars, "low visibility" type operations, as well as major wars. The shift in emphasis to include political-social factors requires a revision in training considerations, educational emphasis, and career patterns. A passive political-social orientation must give way to active concern with political-social revolutions. To properly fulfill these kinds of roles, the military must train political sociologists to operate at the action or "people" level, as well as at the strategic planning level. The intellectual and orientation gap between this type of concern and that oriented towards the movement of divisions and armies, logistical trains, nuclear war, and amphibious operations is obvious.

> As an institution the army has been, by virtue of several less than popular incidents (Cuba, Dominican Republic, Vietnam), forced to look at how it might achieve its mission without the traditional deployment of troops. This immediately underscores the importance to the military (Army) of public-political opinion. The concepts of nation-building and institution-building bespeak concern with civilian society. . . . Vietnam would seem to represent a "straw on the camel's back" in forcing the military to a role which is not solely based on persuasion by violence.(14)

What is the significance of these factors to the military institution? Although legacies of the Cold War, such as the stationing of troops in Europe and the standing commitment to South Korea, remain in one form or another, these need to be tempered by some attention to advisory roles, the requirements of military assistance, and low intensity conflicts, which by their very nature involve the military in political-social spheres of activity. Proper training for these roles include knowledge of political systems, social and cultural factors, and some understanding of political-social roles and their impact on nation-building. The political nature of such training is obvious.

## DOMESTIC CONTINGENCY MISSIONS

The frequency with which domestic dissent developed into domestic violence during the Vietnam period suggested to the military that it had to be prepared for missions of domestic law enforcement. Military involvement in such situations reinforced the need for political-social understanding and perspectives. Deployment of troops for any domestic disturbance, whether in urban areas or on campuses, raised the problem of proper conduct and the need for enlightened leadership techniques. These can be more difficult and complex than conventional battlefield situations. The unpredictability of civil-military confrontation, and the political ramifications associated with the outcome, imposed restraints and required a judicious use of force, persuasion, and psychological techniques without resort to weaponry.(15)   The events at Kent State were a case in point.

The possibility of troop deployment within the United States required intelligence on target areas. However, intelligence activity within the United States by various agencies of the military raised a controversy regarding its propriety. Although not specifically considered here, it is important to note the political sensitivity and political "intrigue" with which such activity is tinged. Stemming from background investigations for security clearances of both military and civilian personnel, this activity gradually encompassed dissident groups and individuals. In turn, such information was used to develop studies on various urban areas for purposes of identifying targets for possible troop deployment. This required troop commanders and staffs to become familiar with urban settings, socio-economic groups, areas of dissidence and tension, and political considerations for each of the target areas.

It was felt that contingency missions would also require the military to become involved in environment issues, such as disaster area activities, pollution control, aftermath of military mishaps, and civil defense operations.(16)   A reduction in international commitments would have allowed some shift of attention to such domestic assistance missions. Domestic assistance missions involve close association between military men and civilians, and military personnel and civilians in affected areas. These types of missions are removed from battlefield motivations and demand skills and understanding essentially civilian in content.

However, the emergence of a dominant traditionalist military posture and professional perspective (for a variety of reasons discussed earlier), has reduced serious concern with formal military involvement in domestic contingency missions, contrary to the views held by some immediately following the Vietnam War. Yet, as a number of events have shown, the military remains closely wedded to its domestic environment and must be prepared to perform accordingly. In this respect, this reinforces the need for an appreciation and understanding of the political consequences of domestic involvement.

This is not intended as a catalogue of future missions, but rather to point out that the direction in which the military needs to move with respect to domestic relationships and potential areas of commitment. These are inclined to require a political awareness at all levels within the military. Troop

commanders and junior officers, particularly, require a sensitivity to the "politics" of any situation involving civil-military
relationships.

## DOMESTIC POLITICAL CONTEXT:
## ANTI-MILITARY SENTIMENTS

The military is operating in a vastly changed domestic political
context. An important part of this change evolved from the
antimilitary sentiments that surfaced during the latter years of
Vietnam. This created in the minds of many, a rather distorted image as to the relationships of the military to the
problems of U.S. society.

> The Age of Aquarius is not a happy time for the
> U.S. military establishment.

> Flower children are in the streets. Wars are un-
> fashionable. In circles of the New Left, men in
> uniform have come to symbolize the corruption of
> American life, the distortion of national priorities,
> the darker impulses of the American soul.

> In colleges and high schools, new heroes have
> emerged whose battle cry is "Resist!" Politicians
> decry militarism, priests and doctors and lawyers
> encourage draft evasion, military recruiters are
> driven from college campuses, ROTC buildings are
> stoned and burned.(17)

A diminished military image of the early 1970s was
reflected in the media: in popular films as well as the printed
word. The popularity of the anti-hero or non-hero, as manifested in films such as Catch-22, the Lost Command, and
M.A.S.H., reflected the military image held by certain groups
within society. Even a film such as Patton portrayed a
militarist in the most militant sense appealing to the popular
concept of the military mind. The My Lai massacres, the
alleged graft and corruption associated with the highest circles
of senior enlisted men, the charge of military-industrial col-
lusion, and the stress of the mass media on military activities
within Vietnam, created the type of image which made honor,
duty, country, sound hollow during the Vietnam era. Similarly, a number of publications expressed strong suspicion of
the military establishment, pinpointing waste and mismanagement, and portraying inflexible and immature military perspectives.(18) In any case, there appeared to be a cultural
ingredient which accepted as "real" the futility, rigidity, and
unenlightened quality of military life.

The attitudes thus expressed detrimentally affect the views held by the military with respect to public esteem and prestige.

> Such public attitudes serve to depreciate the image that the professional officer holds of himself. As long as the military was relatively isolated from civilian society, and comprised no more than a small homogeneous organization, prestige and self esteem rested more on internal standards. What the public thought mattered less. . . . Today's greater civilian contacts, and not necessarily more stable image depends to a greater extent on public attitudes and popular opinion.(19)

The military ideology is legitimized by its extension into and acceptance by society. This ideology is based on devotion, duty, honor, country, and its expected acceptance by the public as realistically reflecting military motivations; i.e., the legitimacy of military values. Pressures stemming from the Vietnam War generated societal perceptions, making the legitimacy of military values suspect in the eyes of many young people.(20) Additionally, society in general developed an ambivalence regarding military service. Some of these attitudes manifested themselves during the years of our Vietnam involvement in declining ROTC enrollments and thousands of draft dodgers and hundreds of deserters.(21)

This is not to suggest that there existed then (or exists now) a mass disapproval of the military. On the contrary, various Gallup Polls showed that the military enjoyed a generally favorable image, even if an ambivalent one. Nevertheless, the trend suggested an increasing antimilitary character of certain groups, primarily associated with the college and university youth.(22) This probably was true with respect to the attitudes of those in the academic community. Although this group may be relatively small, its influence is important, since it is the attitude of the academic community - the intellectuals - that the military elite is most sensitive to with respect to image, esteem, and reputation.

While such anti-military sentiments may have diminished, considerably with the fading of the Vietnam War into history, resentment of the military remains just beneath the surface. For example, president Jimmy Carter's call in 1980 for registration of youths between the ages of 19 to 21 sparked some opposition among youth groups, even though registration is a far cry from a return to the draft. Moreover, the composition of the volunteer military reflects the fact that middle class youths and those who are college qualified rarely choose the military service as a career. Thus, a return to the draft in all but the most clearly perceived situations of national security is likely to provoke anti-military sentiments reminiscent of the Vietnam period.

Additionally, manpower requirements for the military during Vietnam included groups from within this youth culture. As more young men were inducted or commissioned through the ROTC, the traditional orientation of the military was increasingly diluted by the general ambivalence and hostility toward military service. In a Department of the Army commentary, the following were noted regarding this phenomenon:

> . . . The process of expanding by only adding young men to the army has resulted in a "civilianizing" of the Army. This was described variously: "ARs and other traditions are no longer sacrosanct," "they believe everything is possible," and "rank is not so awesome." This turn is viewed as both good ("We're finally daring to ask why") and bad ("tradition serves to bind us together and results in esprit de corps - you hear people talk about high morale in Vietnam but you don't hear much about esprit"), (3) Movement and the new blood has apparently established the idea that there is a definable limit to what a man should and could be required to submit himself to in terms of exposure to hostilities (if you're wounded twice you deserve reassignment to more protected duty or if you have completed 4 to 6 months with a platoon you have grounds for being reassigned to less hazardous duty).(23)

The surfacing of these societal attitudes during the Vietnam period, particularly with respect to the academic community, had some repercussions in the military. Partly as a matter of self-defense, partly as a manifestation of frustration and disgust over the distorted images perpetuated in the public mind, and partly as a result of the societal turmoil spilling over into the military establishment, the military showed serious concern, if not outright disaffection, from society.

In domestic political processes, the military was placed in a position in which it had to defend itself in political terms not only with respect to other governmental institutions, but with respect to its relationship to society in general. In addition, problems of society extended into the military establishment and required a level of understanding and appreciation unknown in the military culture. These problems did not lend themselves to solutions through traditional military methods. Rather, solutions in light of the new environment required political means.

The outcome of these conflicts was directly related to the
political acumen of the participants and, in the case of the
military, were contingent upon the ability and performance of
professional soldiers who were politically aware, politically
knowledgeable, and attuned to the requirements of the political
system.  The problems with the military (both intra- and
inter-service) were similar in nature.  The competition for
scarce resources, preferential assignments, career opportunities, and promotions perpetuated and sharpened competitive
drives and lead to a resort to political techniques.  Similarly
inter-service competition stemming from these considerations
spilled over into the external sphere with services making
alliances and seeking support for other political institutions to
serve particular service interests.
    The experience of the Vietnam War and the historical
evolution of American civil-military relations make it clear that
latent anti-military sentiments exist.  These can surface
dramatically and become major factors in the political system
when events occur or when the use of the military instrument
takes place, which are contrary to the perceived program or
policy that the United States ought to pursue.  Such sentiments are quickly subdued however, if the military instrument
is used in a crisis threatening America's national security and
is perceived as such by the people.  In any case, the credibility of the military institution and the profession is one that
cannot be taken for granted by military men.  It must be
carefully examined and nurtured.  At the same time professionals must be prepared for negative domestic reaction, if the
military institution is used in ways inconsistent with prevailing
public opinion.  Unfortunately, it is the latter situation that
occurs frequently.

## THE IMPACT OF DIMINISHING MILITARY RESOURCES

Disenchantment with the decision-making process and concern
over the dominance of the defense establishment moved a
number of Congressmen to demand reduction of defense
budgets and closer control and supervision over defense
activities.  This led to an emphasis on domestic non-military
priorities and reduced allocations for the military.

> It seems clear that - without either stumbling into a
> deep recession or renewing the inflationary boom -
> the nation is successfully negotiating a massive re-
> deployment of priorities and resources, from an
> economy based on defense and business investment
> to one directed more toward consumption, housing
> and social welfare.  . . . Despite Cambodia, defense

> production has declined at an accelerating pace, and
> so it will begin to level out next year. . . . The
> real volume in the purchase of goods and services
> for national defense will decline about as much in the
> coming eighteen months as in the past eighteen - $20
> billion in all over the three years. The sharpest
> part of the drop is under way now, indeed with
> virtually all the cutbacks in procurement to be
> completed this year.(24)

The downward trend of defense appropriations began a decade ago and was only recently reversed (primarily as a result of the Soviet invasion of Afghanistan). In 1971, for example, the President called for a defense budget of $ 71.8 billion, a reduction of more than $ 5 billion from the previous year. Although the 1971 defense budget represented more or less a transitory period (a shift from a war footing), with few indications as to programs and selection of tactics and strategy for the future, the trend seemed obvious.(25) The defense establishment was going through a process of retrenchment with a concomitant reduction in manpower levels, reduced overseas commitments, and restricted options regarding use of military forces.(26)

In the past, the dominance of the military in budgetary matters minimized the type of inter-service competition associated with the era of Secretary of Defense Wilson. A relatively large allocation of resources allowed the military services to acquire virtually all the hardware desired. With the decrease of resources available to the military after Vietnam, competition increased as the services vied with each other for scarcer resources.

Additionally, the military now has to seriously compete with other agencies of the Federal government for resources. Consequently, the military finds itself in a position in which it has to defend its policies and programs to a suspicious Congress, while at the same time each service must guard itself from encroachments by other services. The suscepti- bility of this type of situation to political manipulations and political alliances is obvious. Politically astute and technically knowledgeable officers will be a sine qua non for the effective representation of the military in external political activities and for inter-service competition. By necessity, the military engages in the "kinds" of politics, and on a scale and in- tensity, characteristic of politically-inactive interest groups. Additionally, the military needs to develop political orienta- tions, perspectives, and communications characteristic of political institutions. As suggested earlier, these "kinds" of politics were part of the military institution during the past two decades, but the new environment in the aftermath of Vietnam necessitated an even more politically-oriented military if, in fact, the military was to "survive" in the game of domestic politics and increasing inter-service competition.(27) On this point, it is interesting to note that some observers in the late 1920s argued that the military had become too effective in its political dimension.

The reduction in resource allocation was also reflected within the services themselves with respect to job assignments, promotions, and career patterns in general. Traditionally, there has always been the "politics" of career pursuits within the military (intra-service). With the changing environment, this political factor is perpetuated by the increasing competitiveness within the military profession.

One observer of the naval service has noted:

> The system itself is over-competitive in ways harmful to espirit by sacrificing the subordinate to the personal drive toward promotion and preferential assignment by the senior. A full career can generally be made only over the bodies of outstanding and immensely able and uncomplaining senior enlisted men and junior officers. . . . Furthermore, reduction of forces will not alleviate the drive for choice assignments, but will only aggrevate the competition among rising officers for the still more scarce and even more necessary command assignments. More than ever, reputations will be made at the expense of the inferior, the long-suffering skilled enlisted men and junior officers.(28)

It should be added that reputation and careers are also made over the bodies and at the expense of contemporaries, who are less skilled at the political game, especially with respect to relationships within peer groups and with higher ranking officers and civilians within the governmental structure.(29)


                              TOWARD A NEW BALANCE


In light of the dynamics created by the changing domestic political context and the internal tensions within the military, a reappraisal of professionalism is necessary. Perceptions of a monolithic militaristic establishment, geared to a hierarchical and self-perpetuating oligarchy, must be tempered by the recognition that there are within the military conflicts of views and opinions concerning values; that there is disagreement regarding the shape of the emerging military establishment; that there are "self-evaluations" within the military regarding its political role, both from the institutional and individual

points of view, even if these have resulted in a more traditionalist posture.

The military must do more than give lip service to the
needs for change, however. Recognition of the changing
climate and realistic response is needed in light of the increasing "politicization" of the military. A more flexible and
innovative orientation must be accompanied by more effective
institutional response to political and social demands from
within and without. Traditional military ethos with its hierarchical arrangements and inherent class lines may not be the
most effective response.

Neither the military not civilian should take solace in the
all-volunteer military. Although some problems were solved by
the establishment of an all-volunteer military, it is by no
means a panacea to some of the problems identified here, nor
is it likely to drastically change the direction of politicization
suggested in this discussion. A number of military men and
civilians alike are not convinced of the advantages of the all-
volunteer system, at least in the statements and analyses
presented so far. Questions of enlisted composition, retention
of specialty grades, the role of women, and professional
motivations suggest some of the questions that need further
exploration and resolution.

It should not be assumed that the military will remain
politically passive under pressures of internal and external
forces. The unquestioning acceptance of decisions by civilian
institutions, although a popular myth as far as the past two
decades are concerned, will recede further into the background. Decisions by civilian institutions which do not
account for military interests are likely to evoke a high degree
of political reaction and power-play to protect military interests. With the broadening scope of the political environment, the military is more likely to become involved in political
gamesmanship and resort to political techniques in furthering
its goals. Reinforcing this will be the political nature of
problems that the military was faced with in the Vietnam era,
and that continue into the 1980s.

This is not to suggest that professionalism in the traditional sense has ended. Rather, it is suggested that professionalism must now incorporate considerations of political skills
as part of the individual role, and political effectiveness as
part of institutional patterns. In other words, a new military
ethos need to be developed whose institutional role and
professional status is tempered by political consciousness.

As the effects of the Vietnam War have receded, antimilitary sentiments have diminished. Similarly, the dissatisfaction of military professionals with their status in society and
their negative perceptions regarding society's attitudes towards
the military became less strident and more accommodating.
Nevertheless, the characteristics of the environment that

evolved in the aftermath of Vietnam indicate a basic change in the relationship between military and society and one that cannot be dealt with in traditional terms.

In the process of this changing relationship, the familiarity and security of traditional relationships and institutions have given way to uncertainty as to the role of the military in a democratic society and ambivalence within the military as to proper response to pressures from within and without. This uncertainty and ambivalence are compounded by the fact that responses and initiatives must include a political dimension. This relatively new dimension both within the military and between the military and society requires new initiatives, imaginative intellects, a flexible mental posture, and realistic perceptions. No greater mistake can be made by military and civilian alike than to assume that nothing has changed since Vietnam or that standard military solutions will be adequate.


NOTES


1.   Samuel P. Huntington, The Soldier and the State. New York:  Vintage Books, 1964, p. 259.
2.   Ibid., p. 345.  See also Townsend Hoopes, "Civilian-military Balance," Yale Review, Vol. 43, December 1953, pp. 218-234.
3.   Morris Janowitz, "Organizing Multiple Goals:  War Making and Arms Control" in Morris Janowitz (Ed.) The New Military.  New York:  Russell Sage Foundation, 1964, p. 22.
4.   Kurt Lang, "Technology and Career Management in the Military Establishment" in Morris Janowitz, Ibid., p. 77.
5.   Harold Lasswell, Politics.  New York:  Whittlesey, 1936, p. 1.
6.   George Catlin, A Study of the Principles of Politics. New York:  The Macmillan Company, 1930, pp. 68-69.
7.   V. O. Key, Politics, Parties, and Pressure Groups. New York:  Thomas Y. Crowell Company, 1960, Fourth Edition, p. 5.  References to Lasswell and Catlin are also taken from Key.
8.   A survey was conducted by the Navy in an attempt to ascertain differences in attitudes and opinions between officer candidates and senior officers in the Navy as represented in the Naval War College.  Although no generational gap was detected, a difference was found in "the overall distribution of attitudes between the two groups. . ."  The younger officers tended to be more liberal and concerned with domestic issues and social justice than with international problems.  In conclusion, the author states, "This is not to say, however, that the new generation of officers sees the world through the same lenses as their seniors.  As seen

here, they do not, and if we are to continue to have close rapport between our commanders and their officers, it is necessary to understand just what the differences are." See Commander James A. Barber, Jr., U.S. Navy, "Is There a Generation Gap in Naval Officer Corps?" in Naval War College Review, May, 1970, pp. 24-33.

9.  There are exceptions to this. For example, in a report by the New York Times, November 2, 1970, it was noted that Major General Bernard W. Rogers, Commander of the Fifth Infantry Division at Fort Carson, Colo., had instigated a number of procedures recognizing the existence of new pressures within the Army. This included such things as abolishing reveille and opening an on-post coffee house. It was noted that re-enlistments almost doubled and absent without leave cases were reduced to almost zero. Subsequently, a number of ranking officers have attempted to incorporate new ideas into traditional procedures. However, it is a stretch of the imagination to assume that this represents a significant and permanent acceptance of the "modernist" position.

10.  Thomas Fleming, "West Point Cadets Now Say 'Why Sir?'" in New York Times Magazine, July 5, 1970.

11.  Hugh Mulligan, No Place to Die: The Agony of Vietnam. New York: William Morrow and Company, Inc., 1967, p. 318.

12.  On this point, see, for example, Walt W. Rostow, "Countering Guerrilla Attack," in Franklin Mark Osanka (Ed.) Modern Guerrilla Warfare. New York: The Free Press of Glencoe, 1962, pp. 464-471.

13.  These comments were taken from an informal paper provided to the author by Department of the Army personnel stationed at the Pentagon. In the main, this consisted of a small team of officers in the middle rank group who were attempting to assess personnel requirements and motivations in the light of evolving Army missions and experience. This was not an official study, but did incorporate much of the current thinking with respect to the future Army. (Dated 1969; no other documentation available). Hereafter referred to as Informal Paper.

14.  Ibid.

15.  For an interesting historical survey of the role of the military in domestic disturbances and implications for the future, see Martin Blumenson, "On the Functions of the Military in Civil Disorders," Roger Little, ed., Handbook of Military Institutions. Beverly Hills, Cal.: Sage, 1971, pp. 475-517, in which the author concludes that the "conduct of civil disturbance control operations taxes leadership skills just as fully as, and in some ways more uniquely than, combat operations." (p. 506).

162 BEYOND THE BATTLEFIELD

16. See, for example, Army Times, March 17, 1971. In an article, "Infantry School Teaches Environmental Course," it was noted that "The course is aimed at the tactically oriented officer whose career will encompass problems which will be mostly non-tactical in nature."

17. Richard Harwood, "Troubled Times for the Military," in the Chicago Sun-Times, July 19, 1970, Section Two, p. 1. In a recent survey by the Gallop Poll, it was found that nearly 30 percent of those surveyed gave the Pentagon a "highly unfavorable" rating. See Chicago Sun-Times, August 9, 1970, Section Two, p. 12.

18. See, for example, William Proxmire, Report from the Wasteland. New York: Praeger Publishers, 1970; Robert Sherrill, Military Justice Is To Justice as Military Music Is To Music. New York: Harper and Row, 1970; Seymour M. Hersh, My Lai 4. New York: Random House, 1970; Townsend Hoopes, The Limits of Intervention. New York: David MacKay Company, Inc., 1970.

19. Janowitz, The Professional Soldier, p. 226.

20. An example of this is reflected in attitudes expressed in an informal survey taken of 50 college students from a relatively conservative Catholic, urban university predominately comprised of students representing the low and middle class socio-economic structure. According to 36 students, the military image was tarnished primarily due to the military's involvement in Vietnam and the military-industrial complex. In rating the status of the military with respect to other professions in society, the following order of preference was indicated: doctors, lawyers, priests, teachers, social workers, policemen, and military.

21. See "R.O.T.C. Protests Worry Pentagon" in New York Times, May 31, 1970, p. 4, in which there was a reported decline of 41 percent in R.O.T.C. enrollments in 1970.

22. Some sources indicate that this antimilitary attitude varies with the sections of the country. In the East, the most militant antimilitary sentiment prevails, while the South, Midwest and Rocky Mountain Area retain a favorable military attitude. This would have to be qualified by the attitudes of college and university students in large urban areas such as Chicago and the activities on the campuses of Northwestern, Chicago Circle, and University of Chicago. It is also noteworthy that two of the three Academies are in the East. The Academies judge their reputation on a criteria established from Ivy League and equivalent schools. See Harwood, "Troubled Times" and Fleming, "West Point Cadets."

23. Informal Paper.

24. The New York Times, July 1, 1970, p. 40.

25. See Charles L. Schultze, et al., Setting National Priorities, the 1971 Budget. Washington, D.C.: The Brook-

ings Institution, 1970, pp. 17-54 for an excellent analysis of the defense budget for 1971.

26. "Pentagon Moving to Reduce Forces" in The New York Times, June 7, 1970.

27. An example of this type of activity was reported in the opening of a special command post in the Pentagon, nicknamed Tranquility Base, for the purposes of providing information on the Safeguard program to senators preparing for the debates on the Safeguard Anti-Ballistic Missile system. See Chicago Sun-Times, July 22, 1970, p. 84.

Another example of the types of politics generated in such situations is the report and recommendations by President Nixon's Blue Ribbon Defense Panel headed by Gilbert W. Fitzhugh, board chairman of the Metropolitan Life. In an article, "Panel 'Shakes' Army," the Army Times, August 12, 1970, reporter Gene Famigliette reported that the panel recommended sweeping changes "which would result in a major military upheaval . . ." to include downgrading the Joint Chiefs of Staff. Also, the article notes the panel was "composed mainly of executives unfamiliar with military matters." Predictably, it was concluded that the "chiefs and their supporters in Congress are likely to agree with McNeil and block any move to downgrade the role of top military men. Fitzhugh acknowledged that the present chiefs are 'less than enthusiastic' about his group's proposals." This situation portends a period of political maneuvering and bringing to bear a range of political techniques and political power of the military in an attempt to negate the more objectionable parts of the Fitzhugh proposals.

28. Paul Schratz, "Arms Control and the All Volunteer Armed Force" pp. 2 and 6, paper delivered at the annual conference of the Inter-University Seminar on the Armed Forces and Society, October 9-11, 1969.

29. On this point see Janowitz, The Professional Soldier, pp. 293-302.

# 9 Changing Dimensions of Military Professionalism: Education and Enlightened Advocacy

Steeped in the classic concepts of "Duty, Honor, Country," military professionals perceive the nature of professionalism as self-evident. Academic scholars, on the other hand, analyzing and assessing military professionalism from a variety of disciplinary perspectives and intellectual themes, differ in their analyses of military professionalism. While most military men tend to accept the traditional and clear focus of the profession, "success in battle," scholars seek to understand the impact of an increasingly complex domestic and international social order on the military profession. The simplicity of one is countered by the complexity and, at times, unintelligibility of the other. The result is ambiguity, professional unease, debate among scholars heightened by intellectual criticism of military professionals, and a latent professional distaste for the scholar's intrusion into an honorable profession.

Searching back over the 100-year period since the Civil War, it is difficult to find one conceptual scheme as the basis for military professionalism. To be sure, the fundamental basis for the profession of arms in the United States rests on "Duty, Honor, Country." More in name than in fact, these concepts have nurtured professional pride, distinguished between civilian and military professions, and perpetuated an internal cohesion in the military profession. The fact remains, however, that the concept of military profession is still difficult to define, since it is clouded in emotional issues and at best is only slightly susceptible to empirical analysis. Dealing with attitudes and images, obscure boundaries, and a number of political-psychological facets, military professionalism is, in the main, an amalgam of ambiguous, pseudo-scientific rationale, traditional heroics, and organizational politics. Over the past two decades, there has been a significant amount of literature focusing on the nature of military professionalism. This literature, stemming not only from academic studies but from the pens of a small group of military scholars, covers a variety of perspectives ranging from the social origins of military professionals to the issues of the military as a profession. The Vietnam War, the turmoil of the 1960s, and the spin-off from Watergate have contributed in no small measure to the increased intellectual concern with professionalism.

However, the preponderance of studies on the military profession rarely focus on politics and professionalism. Those that do are considerably influenced by Samuel Huntington, author of Soldier and the State and the Garrison State thesis.(1) In this respect, many political scientists tend to presume that the military institution is separate from the political system, except in an abstract sense. Thus, the military is thought to be a separate system, isolated from the mainstream of politics and political life. This view is reinforced by the idea, particularly among the liberal-oriented, that the military institution is fundamentally antithetical to a democratic political system. Hence, the frequent outcry that military men have no business publicly commenting on policy, nor do they have any business becoming involved in "politics" in any fashion. As a result, research on the military institution and military professionalism tends to be limited to internal military matters or viewed on a broad and highly general level with regard to civil-military relations and policy, to the neglect of political attitudes, political roles, and the politics of military professionalism.

This is a curious oversight, since the importance of the political dimension seems clear in light of the external environment in which the military must operate, the nature and politics of the domestic political system, and organizational politics. The purpose of this chapter is to suggest an approach that focuses specifically on these matters, while exploring their ramifications on military professionalism.

In this context, this chapter is based on two premises regarding the military profession. First, regardless of the debate centering around the status of the military as a profession, it is presumed that the military is indeed a profession. This presumes that it has the attributes generally associated with civilian professions. Additionally, the uniqueness of the military profession is perceived to be based on three important characteristics: the concept of ultimate liability, the state-profession relationship (i.e., the state as the sole client), and the concept of honor. Many of these matters have been discussed in detail elsewhere in the literature.(2) In brief, many military men feel that military professionalism may, in the final analysis, demand that the military man give his life in the performance of his duties. Moreover, it is presumed that the profession serves only one client - the state, and that this client can demand total commitment. Finally, the cohesion and status of the profession is based in no small part on the concept of "honor"; that is, a presumption that the prestige of the profession rests on a clear sense of right and wrong, and collective esteem in the context of fame, glory, and respect.

Second, the military professional refers primarily to the officer corps. Regardless of the importance of the enlisted structure (to include quantity and quality), it is the relationship between the officer corps and the state that is fundamental to the nature of civil-military relationships. Indeed, it is the officers corps that sets the "pace," provides professional standards, and creates the professional image.

Before we explore the matters associated with the purpose of this chapter in greater detail, it is necessary to briefly examine the liberal-traditional alliance and its consequences to the military profession. It is this perspective that provides an intellectual rationale which reinforces popularly held narrow views about the military profession, and limits professional dimensions.

## THE LIBERAL-TRADITIONAL ALLIANCE

The liberal-traditional alliance rests on the presumption that military professionalism is defined in terms of "purely military matters." From this flows the conclusion that there is a body of knowledge and skills that are uniquely military and that such knowledge and skills are the monopoly of the military. Indeed, most of the major attributes that scholars have historically associated with the military profession are part of this presumption and outlook. Moreover, since the practice of military professionalism can only be accomplished by serving the state, the institution becomes the embodiment of the profession.

As a result, purpose, training, career success, and standards of performance are determined exclusively by military criteria. The uniqueness of the profession and its exclusive rights on military matters nurtures a military socialization and "education" that is coterminous with the perceived traditional purpose of the profession - success in battle. In simple terms, professionalization remains fixed in the "Follow Me" concept and "Can Do" provincialism.

A narrowly defined military professionalism confined to purely military matters serves a particular purpose. For the liberal political heritage, it insures (presumes) civilian control and a non-political military. For the traditional military orientation, it insures (presumes) a total focus on specific military skills and training as the proper career orientation. The consequences of the liberal-traditional alliance, however,

prevent the military professional from developing a broad
intellectual awareness of the political-social environment in
which he must operate, while insisting that he intensely and
solely concern himself with immediate problems of a clear
military content. In other words, the military must not
"dabble" in those things political, nor must it concern itself
with developing the kind of intellectual awareness that is likely
to carry the military man beyond the confines of traditional
professionalism. The involvement in politics (and the serious
study of politics) must be avoided. This can be done to a
great extent by keeping the military man busy on military
things (skill acquisiton and training leave little time for
serious education), while reminding him that professionalism
and politics do not mix - for any purpose.

In sum, according to this view, there is a distinct
separation between politics and professionalism (indeed,
between the military and society). Thus, while the liberal
tradition would limit legitimate military activity to a relatively
narrow area of what is perceived as clear military matters, the
traditional element in the professional officers corps would
insist that military career development be determined by those
pursuits that are clearly military in nature and focused in the
military institution.(3)

Our argument rejects these perspectives. In brief, it is
our contention that the military is, among other things, a
political institution. Indeed, an important part of the military
professional's area of competence and operations is "political."
We reject the thesis that military professionals are somehow
more professional if they remain aloof from and isolated from
"politics." Not only has this thesis proven questionable over
the past 20-year period, but it appears increasingly unrealistic
in projecting towards the future. Moreover, to presume that
somehow military professionals are not affected by politics of
our system or that their political preferences, behavior, and
attitudes, are unimportant is to ignore political realities. To
conduct research or analysis on an implicit presumption that
the military institution should do only military "things" is to
accept an intellectual parochialism that ultimately distorts the
nature of the military institution and the concept of military
professionalism.

Additionally, it is our contention that the close relationship between politics, war, and the military profession
requires a perspective and educational base beyond the traditional concepts of "winning wars" and skills related only to
immediate military concerns. In light of the range of possible
military operations and their political and social ramifications,
it is simplistic to presume that military professionals need only
be concerned about the "grand battles" of World War II.

Finally, the nature of democratic systems, while inherently antithetical to the military ethos, nevertheless requires

understanding and astuteness by military professionals if they
are to serve the democratic state and reduce the inherent
tensions between military and society to acceptable proportions. These three perspectives - politics of the military,
politics of war, and democracy and the military - require an
educational and intellectual perspective that can best be served
by the kinds of scholarly inquiry and analysis provided in
graduate education. In the remainder of this chapter, we
focus on these distinct, yet interrelated elements of professionalism and how they relate to the military posture and
strategic requirements of the 1980s.(4)


## MILITARY AND POLITICS


Earlier in this volume, an examination was made of the political
aspects of military professionalism. As we noted, it was
during the period following World War II that politics became
an important part of the military profession and the institution,
even if denied by the majority of military men.(5) The changing political and social patterns of American society and the
role of the United States as a superpower drew the military
closer to society and required a political consciousness on the
part of the profession.
      With the end of the post World War II era, marked by the
American withdrawal from Vietnam, a number of internal and
external forces have again affected the character of the
military profession as well as the institutional posture. These
forces acted as catalysts to changes that have, among other
things, generated a highly expanded and sharpened political
dimension which the military finds difficult to avoid and a
dimension to which the military finds it difficult to respond.
      This political arena has not generally been acknowledged
as a legitimate concern for military officers; that is, it has not
become an element of the professional ethic in the same sense
as other military expectations and specialties. Many professional military men still view "politics" as something
denigrating professionalism - yet virtually every officer in the
middle rank years and beyond is immersed in military politics.
Indeed, there is a multi-dimensional nature about politics and
the military profession.
      Politics exist between individuals, individuals and groups,
within groups, between groups, and between groups and the
government or decision-making machinery. In this respect,
military politics can be viewed from at least three levels:
intra-service, institutional, and systems. Intra-service
politics has to do with individuals and small group interactions
within a particular service (i.e., emerging elite politics,
careerism). Institutional politics concerns itself with politics

between the services and/or ad hoc military task forces and commissions with the military decision-making machinery. This may also include political linkages with political actors outside of the military establishment. Systems politics refers primarily to the politics that the military system as a whole engages in with respect to the decision-making machinery and political actors of the political system (i.e., military politics and the defense budget).

Distinguishing between these various levels of politics however, is not truly reflective of political realities. The levels of politics are intermingled and interrelated to a degree which makes it difficult to identify where one begins and the other ends. Yet upon closer examination, the general thrust of each of these "kinds of politics" is apparent.

Few would deny the existence of intra-service politics. This has been debated at length, particularly in the aftermath of the Vietnam war. The concerns with careerism, political ethics, and concepts of the emerging elite and the protege system reinforce the view that internal dynamics of the military profession are in no small way associated with "office" politics - politics associated with choosing the most expeditious path to a successful career, and adopting the means, the informal linkages to the "power" structure, and the proper career posture to achieve the career goals. Thus, officers engage in "power" politics within peer groups and between subordinate and superior, establishing the basis for gaining prestige and status, and hence favorable career postures. The politically astute officer not only readily identifies who is "important" for his career, but also learns how to manipulate relationships to place him in the most advantageous position. Access to and knowledge of power centers within the military are essential for these purposes. Moreover, the nature of the competitiveness within the military makes it highly susceptible to informal lines of authority and lends itself to manipulation by individuals and "elite." (6)

Institutional politics refers primarily to inter-service matters. However, as most would concede, inter-service politics is not limited solely to politics between the military services. It encompasses a variety of federal departments and coalition-building by services with other political actors to support a particular position against or with other services. It would seem, therefore, that institutional politics, rather than inter-service politics, is a more appropriate label. The most visible aspect of these politics is in the Pentagon where Action Officers scurry around seeking the necessary data and support to reinforce their Services' (Service Chiefs) positions. Such activities are not limited to data gathering and rational analysis, but involve "consensus"-building, negotiations, bargaining, and compromises. Mission assignments, for example, invariably lead to impact on resource allocation, manpower levels, and acquisition of advanced weaponry.(7) Thus, Services are particularly sensitive to debate on missions. The ultimate decision, however, rests in no small part on "politics" rather than on precise military criteria. It is general knowledge that similar situations occur daily not only at the Pentagon but in virtually every area in which Services must operate, resulting in conflicts over allocation of resources, weapons technology, manpower, and status.

On the systems level, the military, by the very nature of its organizational purposes, is involved in political activities to protect its interests, acquire the necessary resources, and maintain its position vis-a-vis other institutions. The environment in which these political activities take place is characterized by complex power manipulations, which are, by and large, obscured from public view. In this respect, the military in the United States does not necessarily engage in aggregation or articulation of interests in a manner normally associated with political parties or interest groups. The military plays a more sophisticated political role, in which the facade of political neutrality is maintained while attempts are made to manipulate and influence political institutions and decision makers. The outward manifestations of this political activity is accomplished through a network of institutions, both formal and informal, and through a series of interlocking, pervasive, and personal relationships. While the charge of "old boys" school may be too harsh, there is nevertheless an "elite-like" association which funnels a military perspective and channels military pressures to the proper decision makers. Such activities also serve as a means of interpenetration between military and civilian sectors.

Additionally, the military is faced with a political environment which requires responses not solely or even predominantly from the perspective of military interests. The supervision and control over military facilities in the United States is one example. As Goodpaster notes:

> Within our own country, the decisions concerning such facilities (military facilities) reflect everything from military need and operationally advantageous location to the availability of transportation and labor and seniority and influence of key members of congressional committees. A constant give-and-take between opposing interests lies behind these decisions; service efforts to reduce or eliminate less productive facilities frequently clash with congressional opposition to cutbacks harmful to a particular congressman's district. The range of considerations is, to say the least, interdisciplinary, and the need for knowledgeable treatment of the issue, in a context of good will and understanding of the polit-

ical process, without sacrifice of the dictates of the economy and effectiveness, calls for education in complex forms of management analysis and decision making.(8)

Another example is the question of the stationing of large units from overseas upon their return to the United States. The political pressures brought to bear upon the military by Congressmen, bureaucrats, and interest groups for a politically acceptable decision is typical of the "politics" involved in such a military decision. The stationing of large units in one or the other part of the country has an impact on the economy of that region, and is indeed a legitimate concern of politicians and interest groups. Should such matters be considered in the "military" decision of troop stations?

In sum, the basic political character of the U.S. military is not that it is apolitical, but rather that it is a political institution, among other things, and is involved in the political processes of our system. Although this involvement has tended to remain on the level of "low visibility," it permeates many of the formal and informal institutions of the political system. The fact that the U.S. military is considered a professional organization does not necessarily inhibit its capacity to act in the political environment. Moreover, the very nature of the institution is such that politics, career interests, and service roles are intermixed.

## CHANGED CONCEPT OF WAR

It has been popular to presume that politics are left to politicians and wars to generals. This cliche has long been outmoded. To presume that military professionals, for example, should remain unconcerned about the political and social conditions of potential aggressors, and that the military professional should not be involved until the first shot is fired is to neglect the lessons of modern war.

The purpose here is not to examine the details of strategic issues and the nature of warfare. More simply, it is to suggest that at least three elements of modern war warrant - if not compel - a political dimension to warfare that should be a legitimate concern for military professionalism. These include the issues associated with military intervention, deterrence, and the aftermath of warfare. In each of these cases there are political and social necessities governing military involvement. Moreover, traditional styles of command resting on a singular military perspective may not be adequate.

As one observer has noted, "The traditional pattern of centralized command in battle is no longer possible; com-

manders must be more flexible, familiar with a wide range of
techniques of combat, <u>above all more highly educated</u>; they
cannot be expert in all fields now relevant to their job but
they must be able to handle and digest expert advice."(9)
(Underlining added for emphasis.)

## Military intervention

Intervention by U.S. military forces, regardless of the
nature of war and geographical area, requires serious analysis
and detailed attention to the consequences of intervention.
These are not matters that can be considered from a purely
military perspective. The explosive nature of "nationalism,"
the fragile nature of many political institutions in target areas,
and the possibility of popular reaction by segments of the
populace, all pose exceedingly difficult non-military issues with
significant military ramifications.

Indeed, military intervention may generate serious
political repercussions and ramifications which can become
entangled with military operations, not to mention possible
reaction in U.S. society. Moreover, military intervention may
necessitate restricting the maneuverability and firepower in
military operations on purely political grounds. In such an
environment, the military professional is also likely to be
confronted with problems associated with the political-social
fabric of the society of the area of operations.

The intellectual perspective to understand and appreciate
the inter-penetration between military and civilian elements,
and the political and social consequences of military intervention cannot be achieved by theoretical studies on a one-time
basis. This can best be acquired by a grasp of the tools of
political-social analysis. Thus, from the time of planning,
through execution and aftermath, the military professional will
find it extremely difficult to limit himself solely to the military
element. He must be able to assess the political-military and
social inter-relationships, and their consequences on his own
military efficiency. Such knowledge is developed over a period
of time and requires serious study with intellectual tools that
are rarely part of traditional military education and training.

## Deterrence

It has long been recognized that successful deterrence
rests on two considerations: capacity of the military instrument and credibility. Thus, not only must the military be
capable of inflicting damage that is unacceptable to the enemy,
but political leaders must be prepared to use the military
instrument in this capacity. To insure that the potential
enemy does not miscalculate or is not tempted to instigate a
major war, the United States must be in a position to engage

in a judicious mix of political maneuvering, psychological warfare, and military shows of force (used here in the broadest sense). In sum, deterrence seeks to prevent military confrontation. "Essentially deterrence means discouraging the enemy from taking military action by posing for him a prospect of cost and risk outweighing his prospective gain . . . deterrence works on the enemy's intentions; the deterrent value of military forces is their effect in reducing the likelihood of military moves."(10)

Equally important, deterrence requires understanding of the potential enemy's political and social character, and the ability to "read" the potential agressor's political and military maneuvering. In sum, much of the success of deterrence goes beyond the calculus of weapons and military manpower. It also depends upon the subleties and political nuances of political-military maneuvering as well as a perceived military capability. Since the military institution is an obvious element in such considerations, it logically follows that the military professional should have knowledge of these matters and the environment in which he must operate.

In this light, perhaps the military profession needs to do more than base its professional ethos on "success in battle." As Von Baudissin notes: "To seek to centre the image of the armed forces solely on the 'fighting man' would run counter to, 1. the spirit of deterrence, rightly understood, and with it the security policy function of the armed forces. . . ." 2. the fact that the position of 'fighting man' is only a staging post or ancillary function for all officers."(11)

And as Abrams points out,

The shift to an over-riding strategy of nuclear deterrence has placed the military in an anomalous, not to say philosophically absurd, position. Armed forces are now maintained in order that armed forces shall not be used; their major commitment is to psychological warfare waged by politicians; and the object is of course to prevent military action. Soldiers are asked to develop a professional ethos in line with the new technology of violence and at the same time to accept the almost total illegitimacy of the most advanced technology relevant to the goal for which the profession ostensibly exists.(12)

Deterrence strategy thus not only contradicts the traditional concept of military utility, but also adds a political dimension to professionalism, demanding that military men know when not to use military force and when to use it in a non-combat function.

Disengagement

It is likely that military involvement in the coming decade will necessitate serious thought of "disengagement." On the battlefield, disengagement from the enemy is a highly complicated and intricate operation, one that only the seasoned soldier can usually accomplish without fear of disastrous results. Disengagement in all but long-term occupation is likely to involve equally difficult, if not more complicated, operations with highly visible political impact. It is difficult to envision, for example, U.S. military involvement in any area of the world (other than areas in which the U.S. military is already operating with ground forces) without serious political overtones in the United States and in the target area. To presume that a Mayaguez type operation or a swift surgical operation in the character of Entebbe (Uganda) can be always accomplished successfully is wishful thinking. To be sure, the Mayaguezs and Entebbes may occur again, but these operations are one extreme end of the military intervention scale. Military interventions in the character of Vietnam and Korea or even Lebanon are also part of the Mayaguez-Entebbe syndrome. For many, considering military intervention in this fashion is at least irrational and at best calamitous, not necessarily for the military outcome, but for the likely political repercussions internally and externally. For military professionals to be able to deal with such issues and contingencies, they must be "intelligent" enough to go beyond military perspectives and understand the predominantly political nature of the military's role.

Disengagement is not just a military affair, since military intervention intrudes upon the political-social environment of the "target area." If military intervention is to secure a particular political goal, it is difficult to see how military men can avoid becoming involved in the process and power of influencing the political structure and social relationships in the area of operations. The disengagement of military forces from an area requires restructuring the political forces and restoring the environment to some semblance of civilian order. This cannot be done simply by ordering a military withdrawal. Even if the sole concern was purely military, it is difficult to conceive of a military disengagement that could be "clean and surgical" - the reaction of segments of the populace and popular forces would always be a crucial concern. Finally, military professionals need to consider the political and social repercussions of military disengagement from the area. The withdrawal from Vietnam, for example, has left some deep questions regarding military impact, the conception of counter-insurgency, and our own sense of accomplishment.

In sum, the concept of war in the 1980s is sufficiently different from the past to make irrelevant the traditional division of labor between civilian and military roles. As the military learned in Vietnam, the ability to handle non-military aspects of war successfully goes beyond traditional military skills. The extent and relationship of these non-military problems and the demands on the military profession seem clear in our brief examination of deterrence, defense, detente, and the potential use of military force outside the continental United States. Thus, the wars of the future are likely to be an inexplicable mix of political, social, economic, and military factors. This will probably be true for all types of conflicts, ranging from nuclear war to limited military intervention. While the non-military issues surrounding any type of military action are an important part of all professionals' intellectual dimension, the aftermath of military action is even more important. In such circumstances, to presume that somehow one can clearly identify "pure" military issues and implement pure military solutions is simply to forget the lessons of history or to lack the intellectual dimensions for conceptualizing on such matters.

## Democratic society and the military

An understanding of the American political system, its values and democratic theory, is essential for the military professional if he is to perform his role effectively and in a way acceptable to American society. The problem is a difficult one because in its ideal form, it requires the acceptance and compatibility between a system based on hierarchy, order, authority and another based on negotiations, compromise, pluralism, decentralization, and "liberty and equality." Moreover, demands of institutional loyalty within the profession are countered by the constitutional right of critical inquiry and individual freedom in a democratic society. Too often, the military profession presumes that an efficient democracy is one that is constantly "peaceful" and devoid of inner tensions. More often, a democratic system exhibits tension and disagreement. If democratic theory is examined carefully, one will find a constant conflict between liberty and equality, between individuals and institutions, and between authority and freedom. Somehow, to presume that such conflicts must always be subdued to establish law and order is to misread the "dynamics" of a democratic system. The difficulty of transferring these considerations to the operation of a military system is clear. The fundamental professional dilemma is the need to accept these democratic premises, reflect them in a reasonable way in the military system while maintaining an effective military posture. Such an understanding and appreciation requires more than a cursory study of America's government or a "newspaper" knowledge of politics.

Additionally, understanding of democratic systems and the general value systems they engender can be a reinforcing aspect of civilian control. The proper role of the military in a democratic society and the understanding of values and the operation of the democratic political system provide a rational perspective in which the military professional can perceive his own rule and the limitations of military authority within the system.

As Von Baudissin observes:

In the selection, education and employment of the officers it should always be borne in mind that the military "sub-system" tends to acquire a momentum of its own that runs counter to the political aspect of its executive function. The extent and complexity of security problems make civil control from above difficult, but so too do the military apparat and its attendant complex of armaments. The primacy of politics can only be enforced if it is recognized unreservedly by the majority of officers, or at any rate by those exercising the relevant function. But, over and above this, it is of decisive importance for the credibility of the state and the social order, and also for the effectiveness of the troops, that - even in exceptional circumstances, such as application for force under orders - officers should continue to feel bound by the laws and general assumptions of humanity.(13)

Another manifestation of the inherent tensions between the military and democratic society is in the relationships between individual autonomy and the organizational loyalty. In other words, there is a built-in conflict between individual ethics and institutional norms. Throughout history, the conflict between individual ethics and institutional norms have been characteristic of society. In the military, the professional officer is always faced with the questions of conscience or obeying institutional dictates. Professional stress on the requirements of integrity and institutional goals has normally shaped individual behavior so as to considerably reduce dissent or resistance. In other words, integrity and instant obedience are sine qua non of military institutions. Yet, the question of conscience, and actions contradictory to institutional demands has become particularly sensitive in today's military. The close relationship between personal values, institutional norms, and community value systems is necessary if institutional commitment, professional norms, and congruence with the civilian community are to be maintained. That is, there must exist a harmony between the values of the democratic system and military professionalism - not necessarily a perfect harmony, but at least an adequate commonality of values reinforcing the ideology of the system. When the ethos of the military profession and its behavior move beyond perceived social norms, the military loses its credibility and legitimacy of purpose.

A more fundamental question arises from individual value systems. At what point does a professional officer follow his conscience even if it means violating institutional norms? Can an individual be a professional officer and still not accept institutional demands? Yet professional ethics and military competence are synonomous for many. Can one be ethical and still resist the institution?

There are those who suggest that institutional requirements and professional demands are first and foremost, regardless of individual preferences and attitudes. Thus, institutional goals and success are the necessary criteria for behavior for the military professional. In this sense, these are the "absolutists" who would view individual dissent and resistance as "traitorous" to professional ethics. In contrast, there are those who would argue that individual conscience and "individuality" must be a basic ingredient of professionalism if the profession is to maintain its links to society and if innovative and imaginative officers are to remain professionals. Finally, there are those who argue for situational ethics. The argument is that individual conscience and "individuality" can be part of professionalism, but that they must be subordinate when the institution has adopted a particular policy or has made a decision to act in a certain way. We suspect that many professionals have adopted this latter position. It may be the less difficult of any position to reconcile to individual careers.

The extreme position is taken by those who would argue that individual worth and conscience are foremost and that the institution must respond under any circumstance. We feel that there are few, if any, in the military who realistically accept such a position.

Military men are prone to view the dilemma between individual conscience and institutional demands as unique to their profession (see chapter 10). Yet, the study of history and political philosophy shows that this dilemma has been characteristic of western civilization. Sophocles, for example, in his play Antigone, points out the dilemma between the heroine and King Creon. Resisting the king because of laws which she believed violated the higher law of the gods, Antigone accepted death rather than conform. Socrates, as described by Plato, accepted death for breaking what he considered unjust laws. The play, A Man For All Seasons, finds Thomas More defying Henry the VIII of England. Not only did More place the law of God above that of the king, but he would not reverse his decision even though it meant death. The point is that throughout history, men of conscience, committed to their principles of right or wrong, were willing to accept death rather than institutional demands or unjust laws. An understanding of these historical issues and study of their substantive elements can lead to a broader and more flexible professional perspective. At the minimum, such an analysis will assist military men in appreciating the complexities of the problem between individual conscience and institutional demands, and in recognizing that such issues are rarely solved in absolute terms.

Finally, while the nature of democratic systems may appear to be inherently antithetical to the military ethos, the military is an integral part of the political system. As such, there must be an acceptable way in which the military profession can exercise its functions within a democratic environment. To presume that the military remains immune from the environment and society which it is to serve is simply to deny its very status as a profession. Moreover, in the relationship between society and the military, there are no clear and absolute solutions. Society changes, values change, and previously held assumptions and relationships may prove fragile and incorrect. Workable relationships evolve from an understanding of values, the manner in which the political system operates, and an appreciation of the internal contradictions and tensions between the individual and institutional conformity. While this may not necessarily lead to "answers," it will militate against the kinds of perspectives that establish a rigid set of criteria in absolute terms, thereby leading to consequences which result in institutionalizing a perceptible and dysfunctional gap between military professional behavior and expectations.


## THE EDUCATED PROFESSIONAL


Synthesizing the intellectual demands and conceptual ability to understand and appreciate the professional requirements in the three elements is a difficult matter. To do so, the military professional must be able to apply political-social tools, quantitative analysis, analytical insights, and intellectual sensitivity to the study of domestic and international environment, military force, and consequences of policy.

Again, as Von Baudissin notes:

> . . . the general development of all military decision and action can only superficially be determined in a purely "military" way, for everywhere a considerable part is played by personal preconceptions of a social and political nature. Most officers have to take account of "civilian" factors in making decisions, and

in any case their service actions and omissions have direct or indirect consequences for the public, society and politics.(14)

In brief, the military professional should be able to "think" - not merely military thoughts, but the kind of reflection that is broad in scope and projects beyond military boundaries. Indeed, one can argue that one characteristic of any profession is an intellectual awareness of the world outside the confines of the professional world. The singular channel through which one can achieve this intellectual awareness is through higher education - graduate education, in an environment that exposes the individual to a variety of ideas, analyses, and perceptions not likely to be encountered in a professionally focused environment. The professional military man who has a liberal education is in an excellent, if not the best, position to "think."

This does not necessarily mean that civilian graduate education or education in the liberal arts can only be obtained through non-military educational systems. Yet, the fact remains that the relatively broad scope of civilian type education systems, its stress on conceptualizing, and its relatively free range of intellectual inquiry, makes it more attuned to the kinds of educational necessities required for military professionals than is possible with the education system in the military establishment.

The issue of civilian education for professional officers has primarily revolved around whether or not civilian education is needed to fill certain positions or billets. This has been fueled by arguments over training or education. Exponents argue that acquisition of military skills is the first and foremost need of professionals - that education qua education is at best a luxury few professionals can afford. Proponents argue that education is needed by a number of officers if they are to perform their politico-military positions. At worst, such arguments give rise to charges of ticket-punching. At best, the arguments of proponents presumes the necessity of a small "educated" elite within the professional ranks.

In our perspective, civilian graduate education is an essential element of professionalism. It is neither a luxury nor is it limited to a selected number of billets. Rather, graduate education - or more precisely the intellectual horizons, conceptual perspectives, and interdisciplinary dimensions that are a fundamental part of graduate education - is an important part of professionalism. Every professional who expects to proceed beyond the middle rank years must be "educated."

Higher education provides the necessary background to understand the political environment, both domestically and internationally, and prepares the professional to understand the nature and limits of military policy and military operations. As Yarmolinsky has noted:

Let me go back one step and ask why it is important
for officers to be educated in non-military subjects
beyond the general education they acquire in the
military academies, or elsewhere, in pursuit of a
bachelor's degree; I suggest that the reasons for
this requirement for a large proportion of the officers corps . . . are to be found in three general
areas: in the need for professional skills in what
are essentially civilian professions; in the need for
general background in areas of public policy and
statecraft that impinge increasingly on the daily
work of senior military officers; and in the need to
return, from time to time, to the springs of intellectual inspiration in order for an officer to avoid
going stale, or even sterile, in the middle years of
his career.(15)

Moreover, it has been aptly demonstrated that in our
society, higher education correlates closely with greater
participation in the political system; that higher education
provides a more enlightened view of democratic values and the
political system.(16) But the values and knowledge acquired
in higher education must be nurtured. It cannot be a one
time exposure. It requires consistent long-range reflection
and intellectual nurturing.
A case can also be made for higher education on the
premise that the educated professional makes a better professional. This can be accomplished without jeopardizing the
professional's ability to handle purely military skills. Indeed,
one can argue that an educated officer is in a better position
to integrate military skills with military requirements. Moreover, the educated officer will be intellectually prepared to
understand the consequences of military actions and the over-
arching political and social implications of military operations.

Is there not fundamental antipathy between the twin
purposes of military schooling: between training,
which is either technical or aimed at getting men
accustomed to doing what they are told, or both,
and, education, which must be devoted to helping
men learn to think critically, to establishing their
minds' standards of aesthetic and intellectual excel-
lence against which they will implicitly weigh the
value of what they are told to do?
Indeed there is . . . the truly liberally-
educated soldier is the soldier who can reconcile the
necessity for training and education, and be happy
in both. . . . For it is the man liberally educated,
not the man technically educated, who will be the
most sensitive to the great flux of civil life; it is the

man who is both liberally and professionally educated
who will be the better soldier.(17)

To be sure, these observations on higher education have
their detractors.  With some compelling arguments, some
military men as well as scholars have pointed out the susceptibility of the military to "politicization" - that higher education
inevitably engenders military "politics." It is also argued that
higher education should be limited only to specific positions
within the military and tailored specifically for clear, military
requirements, the argument being that military skills are the
predominant professional concern.  Thus, while concern with
military politics and higher education implicitly requires a close
identification with society, avoidance of politics and concentra-
tion on military skills suggests a "separateness" from society.
This separation, it is argued, will therefore allow the military
to concentrate on being a military "professional."

Of course, there is a valid argument regarding politicization of the profession - if by politicization we mean "partisan
politics" or activities that subordinate the best interests of the
country to the more parochial interests of a particular institution.  In the main, however, the term politicization has been
levelled at virtually any activity that has broad range of
political concerns, from officers who speak out on policy, to
those who advocate the study of politics.  Note, for example,
the conclusions of one writer regarding politicization and the
Vietnam War.  "Corson is an intellectual and a politicized
Marine Corps Lieutenant Colonel, now retired.  . . . He
deserves special attention as a prototype of the military officers who become committed to the liberal-reformist view of
counter-insurgency."(18)  Although the author of this
particular work does not further explain what is meant by
politicization, it is presumed that he means that Corson was
focusing on political-social problems of the Vietnam War -
hence, he was politicized.  The same author states ". . .
involvement in counter-insurgency politicizes the military and
encourages its intrusion into civilian life."(19)  Study of such
insurgency wars and the appreciation of the political-social
factors, according to this author, means that the military will
be involved in some extra-constitutional activities in civilian
society.

In another perspective, General Bruce Palmer, Jr.,
former Vice Chief of Staff of the U.S. Army said, in part:

. . . we have perhaps a paradox.  The necessity
for a military man to understand nonmilitary aspects
has been widely accepted at a time where there is
also a valid need to be highly proficient in strictly
military matters.  We must be careful, therefore,
that we do not degrade the military character of the

art of leadership which we are trying to impart.
This is basic - a military leader must be able to
handle his men in a military unit. Moreover, I
believe that there are pitfalls in becoming too
politicized. Perhaps this has already happened to
our military leaders and as a result has blurred
military thinking.(20)

Here we may presume that politicized means focusing on non-
military aspects, which in turn may cause blurred military
thinking.
    Another view of politicization contends that professional
officers may become committed to a particular position and use
a variety of procedures and means to support that particular
position. Thus, politicizing in this perspective may lead to
internal professional conflict. In any case, politicization
suggests some nefarious scheme that needs to be avoided at all
costs. Equally noteworthy is the fact that higher education
and politicization have been given an implicit cause-and-effect
relationship. Those who study politics, the political process,
and social sciences in general are, in the main, viewed with
suspicion by many professionals rationalizing in terms of the
potential politicization of the educated officer.
    In sum, these arguments rest on the notion that military
men who study politics and become educated will also become
civilianized (politicized) and not be able to perform as military
professionals. Moreover, the arguments continue, educated
professionals may be inclined to use their knowledge to control
and influence the political as well as military system for
"political" purposes.


                    TWO PROFESSIONAL PERSPECTIVES


The debate over these matters is reflected in two predominant
professional orientations: traditional professionalism and progressive professionalism.(21) The former rests on the premise
that military professionals have a specifically defined military
purpose with a clear delineation between military and political
systems. (As discussed earlier, this is a basic part of the
liberal-traditional alliance.) Thus, professional training,
socialization, lifestyle, and career orientations are all directed
towards nurturing the professional ethos: success in combat.
In sum, civilians make policy and military men carry it out.
Domestic politics and institutions have very little relationship
to the military role.
    The perpetuation of this traditional professional per-
spective rests on a relatively uncomplicated view about
the operation of the political system and a latent sentiment

regarding the military as "separate" from society. One of the consequences is a perception of the world viewed in military terms, with little attention paid to political-social relationships, non-military dimensions, and the broad consequences of military policy. In the complexities of the modern age, to presume that the destruction of a particular target has no political and social ramifications or is divorced from the total political strategy of the war is to view war and conflict in terms of a bureaucratic, incremental, and engineering approach, one that considers war and politics an administrative and managerial rather than a political and social phenomenon. For a profession that prides itself on dealing with people and is basically a political-social institution, this is an odd perspective.

Progressive professionalism, on the other hand, presumes that military professionals need to have some knowledge of foreign policy and the policy uses to which military instrument may be used. (This perspective receives little support in liberal intellectual circles and indeed is viewed by some military men as primarily "rhetorical.") Progressive professionalism is at best a modestly cautious and sometimes misleading approach to the fundamental issues facing the military profession. Demanding that military professionals study "politics" is a charge without clear direction; nor does it provide the rationale for professional dimensions. Moreover, such a perspective appears to remain rooted in traditional professional ethos rather than in a forward looking perspective. Indeed, simply to study politics outside intellectual discipline, scholarly demands, and conceptual rigor is to develop a false sense of intellectualism and faulty perspectives. It is just such a pseudo-intellectualism that has placed military professionals in situations which reveal their inability to deal with civilian counterparts or to logically and systematically counter arguments and perspectives of civilian intellectuals and academicians. Few advocates of progressive professionalism, however, provide a method by which military professionals can acquire the necessary intellectual awareness and expertise to properly assess the political, social, and economic factors. The presumption is that after one reaches a certain rank and completes certain senior level schools, one automatically becomes knowledgeable in non-military factors, political analysis, and inter-disciplinary perspectives.

To be sure, there is rarely a clear delineation between the two. Nevertheless, one or the other perspective tends to dominate the thinking and perceptions of military men. Rarely does either type of professional perspective appear in its extreme form. That is, few military men advocate complete isolation from domestic politics and society; and few advocate a professionalism inextricably immersed in politics. Yet distinctions are recognizable within the profession (see Chapter 8).

## A NEW APPROACH

If one accepts these views, what needs to be done? We are not suggesting a drastic overhaul of the profession. What is necessary is the development of a true spirit of intellectualism conditioned by military realities. Such a professional ethos will foster an understanding of the proper role of politics and the military, the limits of legitimate political actions, the intermix of political-military purposes, and the need for identifying and assessing priorities be they military or civilian. In brief, the profession must adopt a broad intellectual dimension and an enlightened advocacy role.

At the minimum, we feel that concepts associated with the following need to be part of every professional's intellectual baggage:

- Sense of history
- Conflicts within society between individual rights and system imperatives
- Understanding of ideals and actualities of the American political system
- Understanding of the role of the military in a democratic society
- Political consequences of military decisions and military actions
- Moral and ethical issues of professional service and standards of moral behavior
- Problems of political change and economic development

These are not courses of instruction, but of intellectual insights and understanding. Some are acquired by individual professional efforts, but in the main, the military system should create the opportunity for the professional to explore such matters as a normal part of the professional development.

As Goodpaster states,

The effective command of complex military units and organizations remain as much an art as a science. Development of the capacity for exercising command effectively is advanced by studies ranging from history and the understanding of the human condition to ethics and psychology of leadership, before the processes of decision, the capabilities of weapons, the elements of alliance relationships, the thought patterns, culture and doctrine of possible opponents, and the whole gamut of professional military knowledge are even broached.(22)

To achieve these goals, a number of changes within the military profession are necessary. First, the profession needs to broaden the concept of military education to include a wide ranging graduate education experience. This can be accomplished in a variety of ways including fully funded education, a more "university" type environment in the highest level senior schools, and a broad political-social perspective in tactical and strategic considerations.

Second, the military profession must recognize a legitimate political dimension to the profession. On one level, the study of politics should be part of the professional's military education. On another level, the profession needs to provide intensive as well as extensive education and skills in politics and political analysis. Part of this thrust can be achieved by adding political specialties to those studies now available to officers as a secondary MOS. These specialties are not primarily concerned with intelligence evaluation; rather, the concern is with policy evaluation, political power, political-social groups and relationships, and the general operation of the political system. In the foreign area, intensive study would be concerned with development, revolution, comparing political systems, internal political-social dynamics, and the resulting policy of foreign systems.

The essentials of this specialty are a social science background with particular emphasis on analytical tools and evaluation methods. Thus, while the broadly-based liberal education thrust would be a part of the "generalist" career pattern, these specialties provide an exceptional educational base for knowledge and skills in "politics."

The point is not that the military professional should become a politician, but rather that it is necessary for the professional to become much more politically astute, knowledgeable, and sensitive to political imperatives of domestic and international societies, among other things. As a matter of fact, one cannot help but wonder why the military profession has not made this a serious part of the professional socialization and education. Since the end of World War II, some of the highest ranking military men have made it clear that politics is a way of life once one enters into the emerging military elite.(23) Our notion goes beyond this, however, emphasizing that the political role is an inherent part of the total professional world. This does not envision partisan politics, but an enlightened professionalism that is thoroughly grounded in the principles of democratic theory. Indeed, we are convinced that an educated and enlightened professional provides the best safeguards for democracy and for the profession itself. For those who fear an educated military professional and his role in the political system, we can only point out that it has not been demonstrated that education, enlightenment, and political involvement necessarily leads to a

denigration of professionalism. On the contrary, it is the
pseudo military intellectual who is to be feared.

The acknowledgement of this political dimension will
provide an opportunity for the profession to project a realistic
and effective voice in the political system within the legitimate
bounds of a broadened professional ethos. Additionally, it will
allow some "individuality" in the search for professional satisfaction and purpose with recognition that individual ethics and
values are a component of professionalism. The institutionalization of healthy skepticism, reasonable inquiry, and legitimate
dissent would do much to reinforce the "worth" of the
individual while providing a momentum to innovation, imagination, and self-examination.

A more "open" system of communications should be
established between officers who are involved in political-
military matters, officers in all ranks concerned with such
matters, and long-range planning staffs at the various senior
level military schools. Perhaps this kind of channel - i.e.,
the political-military channel - could sitmulate serious military
thought on military policy, provide opportunities for professionals in sensitive political-military areas to state their views
without being accused of opposing policy, and provide realistic
input to the policy process that is not limited to a narrow
group of Pentagon officials.

This can only be implemented if a distinction is made
between disagreement with policy and its execution. As the
Singlaub affair demonstrated, too many civilian leaders presume
that speaking out on policy is the same as lack of execution of
that policy. Nothing could be further from the truth.(24)
There is nothing incompatible between exact execution of
policy, dissatisfaction with it, and a personal opinion regarding its validity. As we learned in the Vietnam War, lack
of internal criticism of policy, the muting of professional
officers and civilian elites, often leads to a policy that is
inadequate and ineffective, perpetuated by those favoring the
policy, and institutionalized to such an extent that disagreement is tantamount to "treason."

Finally, with the recognition that education is essential
and that there is an important political dimension, the military
profession needs to adopt an "enlightened advocacy" posture.(25) This is not based on roles - although this may be
an important consideration - but rather with the intellectual
dimension of professionalism. In this sense, "enlightened"
simply means horizons and perspectives that are not bound by
military considerations, horizons and perspectives that consider
social and political implications of military decisions, and appreciate the need for priorities that intermix civilian and
military considerations.

Such perspectives and horizons are best acquired by the
education characteristic of the better universities of our coun-

try. The kinds of intellectual challenge and critical inquiry common to the graduate education environment is an effective way to accomplish the professional goals suggested here. Enlightened advocacy, therefore, presumes not only the advocation of a particular position or point of view, but also that this be done with sophistication and maturity - a sophistication and maturity, it might be added, that rests on an educational foundation in the best intellectual tradition. Enlightened advocacy will not necessarily solve all of the problems now apparent in the search for acceptable concepts of military professionalism. Nevertheless, for the military profession to deal with itself, the institution, and the political system, enlightened advocacy may be a reasonable solution. Integration of non-military education in the liberal arts tradition, combined with a particular development of military skills, is the kind of thrust that the profession ought to adopt in preparation for the wars of the 1980s. To reiterate, this may be a reasonable professional perspective, but it is one that requires continuous nurturing and knowledge. As Goodpaster succinctly points out, "The most advanced academic and intellectual insights are no more than a necessary starting point."(26)

Obviously, what is suggested here is not an easy alternative for the military profession. It requires not only an institutional change but a differing professional spirit. It will be difficult, for example, to rationalize the enlightened advocacy perspective in cost-effective terms; that is, it is almost impossible to assess the impact of this perspective in terms of dollars and cents. Cost effectiveness can rarely measure subjective factors and leadership effectiveness. What is more difficult is to "sell" such an alternative to those whose immediate concern is operational effectiveness now, over and above all else.

It will be still more difficult to change the traditional professional view of the world. While there is a valid argument to maintaining the "military point of view," it is clear that its meaning needs to be expanded. As we have stated earlier, a traditional (and narrow) meaning seems inappropriate, not only historically but for future military considerations. To reiterate, the military point of view tends to be incrementalist, engineering oriented, and lacking in sensitivity to subjective considerations.

Perhaps one of the sharpest critics of this military thinking process is voiced by I.F. Stone, in his examination of the Vietnam War:

In reading the military literature on guerrilla warfare now so fashionable at the Pentagon one feels that these writers are like men watching a dance from outside through heavy plate glass windows. They

188 BEYOND THE BATTLEFIELD

see the motions but they can't hear the music.
They put the mechanical gestures down on paper
with pedantic fidelity. But what rarely comes
through to them are the injured racial feelings, the
misery, the rankling slights, the hatred, the devotion, the inspiration and the desperation. So they
do not really understand what leads men to abandon
wife, children, home, career, friends; to take to the
bush and live gun in hand like a hunted animal; to
challenge overwhelming military odds rather than
acquiesce any longer in humiliation, injustice, or
poverty. . . .(27)

One basic issue then is how to equate the military
necessities with a position of enlightened advocacy? For those
looking at the future through heavy plate glass windows, it
will be impossible to rationalize and justify such a position.
And here is the paradox: to appreciate the need for such a
professional perspective will require professional military men
who are enlightened and educated. There is little evidence to
suggest that such military professionals exist in sufficient
numbers or have the necessary power to influence the
profession at this period of time.
     In any case, there is indeed a military point of view. We
argue that the military professional is in the best position to
provide this military point of view. But to presume somehow
that the military perspective should not include the bringing to
bear of a military intellectual focus that appreciates and
understands the consequences of military decisions upon the
political and social life of the system is to deny the very
criteria of a "profession." Thus, those who argue that the
military men should focus only on providing the best military
judgement upon <u>military</u> problems are dealing in half-truths.
Moreover, such arguments forget at least one lesson of Vietnam: the inadequacy of a purely military solution to revolutionary war. In this respect, to blame civilians for not making
proper civilian decisions is simply to presume that traditional
professional perspectives are correct in any war and relegates
strategic thinking and "intelligence" solely to civilians.
     Consideration of non-military factors is too often viewed
by professionals as something that can easily be added to the
commander's operational orders, revealing a rather simplistic
view of the matter. Understanding and appreciating non-
military factors, like being inter-disciplinary, is primarily a
product of the mind. It is a mental process, broad in scope,
that weighs the limits and restraints of the broader environment, and the relationship of the military mission in these
terms.
     What this new perspective argues for then is an educated
military man who is an enlightened advocate. An educated

professional military man will not necessarily lead to a civilian-military utopia. After all, the essence of the military pro-fession makes it anathema to a liberal democratic society. Nonetheless, enlightened advocacy will provide a close link between the intellectual dimensions of military professionalism, the democratic need, and civilian elite. It may not lead to a closer linkage between the various military and civilian structures. But it may provide the best environment to achieve an intellectual empathy and understanding between military and civilian elite and military and civilian professions.

Not all professionals need to be men and women for all seasons, but the fact remains that the pursuit of higher education and the recognition of its importance as fundamental to professional competence will have a profound impact on the professional character, spirit, and image. Moreover, it will enhance the profession's ability to deal with the political-military environment of the 1980s. Education as used in this context does not stop with formal education. Opportunities must exist to exercise the mind and utilize the intellectual knowledge. At a minimum, this requires professional recogni-tion of the value of education in the total professional en-vironment.

Equally important, we are speaking here of a long-term proposition. The broadening of professional intellectual dimensions will not come by adding courses to senior service schools or by increasing by x percent the number of military officers attending civilian graduate education. It may require this, but much more: a different concept regarding socializa-tion and education. What is being suggested here is primarily a long-range perspective in which military operations and military schooling include political-social factors and the ability to apply methodological tools for political analysis and policy evaluation as a matter of course. This perspective is only a starting point, since specific answers must be sought by those who accept these perspectives. But it seems to us that nothing could be more dangerous to military professionalism than to develop a world view that is unidimensional, omni-competent, and limited in its intellectual scope.

In the final analysis, we are convinced that the educated military man, skilled in his own profession, and unafraid to commit himself to higher principles, provides the best safe-guard to civilian control and a democratic system. Attuned to broad conceptual thought processes, and with horizons that go beyond the "military world," the professional is likely to be sensitive to the proper place of politics in the profession, concerned about professional ethics, and in a position to develop an intellectual awareness to deal reasonably and rationally with the political environment.

NOTES

1.  Samuel  P.  Huntington,  The Soldier and the State.
New  York:  Vintage  Books,  1964;  and Harold  D.  Lasswell,
"The   Garrison   State,"  American  Journal  of  Sociology,  1946,
pp. 455-468.
2.  See  Charles  C.  Moskos,  Jr.,  "The  Military,"  Annual
Review of Sociology,  Vol.  2,  1976,  for  a  review  of  the  literature.
3.  See  David  W.  Moore  and  B.  Thomas Trout,  "Military
Advancement:   The  Visibility  Theory  of  Promotion,"  American
Political Science Review,  Vol.  72,  No.  2,  1978,  pp.  452-468.
The  authors  note  that  ". . . The Huntington  approach  seems
to  have  been  overtaken  by  events.   The  military,  after  all,
has   become   quite   involved   or   integrated   into   the   decision-
making  process,  and  physical  isolation  of  the  military  from
society  is  no  longer  a  feasible  or  realistic  alternative."   (p.
468).   Yet  many  professional  military  men,  as  well  as  academicians   and   scholars,   would   deny   the   military   the   necessary
educational   and   intellectual   experience   and   opportunity   to
approach  their  "political"  role  from  a  systematic  and  professional   perspective.    In   this   respect,   see   Jerome   Slater,
"Apolitical  Warrior  or  Soldier-Statesman:   The  Military  and  the
Foreign   Policy   Process   in   the   Post   Vietnam   Era"   and   John
Lovell,  "Apolitical  Warrior  or  Soldier-Statesman:   Commentary,"
in   Armed  Forces  and  Society,   Vol.  4,   No.  1,   Fall,  1977.
4.   The  argument  here  is  focused  only  on  one  side  of
the  problem  -  the  military  side.   A  good  case  can  also  be  made
for  the  need  of  civilian  elites  to  understand  and  appreciate  the
military,  an  understanding  that  requires  more  than  ivory  tower
assessments  based  on  historical  stereotypes.   It  requires  a
sensitivity  to  the  demands  of  the  profession  and  a  flexibility  of
civilian  perspectives.   These  are  not  necessarily  acquired  by
library  research  or  one-time  exposure  to  "Generals."
5.   There  were  major  exceptions  prior  to  World  War  II,
since  a  number  of  high  ranking  officers  did  engage  in  politics
as  an  inherent  part  of  their  military  careers.   See,  for  example,   Allan  R.   Millett,   The General, Robert L. Bullard and
Officership  in  the  United  States  Army,  1881-1925.   Westport,
Conn.:   Greenwood  Press,  1975.
6.   See  Sam  C.  Sarkesian,  The Professional Army Officer
in  a  Changing  Society.   Chicago:   Nelson  Hall  Publishing  Co.,
1975, pp. 164-174.
7.   For  an  absorbing  account  of  the  struggle  over  policy
matters   involving   resources   and   missions   in   Vietnam,   see
Robert  L.  Gallucci,  Neither Peace Nor Honor; The Politics of
American Military Policy in Viet-Nam.   Baltimore:   The   Johns
Hopkins  University  Press,  1975.   See  also  Lawrence  J.  Korb,
The   Joint   Chiefs   of   Staff;   The   First   Twenty-five   Years.

Bloomington:    Indiana    University    Press,    1976,    particularly
Chapter Four.
    8.   Andrew J. Goodpaster and Samuel P. Huntington, et
al., Civil-Military Relations, American Enterprises Institute for
Public Policy Research, Washington, D.C., 1977, p. 45.
    9.   Philip Abrams, "The Late Profession of Arms:    Am-
biguous Goals and Deteriorating Means in Britain," European
Journal of Sociology, Vol. VI, No. 2, 1965, p. 246.
    10.   Glenn H. Snyder, Deterrence and Defense:    Toward
a  Theory  of  National  Security.    Princeton, N.J.: Princeton
University Press, 1961, p. 3.
    11.   Lt-General Wolf Graf Von Baudissin, "Officer Educa-
tion  and  the  Officer's  Career,"  Adelphi  Papers  #103,  The
International Institute for Strategic Studies, 1973, pp. 40-41.
See also the interesting paper by Edward Romar, "Reaction
and Reform:    The Political Ideas of Generals Hans Von Seeckt
and Wolf Von Baudissin," presented at the Inter University
Seminar  on  Armed  Forces  and  Society,  Annual  Conference,
Chicago, Ill., October 20-22, 1977.
    12.   Abrams, pp. 246-247.
    13.   Von Baudissin, p. 39.
    14.   Ibid., p. 43.
    15.   Adam Yarmolinsky, "Where Should the Officer Obtain
His  Education?"    Lawrence  J.  Korb  (Ed.),  The System for
Educating Military Officers in the U.S., Occasional Paper No.
9, International Studies Association, 1976, p. 152.
    16.   See, for example, Gabriel Almond and Sidney Verba,
The Civic Culture.    Boston:    Little, Brown and Co., 1965, in
which the authors conclude, among other things, that the more
educated person is more aware of the impact of government on
the individual; the more educated are likely to participate in
the political process than the less educated; the more educated
individual  has  more  political  information;  the  more  educated
individual is more likely to express confidence in his social
environment and to believe that other people are trustworthy
and helpful (pp. 317-318).    Also, the authors state that "In
the United States and Britian, where a large proportion of the
respondents express pride in the political characteristics of
their  nations,  this  proportion  was  higher  among  the  better
educated respondents.    In the United States, 92 percent of
those with some university education responded with political
objects of pride. . . . (p. 67)."    There are many studies on
the relationship of higher education, political participation, and
political attitudes.    See, for example, Lester W. Milbraith and
M.L.  Goel,  Political  Participation.    Chicago:  Rand  McNally
College Publishing Co., 1977; Norman H. Nie, Sidney Verba,
John  R.  Petrocik,  The Changing American Voter.    Cambridge,
Mass.:    Harvard  University  Press,  1976;  Sidney  Verba  and
Norman  H.  Nie,  Political Participation in America:    Political
Democracy and Social Equality.    New York:    Harper and Row,

1972. The preponderance of evidence in the literature suggests that the higher educated person in a democracy is likely
to have a stronger commitment to the democratic creed and a
higher concern with individual rights and values.
        17. Josiah Bunting, "The Humanities in the Education of
the Military Professional," in Korb, p. 158.
        18. Equal Ahmad, "Revolutionary War and Counter In-
surgency," David S. Sullivan and Martin J. Sattler (Eds.),
Revolutionary War: Western Response. New York: Columbia
University Press, 1971, p. 20.
        19. Ibid., p. 46.
        20. Address by General Bruce Palmer, Jr. "Leadership
Challenges for a Multi-Role Army," United States Military
Academy, West Point, N.Y., June 26, 1969.
        21. These views are best reflected by General Douglas
MacArthur, General Maxwell Taylor, and the late President
John F. Kennedy. At his famous address to the Corps of
Cadets at the United States Military Academy in 1964, General
MacArthur, in articulating traditional professionalism, said, in
part, "Your mission remains fixed, determined, inviolable - it
is to win wars. Everything else in your professional careers
is but corollary to this vital dedication." The General went on
to state emphatically that concerns about governmental
processes, internal domestic issues, civil rights and liberties
were great national issues but not for the participation of the
military professional nor for military solution.
        Progressive professionalism is best represented by the
perspective expressed by General Maxwell Taylor who argues,
"For the sword to be an effective instrument of foreign policy,
its forgers must have some understanding of the purposes to
which it may be put, hence, know something of the future
goals of national policy and the obstacles to them which may
have to be resolved by military force." See Maxwell Taylor,
Swords and Plowshares. New York: W.W. Norton and Co.,
Inc., 1972, pp. 254-255.
        Supporting his point, Taylor quotes from John F.
Kennedy's speech to the West Point Corps of Cadets, "The
non-military problems which you will face will also be the most
demanding - diplomatic, political and economic. You will need
to know and understand not only the foreign policy of the
U.S. but the foreign policy of all countries scattered around
the world. You will need to understand the importance of
military power and also the limits of military power. You will
have the obligation to deter war as well as fight it." The
"politics" of this charge is self-evident.
        The policy and political needs of the military profession
and their relationships to education was recognized over two
decades ago by two scholars, John W. Masland and Laurence I.
Radway, Soldiers and Scholars; Military Education and National
Policy. Princeton: Princeton University Press, 1957. They
wrote that military leaders,

. . . are required to understand, to communicate
with, and to evaluate the judgement of political
leaders, officials of other executive agencies, and
countless specialists; they must make sound judge-
ments themselves on matters which affect a wide
variety of civilian concerns. They are called upon
to evaluate the motivations and capabilities of foreign
nations and to estimate the effects of American action
or inaction upon these nations. And above all, the
new role of military leaders requires of them a
heightened awareness of the principles of our democratic society [p. vii].

22. Goodpaster, p. 46.
23. See, for example, Matthew B. Ridgway, Soldier: The
Memoirs of Matthew B. Ridgway. New York: Harper and
Row, 1956; Taylor, Swords and Plowshares; William Westmore-
land, A Soldier Reports. Garden City, New York: Doubleday
and Company, Inc., 1976; Elmo Zumwalt, On Watch: A
Memoir. New York: Quadrangle Books, 1976.
24. Major General John K. Singlaub, Chief of Staff,
U.S. Forces in Korea, was quickly removed from his post in
the Summer of 1977 for suggesting to a reporter that President
Carter's decision to remove U.S. ground forces from South
Korea would create a dangerous security problem in the area.
It is interesting to note Ridgway, Soldier, p. 270, on this
point.. ". . . and this is the essential point – I said that the
civilian authorities must scrupulously respect the integrity, the
intellectual honesty, of its officers corps. Any effort to force
unanimity of view, to compel adherence to some politico-military
'party line' against the honestly expressed views of responsible officers, I pointed out, is a pernicious practice which
jeopardizes rather than protects the integrity of the military
profession."
25. While there has been some cautious support of an ad-
vocatory role (not exactly in the sense of advocacy used here)
– that is, military men defending public policy outside of
military circles – these have been qualified by rigid restrictions. For example, see John R. Probert, "Vietnam and
United States Military Thought Concerning Civil-Military Roles
in Government," in Charles L. Cochran (Ed.), Civil-Military
Relations. New York: The Free Press, 1974, pp. 140-151.
26. Goodpaster, p. 45.
27. I.F. Stone, In Time of Torment. New York: Vintage Books, 1968, pp. 173-174.

# IV
## Challenge to Professionalism

# Part IV
## An Introduction

This part reviews the nature and character of the new challenges to the military profession that range from the political-social to the technical factors and moral and ethical issues. The selections point out that for too long the profession has presumed that the professional challenges are primarily rooted in the technicalities of the battlefield environment. Yet battlefields of the future and the nature of modern conflicts do not lend themselves to "military" solutions alone. This is one lesson that the military profession and the institution should have learned by the Vietnam experience. But from all indications, attention of the military profession is again focused primarily on the European scene, with little attention to the non-European areas in which conflicts are more likely to occur or to the political-social elements of conflict. What is also stressed in this part is the moral and ethical dilemma faced by the military professional when involved in low intensity conflict or in wars that are non-European in nature. Liberal democratic systems expect a degree of moral and ethical behavior on the battlefield by their military men as well as the support and perpetuation of moral and ethical principles of democracy. Military professionals have tended to respond by simply assuming that they are the implementors of policy and, therefore, not responsible for political or moral consequences or for its moral and ethical substance. This is a reflection of the traditional professional perspective that seeks to fall back on well-worn relationships, stressing clear delineations between military and society. The final selection is basically a challenge to the military profession in terms of the new demands of leadership. If military men are to be effective leaders, they must be educated and socialized into a new professional posture that has accepted, digested, and incorporated the political-social elements and intellectual horizons demanded by the domestic and international environment.

# 10 Moral and Ethical Foundations of Military Professionalism

It has been said that war and politics have their own morality. If this is true, politicians and military men share a common dilemma: the problem of reconciling their individual moral and ethical principles to the larger objectives of war and politics. Yet, if we assume that war and politics are simply the larger universe of individual morality and ethics, then we have placed ourselves in a moral and ethical box from which we can extricate ourselves only by jeopardizing our sense of autonomy and self-esteem. Nowhere is this dilemma more apparent than in the military profession. Politicians in general seem to recognize the difficulty of equating politics with the individual "writ large." Military men, however, tend to presume that individual morality and ethics and those of the profession must coincide, even though military men as well as politicians are rarely placed in a position in which distinctions can be made between clearly evil or good alternatives. This "either/or" absolutism makes it difficult for military professionals to seriously undertake imperfect positions, fearing that less than absolutism will expose them to charges of advocacy of less than the highest moral and ethical standards. As a result, a unique posture is adopted.

> The fact is that it is necessary and moral to do things in politics that would be unjustifiable in the circumstances of private life. The political order has exigencies and complexities that have no part in private life. Thus, moral behavior there will be correspondingly more difficult to judge. . . . The problem is that because it is more difficult, the moral dimension tends to be dropped. As a result, politics often gets done without conscience. Outside of last-resort matters, then, it appears that one

199

enters a moral free zone where conscience can be
dropped before entering.(1)

For a profession striving for philosophical guidelines in
absolute terms, the impossibility of the goal makes it expeditious to acknowledge a moral free zone as a rationalization
for reconciling the gap between military behavior, morals,
ethics, and military purpose. Furthermore, such a perspective
alleviates the need for serious philosophical reflection. The
fact remains that the professional stress or integrity, obedience, and loyalty builds an antagonism into the individual-
professional relationship. While individual integrity demands a
sense of self-esteem, honesty, and honor, professional demands may require their subordination in order to maintain the
honor and integrity of the profession. This problem has been
a continuing source of professional tension. In the aftermath
of Vietnam, it became more pronounced.

The volunteer-military era in the United States has added
an urgency to the examination of professional morals and
ethics. Manpower issues, particularly those dealing with
quality of personnel, role of women, attitudes and values, and
the military socialization process affect the moral and ethical
patterns of the profession and the institution. The relatively
rapid turn-over of first-term enlisted ranks will continually
bring into the military a large group of young men and women
with varying ideas of morality and ethics and with back-
grounds linked closely with the political and social structure
of the civilian system. In light of the civil-military interpenetration and the inability of the military to isolate itself
from society's influences, it is unlikely that the military
socialization process can prevent a continuing civilian impact
on these young men and women. With a moral and ethical
background that may differ considerably from the profession,
the infusion of large groups of people can erode the effectiveness of the military and the cohesiveness of the profession. For these reasons, the profession must set clear moral
and ethical patterns, linked with the best in society.

The purpose of this chapter is to critically inquire into
the moral and ethical foundations of military professionalism -
an inquiry intended to re-examine intellectual and professional
perspectives, the dilemmas these pose, and the presentation of
an alternative moral and ethical posture. This is not intended
to be a historical nor philosophical discourse on morality
and/or ethics. There is a great deal of literature on these
matters ranging from the classical thinkers to contemporary
writers. No serious examination of morality and ethics is
completely satisfactory without some references to these and
their historical continuities. While we will touch upon these
matters, our main focus is on the individual professional and
the profession in the modern context.

Finally, we do not intend to seriously examine the specifics of internal professional considerations; i.e., leadership, quality of the enlisted structure, or job performance. These have been extensively examined elsewhere to the detriment of studies on the broader and more fundamental issues of professionalism, morality, and ethics.

This chapter provides no set of answers. It does not delve into metaphysical speculations or philosophical abstractions. Rather, it is based on the presumption that the process of examining morality and ethics as they pertain to the military profession will broaden the understanding of them and allow professionals to come to grips with the dilemmas within the profession and between the military and society. We also believe that serious reflection on morality and ethics will nurture individual and professional integrity.


## AN OVERVIEW OF MORAL AND ETHICAL PRINCIPLES


Moral values derive from "culturally based propositions or generalizations about what befits or does not befit the behavior of human beings."(2) The importance of moral values cannot be overstated since it is an inherent part of human nature. ". . . Moral values make up what we are as persons. . . . Failure here is drastic, not just unfortunate."(3) It follows that moral principles evolve from the larger sense of "humanity" that is, they stem from a universe beyond the immediate world of the individual.

Ethics is, in part, the behavior expected of individuals to conform to these culturally based guidelines. Ethics also presumes that individuals actively seek enlightenment about their moral values and critically examine their behavior in that light.

Some order and priority are necessary in the moral and ethical universe if a coherent environment is to be maintained. The continued functioning of the political system requires such an environment. Order and priority are also necessary if the individual is to develop a sense of personal integrity. A major function of the political system is to integrate moral and ethical standards, establish priorities, and create an orderly environment in which these can operate. First order values are those that are directly associated with life itself - survival and sanctity of life. While philosophers may identify a number of moral vlaues and ethical concerns, we feel that these two are particularly relevant to the military profession, since the purpose of the military, its very existence, is based upon the giving and taking of life.

Other values stem from these, but are of a lesser order. That is, they may be peculiar and unique to a particular type of ideology and culture.

We shall talk about ethics or morality, not as ideas necessarily sacred or "right" in themselves, but merely as widely held values which, rightly or wrongly, receive widespread sanction and approval. We will hold as ultimate values those goals and criteria which seem to us to be most closely in accord with what is real. These ultimate values, which are held by every great religion and which have been advanced by each of the great prophets and religious leaders throughout recorded history, are: love of fellow man, justice in all acts among men, and the self-fulfillment of the individual through understanding and through actions that bring him closer to living in accord with reality.(4)

In this respect, freedom of speech, individual autonomy, justice, and brotherhood may be values engrained in Western liberal democracies, while social justice and the importance of the group and state may be values predominant in non-Western systems. (Interestingly enough, national sovereignties fragment the universal concept of morality and ethics.) In every political system, the values of sanctity of life, survival, and values stemming from these are pursued in accordance with the system's ideological guidelines. In a democratic system, as Frankena notes:

Society must be careful. . . . For it is itself morally required to respect the individual's autonomy and liberty, and in general to treat him justly; and it must remember that morality is made to minister to the good lives of individuals and not to interfere with them any more than is necessary. Morality is made for man, not man for morality.(5)

## PROFESSIONAL PERSPECTIVES

For the individual military professional, the political-social system in the United States imposes moral and ethical dimensions that are further complicated by the ethos and lifestyle of the profession. It is the profession that has the most immediate impact on the everyday life and lifestyle of the member. And it is the professional interpretation of these moral values and ethical patterns that have the greatest impact on the individual's own sense of morality and ethics.
Moral and ethical patterns in the American military profession are manifested in the concepts of personal integrity, duty, honor, country, and officership. Although it is difficult to define these concepts, we offer working definitions to serve as a basis for our discussion.

Integrity (as defined in Webster) is "the quality or state of being of sound moral principle; uprightness, honest and sincere." In broader terms, it means that the individual is an entity in himself; the concept of the "whole man," whose moral values and ethical behavior are derived from the larger universe. It also suggests a sensitivity to other human beings and an awareness of the consequences of the individual's own actions upon other men and upon the environment. Finally, all of these considerations are rooted in the idea that man is a rational being whose values psychically stem from man's uniqueness.

One military scholar has written:

> We forget all too easily the wisdom concerning these matters given to us by almost every moral philosopher dating back at least as far as Socrates, Plato, and Aristotle. The classical Greek conception of the just or honorable man encompassed all of one's human acts. Moral prescriptions are given in broad terms, e.g., "seek the golden mean of moderation between the extremes of too much and too little," or "act in accordance with right reason." Aristotle would advise us not to seek more precision than our subject matter premits; moral philosophy cannot provide the specific conclusions of a mathematical system. We can identify general classes of good and bad human actions, e.g. promise-keeping, truth-telling, lying, cheating, stealing, and so on; but the crucial step to right behavior is not following a rule because it is a rule. Rather one becomes a good man through developing traits of character, by constantly and consistently performing good actions. The critical thing is what kind of person one becomes in the long run, throughout a lifetime. (6)

At various times, duty has been defined as skilled performance, mission orientation, duty above personal interests, and self-sacrifice. In the broader sense, duty refers to the individual's goal in life in the context of his function in the political system. For the military professional, duty presumes a commitment to carry out the dictates of his position and office. In brief, military professionals are expected to achieve their mission regardless of personal sacrifices. Ultimate liability becomes the operational concept.

Honor is both a complicated concept and a simple term. It can be defined in terms of loyalty to the brotherhood of officers, gentlemanly conduct, and personal sacrifice. In simpler terms, it means acting in a fashion to maintain the dignity of office, its repute, esteem, and respect. But above all honor is supposed to be based on moral values and ethical behavior that are rooted in universally accepted values.

The adherence to concepts of integrity, duty, and honor are for purposes of performing the essential professional function, service to the country. What the country demands of the military through its appointed and elected leadership becomes the operating principle for the profession. What the country decides becomes the unquestioned mission for the military. The country (state) is the sole client; professional honor and duty are presumed to be meaningful only in the context of service to the state.

The idea of "officership" is not generally addressed in the literature, but we believe it is important because it distinguishes officers from other ranks. Officership is based on the idea of "special trust and confidence" as spelled out in the oath of office.(7) Officers are appointed by the President and are agents of the executive branch. As such, officers hold a special trust and confidence to perform their duties with a dignity that brings honor to the state. The President "commissions" officers to take on certain powers in the name of the executive and with this commission authorizes them to act in the name of the state. This "commission" goes beyond the credentials of the officer at the time of commissioning. It implies that the officer will maintain and develop his intellectual acuities and performance skills to insure that he can carry out the tasks at any given time or in any given environment while holding this commission.

All of these concepts may appear to be self evident. They are not. The greatest difficulty is in their translation from abstractions to the practicalities and realities of military life. In seeking a solution to this difficulty, the military profession has adopted a parochial perspective which interprets morality and ethics from within the boundaries of the profession rather than from the larger universe. Absolutism in moral and ethical standards qualified by the immediate necessities of military purpose effectively circumvent inherent difficulties in reconciling individuality, the profession, and society, or so it seems. If the military serves society, then its primary value system must evolve from the political-social system it is supposed to serve. One cannot have it both ways - either the military serves society or it serves itself. It is philosophically self-serving to presume that the military serves society yet develops moral and ethical patterns exclusively from the military world. This is one element of the dilemma between the profession and society: the difficulty in relating military vlaues with those of society. It is this that has led to a variety of attempts to clarify and explain the military profession in terms of its "separateness" from society.

THE PROFESSION AS A MORAL
AND ETHICAL COMMUNITY


In the pre-World War II period, when the military was a
"closed" society, there was little civilian penetration of the
military world.  Professionals could reasonably argue that the
military was similar to a church or priesthood with a morality
and ethics of its own.  This perspective was a function of the
politics and social environment of the times, and the relatively
insignificant role played in the political-social order by the
military profession.  World War II changed all of that.  The
military, as is generally recognized, is now an important
political institution with a high degree of civilian-military
interface and civilian value penetration.  This relationship
considerably hinders the professional monopolization of the
philosophical dimensions of professionalism and the "private"
side of professional family life.
     In the years after World War II, a significant amount of
research concluded that the military profession had shifted to
a managerial posture.  The new demands of the nuclear age
and the apparent success of corporations or the entrepreneurial approach to efficiency, took root in the systems
analysis perspective and spread throughout the military
system.  Consequently, a body of opinion developed which
equated military values and lifestyles to that of the entrepreneurial world in society.
     Today we can detect both perspectives, priesthood and
entrepreneurship, within the military and the scholarly literature.  Both perspectives provide half-truths.  There are
segments of the military that can be compared to the managerial and entrepreneurial mind-set, but to presume that this
is the sole thrust of professionalism is to overlook the fact
that in operational units men must still be led.  Command
decisions are not solely or even generally based on a systems-
analysis or cost-effective perspective.  It cannot be presumed
that an entrepreneurial mind-set can be instilled and maintained in a professional system whose client is the state, and
whose performance criteria has little to do with production and
profit.
     It is also unrealistic to presume that the profession is a
priesthood with a monastic underpinning and commitment to a
particular "high calling."  As research and a number of
attitude surveys have shown, individuals become military
professionals for a number of inter-related reasons ranging
from a challenging job to patriotism.  Additionally, these are
usually family men with the same basic drives and desires as
most civilian professionals:  security, a good education for
their children, and social and economic comfort.

One author explained that:

> . . . ideologies and ethics of the profession which
> motivated the officer in his youth, like the ideals of
> the young liberal college student, become qualified
> by the hard realities of family responsibility, job
> status, and retirement security. The middle-aged
> career officer has about the same self-interests as
> any other professional, despite the creeds of service
> and sacrifice. (8)

Attempts to classify the profession into either entrepreneurial or monastic structures inevitably lead to simple
convergence or divergence distinctions. These oversimplifications become particularly glaring upon examining the
differences between profession and bureaucracy. In this
respect, Palumbo and Styskal observe:

> Professionalism is a difficult concept to define; it can
> easily be confused with bureaucracy. Although
> there are many similarities between the two terms,
> there is a major distinction; professional control is
> primarily "horizontal" in that professionals organize
> themselves into voluntary associations for the pur-
> pose of self-control. Bureaucratic control is "ver-
> tical" in that it is achieved through the authority
> structure in an organization. For professionals,
> control is achieved through the sanctions of fellow
> professionals, and code of ethics; for bureaucrats,
> control derives from position. (9)

Lacking formally structured voluntary associations, professional control is attempted through a moral and ethical code
based on integrity, duty, honor, country, and officership.
These concepts are horizontally articulated through personal,
collegial, and "brotherhood" linkages between professionals.
These are, at best, inchoate, with psychological rather than
associational (formal) or structural implications. Vertical
control is exercised through the military bureaucracy which
places professionals in authority over other professionals
through the rank structure. It is this bureaucratic or vertical
structure that also serves as a professional control structure
subsuming (and integrating) the horizontal control mechanisms.
The result is that in the military, lines between professional
and bureaucratic control are blurred. It is this blurring
which precipitates oversimplifications leading to apparently
dichotomous distinctions such as monastic or entrepreneurial
and divergence or convergence. The real issues are not those
to which these oversimplifications seem to be pointing, but
rather the extent of the boundaries for civil-military interface

and the moral and ethical reference points that society provides for the profession. How these are integrated into the military socialization process and how the profession responds are the essential issues. In certain areas, civilian values and ethical patterns govern. In others, values which evolve primarily as a result of the function of the military govern. As the values of the political-social system change and as differing security environments develop in the international arena, the relationships and "mixes" change between civilian moral and ethical patterns and those unique to the military. In any case, the military cannot subordinate first-order values of society nor their ethical manifestations without risking a loss of legitimacy and professional esteem.

We can conclude that the moral and ethical patterns of the military profession must, on one hand, be linked with society, and on the other, stem from the unique purpose of the profession. As difficult as it may be, this requires the linking of a sub-system based on homogeneity of values, a predictable environment, and a controlled socialization process with that of the larger political-social system which is heterogenous, pluralistic in its value system, and which has a variety of sources for socialization.(10)

## PERSONAL INTEGRITY AND PROFESSIONALISM

The horizontal and vertical intermeshing of bureaucratic structure with a professional network contains an inherent dilemma for the individual professional. This is aggravated by the stresses of entrepreneurial forces and monastic isolation. On the one hand, the profession operates through a bureaucratic structure, while proclaiming the virtues of a profession. On the other hand, the bureaucratic/professional system has adopted a number of modern business practices with its entrepreneurial efficiency criteria, while retaining a tendency towards a monastic lifestyle. The individual professional is unable to totally link his moral and ethical principles solely to one or the other dimension. Given the nature of our system, the pervasiveness of the mass media and the existence of alternate sources of socialization and satisfaction (i.e., the church, civilian education, and social institutions), the professional is susceptible to influences external to the profession, albeit in a less pervasive way. Buffeted by these various forces, the individual professional is nevertheless expected to follow the lifestyle and accept the morality and ethics of a profession that primarily evolves from a monastic focus and horizontal network. Although the profession operates within the context of the morality and values of the political-social system, these dilemmas are relieved by adjusting individual lifestyles to the expectations of the profession. Thus, the perspectives of the profession become the dominating morality and ethics for the individual officer. Institutional articulation of integrity, duty, honor, country, and officership are substituted for the individual's own sense of morality and ethics.

Institutionally, it is expected that professional men's first-order values are loyalty to the institution and profession. As Ellis and Moore point out, ". . . the military atmosphere of the West Point culture puts a special premium on obedience to imposed standards of conduct at the cost of internalized ideals."(11)  This circumstance is characteristic of the entire profession.  Ellis and Moore conclude:

> Perhaps more than any other group, the military is victimized by a divided allegiance; on the one hand, they are charged with carrying out dictates of the elected or appointed civilian leaders; on the other hand, as the Americans most intimately acquainted with the implementation of our military policies, they are most likely to have personal qualms about the effectiveness of these policies.  When caught in this moral dilemma, most West Pointers are conditioned to perceive their obedience to lawful superiors as the highest form of duty.  Such a perception is regarded as the essence of military professionalism, for it involves putting personal considerations beneath service, duty above self.  When there is a conflict between what a West Pointer calls duty and honor, then, he is likely to have no ethical answers.  Or rather, he is trained to answer by equating honor with duty.(12)

Reaching essentially the same conclusion, Dixon writes that military men have a basically conservative syndrome:

> It reflects . . . 'a generalized susceptibility to experiencing threat or anxiety in the face of uncertainty.'  It works by 'simplifying, ordering, controlling, and rendering more secure, both the external world (through perceptual processes . . .) and the internal world (needs, feelings, desires, etc.).  Order is imposed upon inner needs and feelings by subjugating them to rigid and implistic external codes of conduct (rules, laws, morals, duties, obligations, etc.), thus reducing conflict and averting the anxiety that would accompany awareness of the freedom to choose among alternative modes of action.'(13)

The demand for institutional obedience and professional loyalty can lead to professional mediocrity and institutional sterility, constraining critical and responsible inquiry, devoid of healthy skepticism. Translated to the lowest ranks, it overwhelms younger officers fostering an uncritical acceptance of anything from above, reinforcing conformity and institutional righteousness. Soldiers have found in every war and in every age, however, that there are incompetents in their ranks who hold positions of responsibility and whose decisions could result in momentous military disasters.

Liddell Hart makes this point:

As a young officer I had cherished a deep respect for the Higher Command, but I was sadly disillusioned about many of them when I came to see them more closely from the angle of a military correspondent. It was saddening to discover how many apparently honorable men would stoop to almost anything to help advance their careers.(14)

Flammer writes, "Armies tend to regard as inherently 'dishonorable' or 'disloyal' any suggestions that important errors were made or that leadership, at least at the top levels, was ever less than sterling."(15) Dissent may be expressed, but it must be done in channels and within the narrow confines of professional loyalty.

One of the most important tests of professional cohesiveness is the ability to sustain and withstand criticism, both from within and without. The crucial test is not when things are going well, but how the profession responds under severe testing. An untested profession cannot claim competence or true professional status. As one scholar notes, "Our judgement or principle is really justified if it holds up under sustained scrutiny . . . from the moral point of view on the part of everyone."(16)

## PROFESSIONALISM AND THE HUMANISTIC FACTOR

Much of the literature on military professionalism deals with skills, technical competence, corporateness, and values intrinsically military in their perspective. While these are certainly valid considerations, there is a major omission. This has to do with the examination of the professional responsibility to the larger political-social system in terms of moral and ethical considerations. This is closely related to the concept of profession as it relates to the wider concern for human behavior and political-social systems.

A professional is not only charged with developing skills and competence in his field, and with a concern for the well-being of the client (the state). The professional must also develop knowledge and awareness of the broader issues of political-social systems and human behavior. All professions are supposed to be humanistic in their perspectives with horizons that go beyond performance competency. This is what the military profession has responded to least and has exposed the profession to charges of "semi-professionalism." It is the nature of the learning process and the intellectual dimension that provide the distinctions between occupation and profession. There is nothing to prevent a carpenter, for example, from reading Plato. But it is unlikely that the carpenter's clients will expect him to expound humanistic insights or debate the issues in The Republic in order to perform well as a carpenter. Military professionals, however, whose client is the state and who are deeply involved in issues of peace and war, can reasonably be expected to have horizons beyond leading battalions in the attack. Reading Plato and examining the problems of rule and the ruled may be a reasonable professional requirement. Understanding the significance of Socrates and the "cup of hemlock" may provide insights into modern moral and ethical dilemmas. Most important, serious thought on such matters is an integral part of the "whole" man concept.

The conduct of war may be the single most compelling professional purpose. The demands of a no-war, no-peace environment, issues associated with the aftermath of war, and the variety of conflicts require a professional dimension not bound by conventional and nuclear battlefield competency. Without a sensitivity to the human factor and intellectual insights into political-social matters, the military may well be a "semi-profession."

The characteristics of the profession (institutional obe-dience and professional loyalty), as we suggested earlier, give short shrift to the humanistic factor and subordinate the moral and ethical issues to the professional demands of performance competency. The "moral free" expediency is an attractive posture since it does appear to provide a rational solution to moral and ethical dilemmas. And as was noted earlier, this approach leads to a simplified decision process, remarkably similar to that described by Simon:

Administrative man recognizes that the world he perceives is a drastically simplified model of the budding, blooming confusion that constitutes the real world. He is content with this gross simplification because he believes that the real world is mostly empty - that most of the facts of the real world have no great relevance to any particular situation he is

facing, and that most significant chains of causes
and consequences are short and simple. Hence, he
is content to leave out of account those aspects of
reality - and that means most aspects - that are
substantially irrelevant at a given time. He makes
his choices using a simple picture of the situation
that takes into account just a few of the factors that
he regards as most relevant and crucial.

What is the significance of these two characteristics of administrative man? First, because he
satisfices, rather than maximizes, administrative man
can make his choices without first examining all
possible behavior alternatives and without ascertaining that these are in fact all alternatives. Second,
because he treats the world as rather "empty," and
ignores the "interrelatedness of all things" (so
stupefying to thought and action), administrative
man is able to make his decisions with relatively
simple rules of thumb that do not make impossible
demands upon his capacity for thought.(17)

Adopting this concept, it is easy for the military profession to accept duty, honor, country, as simplistic guides to
rational action. Nor does this approach challenge personal
integrity. It does accommodate itself easily to the concept of
officership, though, since orders from above become the basis
for legitimate (and uncritical) action.


## SUMMARY AND CONCLUSIONS


In examining these moral and ethical dilemmas, we should not
be deluded into thinking that there is a constant professional
philosophizing about them by all officers. Indeed, if this were
the case, the profession would collapse under the sheer weight
of philosophical inquiry. Professional morals and ethics generally coincide with the individual professional's lifestyle and
philosophical orientation. The characteristics of the military
profession tend to attract those whose moral and ethical
patterns are compatible with those of the military profession.
There are occasions when serious antagonisms emerge between
the profession and society, and/or the individual and the
profession. It is not the frequency with which these occur
that is important, but the depth and seriousness of the
antagonisms.

Without some resolution or accommodation, these antagonisms can erode professional prestige and develop serious
civil-military tensions. Over the long run, it is the profession
that suffers. Equally important, the profession needs to

attract competent, intelligent young men and women. It also
needs to provide an environment that maintains a willing (and
enthusiastic) individual commitment and keep the profession
intellectually and physically challenging. Serious differences
between personal integrity and professional demands or between the profession and society hinders professional vigor
and deters highly qualified individuals from entering the
profession.

The dilemmas and antagonisms between the moral and
ethical patterns of society and the military make for an uneasy
accommodation. This becomes less difficult during times of
clearly perceived crises in which the military is expected to
play a dominant role. At other times, however, the differences between society and the military can become aggravated,
with the profession carrying the major burden of self-analysis
and need for justification.

It is commonplace in some quarters to view the dilemmas
and antagonisms as historical continuities, transitory and cyclic
in nature. It is a mistake, however, to assume that the
present character of society, its technological advances, the
ever-changing security environment, and the propensity for
international conflicts ranging from nuclear exchange to revolutionary wars, can be rationalized away as historical patterns. The changed character of the present era is reinforced
by America's commitment to egalitarian principles. These have
had their impact on the character of the military profession, as
perhaps never before in history. And as we suggested
earlier, in such an environment, neither the monastic/entre-
preneurial or convergence/divergence models can provide a
realistic view.

If we accept the fact that personal integrity is developed
from a variety of sources, not only from within the military,
then there is an inherent tension between the concept of
personal integrity, duty, honor, country, and officership.
Thus, there can be times when the personal integrity of the
military professional is confronted by the contrary demands of
the profession, the institution, and the search for career
success.

We need to recall that moral and ethical dilemmas have
been characteristic of society from the beginning of history.
That such dilemmas occur in the military profession should not
deter military men from recognizing that it is a human phe-
nomena. Equally important military men need to recognize that
such dilemmas rarely have solutions that are valid for all
times.

Upon deeper study and reflection, we will find that moral
and ethical dilemmas are resolved within the intellect and
conscience of the individual. To be sure, such a suggestion
has religious and metaphysical overtones. It may seem expeditious to simply say that it depends on the individual. In

this instance, this indeed is the starting point.  In the final analysis, it is the individual who chooses his profession and develops his own sense of morality and ethics.  It is his own personal integrity that is the measure of the morality and ethics of the profession and society he serves.  The professional is expected to be an educated, rational being, whose professional commitment is not made haphazardly.  The real question is, what kind of moral and ethical pattern best befits the military profession?  One that can integrate the concepts of integrity, duty, honor, country, and officership?

Peter Berger in his book, Pyramids of Sacrifice:  Political Ethics and Social Change, addresses such issues and provides insights which are particularly relevant to the military professional.  Using Max Weber's assessment, Berger identifies the ethics of attitude and the ethics of responsibility.(18) The first is Gesinnungsethik, which can be translated into ethics of absolute ends.  This concept

. . . insists that nothing is ethically valid except adherence to absolute values that permit no modification by empirical circumstances.  In this type of ethics the moral attitude of the actor is all that matters:  If he is morally pure, the consequences of his actions are strictly irrelevant.(19)

On the other hand, Verantwortungsethik, translated into ethics of responsiblity, presumes that the "political actor does not seek some inner purity in adherence to absolute norms, but, often with anguished anxiety, tries to act in such a way as to effect the most humane consequences possible."

This observation leads us to our conclusions regarding the needs of the military profession.  The profession can no longer justify its actions by purity of motive.  That is, it cannot simply rationalize its posture by ethics of attitude; the presumption that ethics of absolute ends (the moral attitude of the actor) is all that counts.  This argument states that if the professional officer is morally pure, consequences are not important.  Such an attitude relieves the individual officer from responsibility for his actions.  In times of war or in performance of particularly serious and onerous duties, this is particularly manifested.  The acceptance of a moral free zone allows the officer to perform with moral purity in the professional context, because such performance can be rationalized from the concepts of duty, honor, country, with little philosophical reflection.  The most damning result is that at a time when professionals are supposed to be engaged in the very purpose of the profession, in performance of their ultimate liability, they tend to negate any moral and ethical standards.

There is a moral and ethical posture that can address these issues candidly and in a framework that reduces the boundaries between ideals and realities. If we accept the fact that human beings are imperfect, that the profession is imperfect, and that we live in an imperfect world, then the most realistic approach is one based on the "ethics of intent" and moral values based on sanctity of life in a democratic context. Ethics of intent combine the ethics of absolute ends with responsibility for the consequences of action. The professional officer, like the political actor which Peter Berger describes, does not exclusively "seek some inner purity in adherence to the absolute norms, but often with anguished anxiety, tries to act in such a way as to effect the most humane consequences possible."

This is not an easy position, either for the profession or the individual officer. It absolves neither the profession nor the individual from responsibility, motive, or the consequences of actions. Equally important, such an approach focuses moral and ethical patterns more sharply at all levels of the profession. If the intent is to deceive, then regardless of the "professional" way in which orders are carried out, regardless of the acomplishment of the mission, the officer is guilty of violating the basis of professional morality and, indeed, personal integrity. If the intent of the officer is simply to advance his career, then regardless of how professionally he performs his duties and accomplishes the mission, he is violating professional morals and his own integrity.

Ethics of intent requires that the profession not only link its values with those of the political-social system, but establish the motivation and environment to engrain such values into the professional milieu. Therefore, it is important that the study of moral and ethical issues become a part of the professional socialization process. As we have said, the concepts of integrity, duty, honor, country, and officership are fundamental to the moral and ethical basis of military professionalism. These are not autonomous to the military profession. Each of these concepts is influenced by and linked to civilian socialization processes and the linkages between the military and society. Civilian values and moral and ethical patterns influence the interpretations and meaning of these concepts. The military, by itself, cannot define these terms as it sees fit without reference to the very political-social system it is supposed to serve.

There may be some who eschew the need for political and national value integration into the military value system. We simply point out that professionalism cannot stand on values and ethics that evolve solely from military technical competence and obedience. If we have learned nothing more from our Vietnam experience and, indeed, from our experiences in other wars, it is that military cohesion and effectiveness is in no small measure contingent upon the political-psychological reinforcement between individual morality and ethics, those of the military profession, and those of society.

It is clear that the moral and ethical patterns of the profession cannot be changed or revised overnight. Morality and ethics are based upon the total socialization process - a process that is deeply engrained within the system and in society. A long-range goal to qualitatively refine the moral and ethical patterns of the military profession requires teaching, study, and example. These are not new techniques. The Christian religion and Confucianism are based on these procedures for propagating the faith and for establishing harmonious relationships.

There is a need to seriously study the dilemmas of a military institution within a democratic society. Equally important, there is a need to seriously examine the theological and philosophical concepts of morality and ethics in the context of the ultimate purpose of the military profession. These must also be examined as they affect the personal integrity and lifestyle of the individual officer. But study is not the only way. One must also be taught the implications of moral and ethical patterns. There are learned men in and out of the military who can address these issues. Service schools need to devote some time in their curricula to the study and teaching of moral and ethical patterns. Learning about morals and ethics should be an integral part of the total professional earning experience.

Finally, a proper moral and ethical environment must be established and maintained by the highest ranking military men and women, and those in particularly important positions, as reference models for younger professionals or professionals-to-be; e.g., ROTC cadets. As one publication noted, "Close examination of our data reveals a tendency in every age group, company milieu, and management level for a man to accept the values of his superiors."(20) This places a heavy burden on senior level military professionals. Decisions affecting their own lives and those of others must be made and evaluated according to moral values and ethical criteria that are rooted in the larger universe of humanity. Most important, the personal integrity of senior officers must be such as to foster a high level of integrity in other professionals. Although it may be difficult, an officer may need to take a stand on personal integrity even if it means standing against the institution.

As one top management official stated:

The pattern and level of corporate ethical standards are determined predominantly by the code of behavior formulated and promulgated by the top management. The rest of the organization, almost perforce, will follow these ethical operating precepts and examples; but in the absence of such norms, the same organization will be motivated by individual, and possibly inconsistent, codes of behavior.

The crucial matter, therefore, is whether or not each individual comprising top management has a well-defined, high-standard personal code of behavior. If each has this clear, objective, consistent concept of ethics - however acquired - he has the yardsticks, the guiding principles, against which to measure the ethical import of his decisions.

The executive whose concepts of ethics are vague, and whose principles of ethics are ill-defined - and possibly even vacillating and inconsistent - is in constant danger of yielding to expediency and even pursuing unethical practices; or, worse, providing an undesirable environment wherein his subordinates can make decisions based solely on their own personal ethical principles, with no frame of ethical reference from the top.

Of course, a well-defined personal code, however high in standards, does not of itself ensure ethical conduct; courage is always necessary in order to assert what one knows to be right.(21)

In the final analysis, though, no code of behavior, efficiency report, or professional socialization process is going to provide the answer to the individual officer who is faced with the dilemma of responding to what he feels is clearly a foolish order or a foolhardy mission, an incompetent superior, or an unethical officer friend. The least challenging course of action (and in our view unethical) is to follow orders from above, obey superiors uncritically, and overlook unethical behavior in one's colleagues. The final decision rests with the individual professional and such a decision will be made by the total man - his moral and ethical principles, his conscience and his sense of personal integrity that evolve from the total socialization process.

Finally, the relationship between the profession and society must be so construed as to accept society as a professional reinforcing political-social base, not as an obstacle to professional purpose. To do otherwise, substitutes the moral and ethical values of the profession for those of society, and makes the military institution a self-perpetuating legitimizer of its own actions. While such a condition may be acceptable to many political-social systems, it is contrary to liberal democratic principles.

In this respect, military professionals as well as society must accept and understand that in its most ideal sense, liberal democratic principles and military values rarely coincide. Indeed, military professionals are incorrectly seen by many civilians as generally outside the mainstream of democratic "life" and values. It is this condition that the profession must understand if it is to deal with the inherent

dilemmas posed by the existence of a profession and an institution that are fundamentally contrary to individual autonomy
and the civic culture of democracy. This understanding is
established and sustained by the continuing inquiry into moral
and ethical issues as part of the individual as well as professional lifestyle and value system. This inquiry is in itself
an enlightening individual experience.

We have emphasized that there is no one set of moral and
ethical answers, but we do not accept the view that situational
ethics is acceptable. Such a posture can easily rationalize any
action on moral and ethical grounds because of the immediate
situation. This simply appears to be another way of accepting
"moral free" activity. We also recognize the difficulty in what
is being suggested in ethics of intent. Military professional
values and those of society will rarely coincide and should not
be expected to do so. But there must be a reasonable, if not
enthusiastic linkage between the universal values, those of the
political system, and military values of personal integrity,
duty, honor, country, and officership. The inherent antipathy between several of these values and their varying interpretations make this a difficult, but not impossible task.

The most we can offer in conclusion is summed up by the
following:

> If it is true that wonder is the beginning and source
> of philosophy, then only these who are utterly
> blase, bored, and superficial are closed to the tasks
> of philosophy. In this sense, then, everyone with a
> mind is summoned to philosophize. Philosophy is
> based on a recognition that human life and its set-
> ting are mysterious. True philosophy is too modest
> to hope to dissipate the mystery; it only hopes to
> enounter it fruitfully.(22)

## NOTES

1. Daniel C. Maguire, The Moral Choice. Garden City,
N.Y.: Doubleday & Co., Inc., 1978, pp. 19-20.
   2. Ibid., p. 20.
   3. Ibid., p. 94.
   4. Edmund P. Learned, Arch R. Dooley, and Robert L.
Katz, "Personal Values and Business Decisions" in Ethics for
Executive Series, Reprints from Harvard Business Review.
This article is from the Harvard Business Review, March-
April, 1959, p. 84.
   5. William K. Frankena, Ethics. Englewood Cliffs,
N.J.: Prentice-Hall, Inc., 1963, p. 98.

218                                    BEYOND THE BATTLEFIELD

6. Malham M. Wakin, "Ethics of Leadership," Sam C. Sarkesian, and Thomas M. Gannon (Eds), Military Ethics and Professionalism, American Behavioral Scientists, Vol. 19, Number 5, May/June 1976, p. 573.

7. For a useful discussion, see John R. Stephenson, "Special Trust and Confidence, Whatever that Means," Research Study, Air University, Maxwell AFB, May 1977, unpublished monograph.

8. James C. Donovan, Militarism, USA. New York: Scribners, 1970, pp. 64-81.

9. Dennis J. Palumbo and Richard A. Styskal, "Professionalism and Receptivity to Change", American Journal of Political Science, Vol. XVIII, No. 2, May, 1974, pp. 387-388.

10. For a more detailed discussion based on empirical evidence, see chapter 2; Bruce D. Russett and Elizabeth C. Hanson, Interest and Ideology; The Foreign Policy Beliefs of American Businessmen. San Francisco: W.H. Freeman and Co., 1975. Bruce M. Russett, "Political Perspectives of U.S. Military and Business Elites," Armed Forces and Society, Vol. 1, No. 1, November 1974, pp. 79-101.

11. Joseph Ellis and Robert Moore, School for Soldiers; West Point and the Profession of Arms. New York: Oxford University Press, 1974, p. 180.

12. Ibid., pp. 176-177.

13. Glenn Wilson (Ed), The Psychology of Conservatives. London Academic Press, 1973, as quoted in Norman Dixon, On The Psychology of Military Incompetence. New York: Basic Books, Inc., 1976, p. 402.

14. Liddell B.H. Hart, Thoughts on War. London: Faber and Faber, 1944, pp. 25-29; as quoted in Philip M. Flammer, "Conflicting Loyalties and the American Military Ethic," Sarkesian and Gannon, p. 593. See also Dixon.

15. Flammer, p. 595.

16. Frankena, p. 95.

17. Herbert A. Simon, Administrative Behavior. New York: The Free Press, 1957, second edition, pp. xxv-xxvi.

18. Peter L. Berger, Pyramids of Sacrifice; Political Ethics and Social Change. New York: Anchor Books, 1976, p. 249.

19. Ibid., p. 249.

20. "How Ethical Are Businessmen?", Harvard Business Review, p. 41. This article reprinted from Harvard Business Review, July-August, 1971.

21. Ibid., pp. 41-42.

22. Maguire, p. 36.

# 11 Military Professionalism and Leadership: Time for a Change?

"To lead is to command." This long-standing military premise has become increasingly imprecise in its conception, obscure in its perspective, and inadequate in its application. Leadership has been traditionally viewed as the art of influencing other human beings to undertake tasks and complete them successfully in a way determined by the leader. In the military, it is accepted that the most visible manifestation of leadership is by command of a unit. Moreover, it is thought that such command is best undertaken by those possessing well known leadership traits, ranging from bearing and courage to loyalty and unselfishness. One result is that military men, particularly those at the junior levels, become socialized and educated into a system that views leadership within a narrowly defined concept of professionalism. Thus, leadership is conceived in military terms with reference to military targets to achieve military goals in a military environment.(1)

Recognizing that the study of leadership and its exercise is a complex undertaking and must deal with a variety of definitions and behavior patterns, it is the contention here that the present perspectives on military leadership are inadequate to respond to the modern security environment in the context of the political-social values of the American political system. This conclusion is based on the observation that leadership must not only deal with the character and personality of the leader and the processes through which he achieves a particular goal, but also with the nature of the environment in which the leadership role must be performed. The term environment refers to the characteristics, values, and expectations of those that must be influenced, both within and without the military institution, and the values and nature of the political system from which the military evolves. Not only has the environment changed from a military to a political-

219

social-military intermix, but those that need to be influenced include both military and civilian. Moreover, the targets are no longer purely military, nor can the tasks be defined in purely military terms. Leadership in the "follow me" spirit may no longer be relevant in such circumstances.

The study of military leadership, as a consequence, has become more complex. The great deal of published material appearing over the past two decades has not clarified the matter to any great extent. In the main, this literature concentrates on the traditional, historical, and organizational elements of leadership, re-emphasizing the military perspective, and applying this in the modern context into a style of leadership appropriate to the command of units.(2)

Since World War II, several seemingly contradictory conditions have developed which should give pause to those advocating the traditional leadership approach. First, the advent of the nuclear age has created a vast range of new weapons with significant battlefield implications leading to a variety of political-social dimensions of deterrence theory and stationing of forces. Second, at the same time, the decentralization of power on the international field and the proliferation of nation-states have developed a complex security environment. Conflicts have taken on a particularly significant political-social ingredient. The survival of the state in any nuclear exchange has become a crucial consideration as contrasted to the wars of the past. In non-nuclear conflicts, the environment for the employment of force is such that political-social factors have become more important than military considerations. Third, the first two developments have created a third: the military institution in virtually all political systems has become an important political actor.

What do these developments mean in terms of military leadership? The traditional perspective of military leadership, as is the concept of Western military professionalism, is so narrowly defined that it is inadequate to meet the demands of the modern political-social setting and security environment. To expect professional military posture and leadership principles to be successfully applied, there must be an added dimension to leadership encompassing the ability to deal with domestic political forces, non-nuclear conflicts, and the sociocultural context of American society. All of these must be nurtured within an expanded and modernized concept of military professionalism. But this does not mean the elimination or subordination of the traditional concerns of military leadership. Rather, new dimensions are necessary which broaden the professional horizons and expand the scope of leadership. Educating military professionals in this new dimension is not reserved solely to the senior military schools or for those who have achieved high rank. These are legitimate concerns at every level and for every contingency.

The purpose of this chapter is to examine the nature of leadership and suggest an alternative concept of leadership. It is not intended, however, that this include a re-examination of the specific elements of leadership. These are examined in a number of publications.(3) What we hope to do is provide an alternative concept of leadership that is developed from a new concept of professionalism; one that is conditioned by domestic political-social forces and the changed security environment.

We need to address several premises on leadership as a preliminary step in this study. First, to understand the concept of leadership in its broadest dimensions requires an examination of the substance and inter-relationships of four elements: the leader, the followers, the situation, and the task. As we suggested, the last three elements have changed from an exclusively military to a socio-political orientation, affecting the exercise of leadership. Second, scholars tend to agree that "any suggestion that leadership can be reduced to some specific ability or set of personal attributes" should be abandoned. "The quality of leadership inheres not in an individual, but in a role that is played within some specific social system."(4) Third, it is useful to distinguish between "leadership" and "headship."(5) The distinction is based on the different sources of power. The power of headship derives from an appointment by the organization or institution. The source of power of leaders comes from within the group to be led. Power is acquired by the leader by virtue of his/her ability to motivate followers towards mutually acceptable goals, sharing of values, and a sense of satisfaction that evolves from task accomplishment and purpose. In sum, headship power comes from sources outside of the group; leadership from within. The ideal military leader combines the two.(6) Fourth, followers, even in the military, play an active role in the leadership equation. Not only are followers the instrumentalities for achieving goals, but they provide the boundaries beyond which a leader dare not go without risking group sanctions. Such boundaries derive from values of society and the way these are interpreted by the group. Fifth, leadership inheres in individuals and not in institutions or organizations; that is, institutions do not lead, people do. When one speaks of the leadership of the military, what they probably mean is the leadership exercised by specific individuals, representing the institution and organization. This is not to deny the need to study the impact of leadership style on organizational efficiency and institutional esprit. Military leadership is rarely viewed outside of the organizational setting, since it is inextricably mixed with the idea of unit mission.

## DOMESTIC POLITICAL ENVIRONMENT

Every military system must operate in accord with the ideology of the political system, interacting with other political actors within that system. The degree and character of the interaction is determined by the values embodied in the ideology. In an authoritarian system, the military's position may be totally subordinate to the party leadership with party control extending throughout the military institution. Yet the military may remain relatively autonomous from the remainder of society. In democratic systems, the role of the military is based on civil-military interaction in which democratic values and political forces are projected into the military system. The pluralistic nature of politics characteristic of these interactions allows little opportunity for the military to totally isolate itself from the system.

The defense budgetary process in our political system is a prime example of these characteristics. Military involvement in congressional hearings, the development of military requirements, and input into the decision process, necessitate response to a number of political factors. Aside from the formal process, however, there are a number of points in the budgetary process where military men have the opportunity to exert influence through informal means utilizing a variety of political techniques. Partisan politics may have no place in the formal civil-military relationship, but there can be intense partisanship when it comes to military budgetary considerations. The point is that military men must deal with a variety of non-military political actors and processes as a matter of course.

As it was noted several years ago,

> In domestic political processes, the military has been placed in a position in which it must defend itself in political terms not only with respect to other governmental institutions, but with respect to its relationship to society in general. Additionally, problems of society extend into the military establishment and require understanding and appreciation heretofore alien to the military culture. These problems will not necessarily lend themselves to solutions through traditional military methods. Rather, solutions in light of the new environment, will require political means.(7)

In this respect, successful leadership styles within the military are not necessarily those needed to deal with domestic institutions and groups. The mind-set of military professionals differs from the mind-set of civilian officials and representatives. Equally important, the experience, and education and socialization processes of military officers are primarily concerned with military leadership <u>within</u> the military institution and understandably so. Such a perspective is not particularly sympathetic or empathetic to the labor negotiator, political broker, or consensus-builder in the political system.

## THE AMERICAN SOCIO-CULTURAL CONTEXT

It is acknowledged by many that military systems reflect, more or less, the political-social system from which they evolve. Authoritarian systems breed authoritarian military systems, democratic systems breed democratic military systems. While there is much truth in such observations, some qualifications are in order, particularly when dealing with democratic systems. Inherent in any military system is the tendency for authoritarianism and bureaucratic conservatism. Even in a democratic system, there are limits to the degree of democratization that can occur without eroding the very basis for the military system. Nonetheless, for the American military system to remain legitimate (i.e., retain the support of society), it must in some degree reflect basic societal values and be in accord with the ideology of the political system. It follows that leadership principles take their cue from professional purpose.

Comparing military systems, as is true in comparing military leadership cross-nationally must, therefore, be done with a great deal of caution. It may be true that leadership principles are universal; i.e., winning battles and wars are fundamental to all modern military systems. But to presume that leadership techniques and processes are also universal is to misjudge the nature and variety of modern conflicts and to presume a simplistic concept of professionalism and leadership. The style of military leadership, as is the case with military professionalism, must take into account the values and attitudes of society. For example, if a society is based on the liberal democratic ethic, military leadership must reflect this. This is of particular importance when dealing with a "citizen" military. This should not be construed to mean that the military must be a perfect replica of society. Yet, it is necessary to recognize that military leadership is inextricably bound to the political-psychological milieu of the society from which it evolves. The egalitarian orientation, the socio-economic leavening, and concern with consensual legitimacy, tend to make the American military system vulnerable to "participatory" politics and the moral and ethical demands of democratic ideology. Moreover, the loyalties of the military as a whole are not wedded to the "regiment." There are a

variety of competing loyalties from the civilian sector of society. These are continually nurtured within the military by
the political and psychological interplay between military and
civilian actors.(8)

The style of leadership in such a context need not
degenerate into consistent concern with consensus-building or
command by committee. Yet, a lack of concern for the
political-social factors will soon isolate a "leader." Firmness,
discipline, and effectiveness are just as necessary in the
military of a democratic system as in others. But the important difference is the way to achieve these in the democratic
context. Leadership style must be within the "rules of the
game" of the political system. Thus, in a liberal democratic
society it may be self-defeating for military leaders to adapt
an uncompromising, unquestioning, "can do," zero-defects
posture.

Leadership in clearly recognized crises is less difficult
than in ambiguous situations. In clear crises, the American
people and the individual soldier are most likely to defer
unquestioningly to the duly elected leader or appointed superior, allowing a wide discretionary use of power and means
to achieve accepted goals. On the battlefield, where survival
may be the most pressing issue, those in leadership positions
are most likely to be obeyed with little hesitation (unless there
are significant aberrations of leadership). The more challenging problem for American military leaders is not in clear
crises, but in ambiguous ones. The fundamental issue is how
the potential effectiveness and spirit of the American soldier
can be harnessed in those situations where military purpose
and roles are complex, contradictory, and ambiguous.


## NATURE OF CONFLICT


The evolution of modern deterrence theory is closely linked to
the development of nuclear weapons. The mutual destruction
capability of these weapons have created a situation in which
potential protagonists must maintain a system of communications
with one another and develop an understanding and appreciation of each other's political-social system and decision-
making process. This is necessary to insure that proper
signals are conveyed and understood regarding military posture and political will. To be a successful leader in such an
environment requires some understanding of the nuances
between military posture, political will, and threat perceptions.
But successful deterrence strategy creates an anamoly, since
military men will find it necessary to develop a high level of
combat effectiveness in order to prevent combat. Leaders will
need to motivate men to train seriously for war in the knowledge that the real purpose of such training is to avoid war.

Non-nuclear conflicts also present a variety of leadership challenges, since such conflicts tend to become enmeshed in the political-social fabric of the adversaries' societies. For a liberal democracy involved in such a conflict, the possibility exists that military purpose and even legitimacy can become eroded. Equally important, policies followed by the government committing ground troops and other military forces to limited war situations can create tension between professional purpose, leadership expectations and behavior, and society. Professional propensities to use military force to its maximum to achieve quick and decisive victory, for example, are mitigated by the tendency of society to demand proper leadership behavior in the conduct of the war.

Much of the concern over such matters can be traced to the American involvement in Vietnam. Subsequently, American military orientation focused on Europe and the battle in the Central Plains with a concomitant decrease in the military's posture to respond to non-nuclear contingencies outside the European context. While recent events may have reawakened interest in non-nuclear conflicts, little seems to have changed in professional education or military leadership to respond to these dimensions.

In this respect, military men may see "military intervention as potentially necessary," while society may question the need for such action (there are occasions, to be sure, when these attitudes are reversed).(9)

> . . . the popular disaffection with the Vietnamese war does not indicate a reversion to pre-Korean attitudes toward limited war. Rather it indicates serious questioning of the premises about the utility of limited war as an instrument of American policy, the premises that originally moved the proponents of limited war strategy and that underlay the original confidence of the Kennedy Administration in America's power to cope with local Communist incursions of all kinds.(10)

In such circumstances, the military establishment and the profession are particularly susceptible to erosion of their credibility, exacerbated by the contradictory demands between society and military purpose. Prevailing leadership techniques and processes tend to reflect these contradictions. In a modern democracy, as in most political systems, there must be linkages between the values and expectations of society and the military. Moreover, democracies presume a high moral quality to values and behavior. Moral quality is also the criteria for determining legitimacy of military purposes and in establishing norms for leadership.

## PROFESSIONALISM AND LEADERSHIP

Professionalism establishes the purposes, values, and the educational and socialization guidelines for the military. Leadership operationalizes these professional principles. Leadership
techniques and processes, therefore, must be in accord with
the professional ethos; i.e., values and moral standards which
in turn must closely parallel the values of society and cannot
be legitimately conceived outside of such boundaries. The
question is what kind of professionalism is necessary to establish the principles and reference points from which effective
leadership can evolve in a democratic system?

The military profession must develop a rationale in which
the military is seen as more than unconditional servants of the
state. To do so requires an understanding and appreciation of
the nature of politics, a sense of realistic and enlightened
self-interest, and perspectives transcending boundaries traditionally associated with duty, honor, country. In the final
analysis, the scope of professional education must be broad
enough to allow military men to deal with environments that are
not exclusively military, and intense enough to understand the
complexities of human motivations and behavior. Such a
charge has implications for civil-military relations and international politics.

In terms of civil-military relations, the military professional cannot realistically isolate himself from the "politics" of
the domestic system without abdicating his professional responsibility and weakening his moral position. As Liddell Hart
points out in his study of German Generals:

> At the same time Seeckt's care to keep his army out
> of politics carried a danger of its own. His attitude
> of professional detachment, and the sharp dividing
> line he drew between the military and political
> spheres, tended towards a renunciation of the
> soldier's potential restraining influence on adven-
> turous statesmen.
>       The Seeckt-pattern professional became a
> modern Pontius Pilate, washing his hands of all
> responsibility for orders he executed. Pure military
> theory deals in extremes that are hard to combine
> with wise policy. When soldiers concentrate on the
> absolute military aim, and do not learn to think of
> grand strategy, they are more apt to accept political
> arguments that, while seeming right in pure stra-
> tegy, commit policy beyond the point where it can
> halt. Extreme military ends are difficult to reconcile
> with moderation of policy.(11)

The military's involvement in external politics also creates new dimensions of professional education.

> We must understand that nowadays the armed forces of a nation are instruments of external politics and must be trained for such activities. In this sense, I say yes to political activity by our military commanders; they must be highly trained in external politics, otherwise they will carry their political naivete into highly sophisticated political arenas, seeing communists under every bush, and, worse still, supporting political losers purely because they seem affluent and respectable on the surface. Military commanders must be trained in armed diplomacy, a training that must start in their early years. Most important, they must be trained in political and social science which is as important as technological education in the armed services.(12)

At a more mundane level, human motivation, professionalism, and leadership can only be balanced and rewarding if they are based on the need to achieve. As Dixon observes, healthy achievement is "buoyed up by the hopes of success." Pathological achievement is "driven by fear of failure," and leads to leadership "traits of dishonesty and expedience . . ."(13)

To develop the necessary professional knowledge to accomplish this balance requires education and training beyond the confines of the existing system. Indeed, part of this may require education outside of the military framework. In the words of Vice Admiral Stockdale:

> Leadership under pressure will often entail being a moralist, jurist, teacher, steward, and philosopher. . . . The final test is that you must be able to act as philosophers in order to explain and understand the lack of moral economy in the universe, for many people have a great deal of difficulty with the fact that virtue is not always rewarded and evil punished. To handle tragedy may indeed be the mark of an educated man.(14)

## CONCLUSIONS

The attitudes and values of a democratic political system and the incoherency of world security relationships have created an environment in which traditional leadership concepts may be wanting. But leadership cannot be seriously assessed or

revised without reference to the nature of military professionalism and its close connection with society.  In this respect,
political and military purposes and policies have become so
intermixed that it is inconceivable, except perhaps in the most
"total" wars, that "purely" military solutions can be identified
for "purely" military problems.  If this be the case, then
"military leadership" in the traditional sense may be an anach-
ronism.  Political-military leadership (or simply leadership) as
a concept may better convey the new dimensions required in
the modern setting.

To "lead," therefore, means the art of influencing people,
both military and civilian, to accomplish a particular goal in a
political-cultural setting that mitigates exclusively military
solutions.  At the minimum, this requires a continuous study
of inter-personal relations and group dynamics, a deep appreciation and understanding of the liberal democratic value
system and ideology as it is manifested in the United States,
and a serious concern for the realities of the American political
system.  Simultaneously, military men who desire to lead must
continually re-examine the techniques and processes in the
exercise of leadership.  Finally, and perhaps most important,
leadership requires that the style of leadership be appropriate
to the instrumentalities (i.e., people) and the socio-political
context in which leadership must be exercised.

In modern times it may not be good enough for military
men who aspire to leadership to be courageous, honest,
competent, and committed to the ideals of duty, honor, country.  In the final analysis, the concept of leadership is an
abstraction.  Isolated from the political-social context in which
it is to be exercised, and ignorant of the character of those to
be led and the purpose for which they are to be led, leadership becomes a meaningless concept.  Perhaps the only sure
thing that can be said of leadership is that it must inspire
others to follow.  This does not necessarily require a particular type of personality or set of techniques.  But it does
require political astuteness, imagination, a mind sensitive to
and experienced in the essentials of human behavior and
human motivation, and the will to undertake some form of
purposeful action to arouse human energy towards a particular
goal.

## NOTES

1.  There are a number of examples relating leadership
to command and to a particularly military perspective.  In
Vietnam, career advancement was in no small measure associated with commanding an American unit.  The attitudes of
many military officers in the post-Vietnam period indicate that

command remains foremost in career advancement and the primary way that leadership can be exercised. The relationship between command and leadership has become intextricably interwoven to a point where a young military officer could say, "The hallmark of officership is effective leadership. Not management, leadership - the human quality which has enabled some men to inspire others to charge up Cemetery Ridge, Pork Chop Hill, or Hamburger Hill, or to fly into target areas at Schweinfurt, Regensburg, Ploesti, or the Thanh Hao Bridge." Major David H. Price, "Thoughts On The Profession of Arms in America Today," The Retired Officer Magazine, May, 1977, p. 36. Also, an important book on military leadership is Taking Command: The Art and Science of Military Leadership. Harrisburg, Pa.: Stackpole Company, 1967, by Colonel Samuel H. Hays and Lieutenant Colonel William N. Thomas. The relationship between leadership and command seems obvious.

2. Most scholars recognize this problem in the study of leadership. The following quote, for example, is from C.G. Browne and Thomas S. Cohn (Eds), The Study of Leadership. Danville, Ill.: The Interstate Printers and Publishers, 1958, and is included in Kenneth J. Janda, "Towards the Explication of the Concept of Leadership," Glenn D. Paige, Political Leadership: Readings For An Emerging Field. New York: The Free Press, 1972, p. 48:

> Through all of the subsequent history of man's attempts to record human experiences, leadership has been recognized to an increasingly greater extent as one of the significant aspects of human activity. As a result, there is now a great mass of "leadership literature" which, if it were to be assembled in one place, would have little organization; it would evidence little in the way of common assumptions and hypotheses; it would vary widely in theoretical and methodological approaches. To a great extent, therefore, leadership literature is a mass of content without any coagulating substances to bring it together or to produce coordination and point out interrelationships. [Introduction, first page].

See also Paul M. Bons, "An Organizational Approach to the Study of Leadership" in A Study of Organizational Leadership. Harrisburg, Pa.: Stackpole Books, 1976, edited by the Associates, Office of Military Leadership, United States Military Academy. On page 17, the author states, "Much confusion in the study of leadership is generated by the multiplicity of definitions. Stogdill (1974) in his massive review of the leadership literature devotes ten pages to categorizing the various definitions of leadership."

3. Hays and Thomas, p. 293. This is an excellent bibliography on the subject of leadership. Also see David L. Sills (Ed.), International Encyclopedia of the Social Sciences. New York; The Macmillan Co., and The Free Press, 1968, Volume 9, pp. 91-113; Glenn D. Paige, Political Leadership: Readings For An Emerging Field. New York: The Free Press, 1972; and R.M. Stogdill, Handbook of Leadership; a survey of theory and research. New York: The Free Press, 1974.

4. Sills, p. 93.

5. Janda, p. 54. Although some scholars decry the distinction between headship and leadership, it is a useful concept if the focus is on the concept of power, its sources, and the relationship between power and leaders. It is used here as a conceptual tool to point out at least one reasonable approach in assessing the leadership role in the context of the political-social environment and the particular military requirements.

6. There is a continuing controversy regarding the meaning of managership and its relationship to the military as an institution and to the concept of leadership. The disagreement is reflected in the following passages:

> A myth has been conceived and is growing that management and command are synonymous. They are not . . . management must be recognized for what it is, a system of bookkeeping that is primarily associated with statistics. Statistics are static. They can do nothing except provide a means of measuring. Command is the relationship between people. People do things. [Price, p. 37]

> Management is an essential component of the military leader's exercise of leadership. . . . Every leader is to some extent a manager. [Hays and Thomas, p. 91]

According to Hays and Thomas (p. 91) ". . . management is the science of employing men and material in the economical and effective accomplishment of a mission." We agree that every leader must be to some extent a manager. However, we would add to this that every manager must to some extent be a leader. A distinct delineation between leader and manager is not only invalid, but it presumes that both leaders and managers are one-dimensional men who somehow can perform tasks and accomplish their missions with no reference to contributing factors and environmental considerations that affect performance.

7. Sam C. Sarkesian, "Political Sodiers: Perspectives on Professionalism in the U.S. Military," Midwest Journal of Political Science, Vol. XVI, No. 2, May, 1972, p. 253. See also chapter 8.

8. As Major Stephen D. Wesbrook points out:

. . . the Army has inherited from society a number of serious social problems. Although the Army has not been the principal source of these problems, they have, nevertheless, negatively affected both its general efficiency in such areas as morale, proficiency and discipline and its combat readiness . . . the Army is currently facing another major societal induced thread to its combat readiness and general military efficiency - sociopolitical alienation. While the manifestations of sociopolitical alienation are not so dramatic as those of racial tensions or drug abuse, its impact may be even more severe. [Stephen D. Wesbrook, "The Alienated Soldier: Legacy of Society," in Army, December 1979, p. 18.]

If the military leader has little conception of the political-social system and the cultural context of American democracy, it will not only be difficult for him to identify values of the system and those that reinforce the military, but it will be virtually impossible to recognize the source of alienation much less try to respond to it. In this respect, it is interesting to note the observation that, "The degree of leadership success is usually linked closely with the success of the group to perform its task. Particularly in the military, unit effeciveness is equated with the effectiveness of the leader. However, some groups succeed despite poor leadership while good leaders fail because of insurmountable odds." (Hays and Thomas, p. 31)

9. Jerald G. Bachman and John D. Blair, Soldiers, Sailors and Civilians, The "Military Mind" and the All-Volunteer Force. Ann Arbor, Mich.: Institute for Social Research, November 1975, p. 62.

10. Robert E. Osgood, "The Reappraisal of Limited War," in Eugene J. Rosi, American Defense and Detente; Readings in National Security Policy. New York: Dodd, Mead and Co., 1973, p. 466.

11. B. H. Liddell Hart, The Other Side of the Hill. London: Cassell & Co., Ltd., 1951, pp. 31-32.

12. Michael Elliot-Bateman, "The Form of People's War" in Michael Elliot-Bateman (Ed), The Fourth Dimension of Warfare. New York: Praeger, 1970, p. 147.

13. Norman F. Dixon, On the Psychology of Military Incompetence. New York: Basic Books, 1976, p. 239.

14. Vice Admiral James B. Stockdale, USN, Commencement Address, 1979, The Citadel, Charleston, S.C., Alumni News, Fall 79, Vol. 35. No. 1, pp. 18-19.

# V

# Conclusions

# Part V
## An Introduction

The two selections in this final part synthesize the discussions and themes presented in the preceding chapters and draw conclusions regarding professional posture and the future. The first selection focuses on civil-military relations. The second addresses the question of what needs to be done in terms of professionalism to meet the challenges of the 1980s. The equilibrium model of civil-military relations places responsibility on both civilians and military men to rethink the whole concept of civil-military relations. The traditional concepts perpetuate traditional military perspectives and simply return to the bygone days when society and the military were presumed to be separate and isolated, and military men did not concern themselves with conflict until the first shot was fired. There is some evidence to suggest an alternative model of civil-military relations and an alternative perspective to military professionalism. These evolve into the modern concepts advocated in this volume. The "equilibrium" model does not eliminate the basic purposes of the military profession, nor those of the military institution. What it does do, however, is to advance a realistic model which takes into account historical precedent and the changing nature of the American political system. The equilibrium model stresses parallelism, friendly adversary, and partnership rather than control, supremacy, isolation, and separation. Resting on the premise that the military system is part and parcel of the political system, the equilibrium model necessitates a professionalism and civil-military relations that expect legitimate political participation in policy and legitimate advocacy of the military point of view. Finally, this perspective rests to a degree on historical evolution of the American military system.

The final selection is a brief and pointed look at the needs of military professionalism. It does not repeat what has already been presented, but the essay does bring together key issues and concepts regarding professional challenges of the 1980s. The essay is not an operational program or laundry list of changes and requirements. Rather, it focuses on the philosophical underpinnings of the military profession. In retrospect, the conclusion is that the military profession is the least prepared of any American institution and sub-system to meet the challenges of the 1980s.

# 12 The Equilibrium Model of Civil-Military Relations

The power and political role of the guardians of the state have been a concern of statesmen since the earliest periods of Western civilization. Fear of usurpation of power by the guardians prompted a variety of philosophical premises upon which the relationship between the guardians and the rulers of the state were to be established. Plato, for example, took care to spell out the legitimate boundaries of the activities of the guardians. ". . . the word guardian in the fullest sense ought to be applied to this higher class only who preserve against foreign enemies and maintain peace among our citizens at home, that the one may not have the will, or the other power, to harm us. The young men whom we call guardians may be more properly designated auxiliaries and supporters of the principles of the rulers."(1)

During most of Western history, the guardians and the rulers had evolved from the same class of people and shared the same values. It was only in the age of the modern nation-state with the beginnings of a professional military that there evolved a "gap" between guardians and rulers. But it has only been in the most recent period of history that much attention and scholarship has been given to civil-military relations as a subject in its own right. To be sure, there have been treatises on the role of the military and military organization. But in the sense of a scholarly subject, civil-military relations owes its inception to the evolution of modern military professionalism and the development of the military institution to a potent, if ambiguous political instrument.

In examining the current literature, three main streams emerge with respect to American civil-military relations: civilian control of the military; the degree of separateness or isolation of the military from society; and the professional concept as unconditional servants of the state. These main streams have

their roots in several presumptions about the military.  First,
the military institution and profession are viewed as a system
outside of the existing political-social structure.  Second,
civil-military relations must seek an "answer" to the problem
posed by the existence of a military system.  Third, the
military is perceived as a necessary evil and society must be
protected from it.  Thus, in the evolution of the American
political system, the concern for liberal democratic principles
has lead to a number of premises regarding the nature of
civil-military relationships which perpetuate a "conflict and
control" model.  However, this represents only one model.

   The purpose of this chapter is to formulate an alternative
model of civil-military relations that is based on "equilibrium"
with an emphasis on "balance," "parallelism," and "friendly
adversary."  Rather than separation, this model argues that
the military and society are an integrated part of the same
political-social system.  Moreover, military professionalism is
perceived in broad terms, including a dimension in which the
military are political actors in a liberal democracy.


## THE SCOPE OF CIVIL-MILITARY RELATIONS


The study of civil-military relations encompasses a variety of
perspectives ranging from the broad landscape of systems
analysis, weapons development, and budgetary processes, to
the very narrow and more mundane concerns with the behavior
of individual soldiers in a local community.  Civil-military
relations can also be addressed from a variety of disciplinary
perspectives:  the sociologist's study of race relations and the
military as a social system; the political scientist's attention to
the impact of the military institution on the policy process;
and the psychologist's study of combat behavior.  All of these
carve out some relevant area under the rubric of civil-military
relations.

   The complexities involved in studying civil-military relations are reflected in the difficulties in arriving at an acceptable definition.  As examples, does civil-military relations
mean relationships between the military institution and the
President?  Between the military and other institutions, the
military elite and civilian elites, or the military elite and the
governing elite?  Does it also include relationships between a
military system and the rest of society?  Or does it mean the
degree of congruence between the values and attitudes of
professional military men and elected leaders?

   Civil-military relations in its broadest sense covers all of
these and more.  Thus, the study of civil-military relations
confronts scholars with problems and methodological complexities characteristic of the study of any type of "system."

There may be much to the argument, however, that the military should be studied simply as another institution within the American political system. Yet, the uniqueness of the military, with its special educational and socialization processes gives it a character and perspective not necessarily compatible with other institutions within the system. Recognizing the imprecision of any definition, it is suggested nevertheless that civil-military relations is the resulting balance between the military and society that emerges from the patterns of behavior and the interaction between military professionals and important political actors, and the power exercised by the military institution as a political actor.

This definition rests on several premises. First, civil-military relations encompasses a multiplicity of relationships and these are not limited to formal constitutional and political power and processes. Second, a military system must be analyzed within the context of the political-social system from which it evolves, including values, morals, and ethics. In this respect, particular attention must be given to the political dimension of professionalism and the linkages these create between society and the military. Third, rarely can the study of civil-military relations avoid addressing the larger issues of the role of the military as a political actor and its impact on the policy process. Fourth, fundamental to the concept of civil-military relations is the character of military professionalism. The values, beliefs, and norms that are the substance of military professionalsim, establish the outlines of military posture vis-a-vis to the political system. It is from this posture that the civilian elite and leaders perceive the nature of their own role and that of the political system with respect to civil-military relations. Thus, a military that deliberately isolates itself from the political process and stresses values that are far removed from the democratic mainstream is likely to engender an ever expanding civilian intrusion into military policy, with little initiative or intellectual input from military professionals.

The study of civil-military relations in this context must include an examination of the character of liberal democratic society as it relates specifically to the military system, the nature of military professionalism, and the characteristics of the military system. From this we can ascertain the "model" that evolves from the interaction of society and the military and determine the necessary military professional posture acceptable in a democratic system.

LIBERAL DEMOCRACY AND THE MILITARY

Thomas Jefferson observed that "A distinction is kept between the civil and the military, which it is for the happiness of both to obliterate."(2)   In a similar vein, de Tocqueville wrote,

> It is in the nation, not in the army itself, that one must look for the remedy for the army's vices. . . . The general spirit of the nation penetrating the spirit peculiar to the army, tempers the opinions and desires engendered by military life, or by the all-powerful influence of public opinion, actually represses them.   Once you have educated, orderly, upstanding, and free citizens, you will have disciplined and obedient soldiers.(3)

These observations are the basis for one major argument in the equilibrium model:   Society and the military need to be conceived as part of the same political system, sharing values necessary to maintain the system.   This is particularly true in the case of a liberal democracy.

In democratic political systems, power is decentralized and diffused, and pluralistic and participatory politics are the rule.   No individual, institution, or group is expected to be outside of the system.   Indeed, a democracy cannot afford to have groups of political actors who are consistently isolated from the political process.   The intent of democracy is to draw all political actors into the political process.   While the degree of political activity and the impact of political actors vary, the key is access to the process.   Therefore, to presume that an institution such as the military, which is not only an instrument of the state, but a political-social sub-system, is separate from the process is to misinterpret the essence of democracy.

In the earliest period of world history, military deeds were considered part of the political history of empires and states.   In The Republic, Plato devoted a considerable amount of discussion to the Guardians and their education.   The major role for the Guardians was to assist in the unity of the "polis."   In The Prince and The Art of Warfare, Machiavelli viewed military problems and policies as part of the broader community.   Even a cursory reading of Clausewitz reveals the inter-relationship between politics and the military.   The works of Mahan, among other things, stressed the close relationship between sea power, national politics, and national security. Without belaboring the point, there is sufficient evidence in history, both of a theoretical and practical nature, which unmistakably shows the relationship between politics and military, and the political and military systems.   The evolution of an industrial age and liberal democratic theories has reinforced this relationship.

A study of the historical patterns of the American political system and its relationship to the military, among other things, indicates that the military has always had a close, even if at times an estranged relationship with society. These have been well researched and presented in a number of publications.(4)   Suffice it to say here that these patterns have never been constant, have periodically and at times dramatically changed from closeness to estrangement and back again, depending on the current issues of the day and the attitude of officials. These shifting relationships, however, are more indicative of a homeostatic equilibrium between the military and society, rather than separateness or isolation.(5) This is not to suggest that individual segments of the military were not (and are not) isolated and separate from society. However, the main thrust of civil-military relations stems from a variety of interactions as noted earlier. These interactions rarely are a result of the existence of isolated segments of the military institution.

The Founding Fathers' fear of "standing armies" is well known. What may be less well known is the extent of the debates on the issues and the philosophical underpinnings of the various positions. It is instructive to briefly examine this period since it does reveal a number of issues that remain relevant today. Equally important, these provide the rationale for an alternative view of the nature of civil-military relations in a liberal democracy.

## Standing armies and democracy

The Declaration of Independence had charged King George V with rendering, ". . . the military independent of and superior to the Civil Power . . ." The American revolutionaries felt that the balance between military and civil power had been destroyed by the British. What the Federalist Papers and the Constitution attempted to do was to restore this balance.(6)   The crux of the debates and disagreements was how this was to be done in the new American republic.

The American attitude toward standing armies was generally set in the aftermath of the Seven Year's War. In order to assist in paying for the great expenses of the war, the British government established policies to insure that the American colonists contributed their share. Not only was this contribution to be used for paying war debts, but it was to be used for the future defense including the support of a British standing army in the colonies. The imposition of a variety of taxes coupled with trade restrictions were in no small measure responsible for the ill feelings toward standing armies held by the American colonists. These carried over into the Revolution and the formation period of the American Republic.

The debate over standing armies centered on two positions: complete abolition of standing armies or the integration
of a small standing army with militia. Arguments for or
against one or the other position generated a great deal of
emotion, echoing similar arguments and emotions regarding the
present day volunteer-military and selective service systems.
As one scholar writes:

> Almost from the moment the Constitution was pub-
> lished in October 1787, it provoked a storm of
> controversy. . . . To Antifederalists, the old anti-
> nationalists, the proponents of state sovereignty,
> those concerned about individual freedom and fright-
> ened by the new union - the Constitution allowed,
> even encouraged, standing armies in peacetime, a
> symbol of the dangerous powers the new government
> would possess. Shortened to a single emotional
> phrase, easily italicized for public use, "standing
> army" called to mind a perfect set of images with
> which to smear the Constitution and inflame popular
> passion. Armies were "dangerous," "the nursery of
> vice," "engines of depotism," the "grand machine of
> power," the "grand engine of oppression," and
> "restringent to the rights and liberties of man-
> kind."(7)

Similarly, de Tocqueville writing 50 years later stated,
"After all, whatever one does, a large army in a democracy
will always be a serious danger, and the best way to lessen
this danger will be to reduce the army. But that is not a
remedy which every nation can apply."(8)

The argument for a standing army was well expressed by
Hamilton in Federalist No. 25. He wrote:

> . . . I expect we shall be told that the militia of the
> country is its natural bulwark and would be at all
> times equal to the national defense. This doctrine,
> in substance, had like to have lost us our inde-
> pendence. It cost millions to the United States that
> might have been saved. The facts which, from our
> own experience, forbid a reliance of this kind, are
> too recent to permit us to be dupes of such a
> suggestion. The steady operations of war against a
> regular and disciplined army can only be success-
> fully conducted by a force of the same kind.
> Considerations of economy, not less than of stability
> and vigor, confirm this position. The American
> militia, in the course of the late war, have, by their
> valor on numerous occasions erected eternal monu-
> ments to their fame; but the bravest of them feel

and know that the liberty of their country could not
have been established by their efforts alone, however great and valuable they were.  War, like most
other things, is a science to be acquired and perfected by diligence, by perseverance, by time, and
by practice.(9)

Madison, writing in the Federalist No. 41, observed:

How could a readiness for war in time of peace be
safely prohibited, unless we could prohibit in like
manner the preparations and establishments of every
hostile nation?  The means of security can only be
regulated by the means and the danger of attack.
. . . A standing force, therefore, is a dangerous,
at the same time that it may be a necessary, pro-
vision.  On the smallest scale it has its inconven-
iences.  On an extensive scale its consequences may
be fatal.  On any scale it is an object of laudable
circumspection and precaution.  A wise nation will
combine all these considerations; and whilst it does
not rashly preclude itself from any resource which
may become essential to its safety, will exert all its
prudence in diminishing both the necessity and the
danger of resorting to one which may be inauspicious
to its liberties.(10)

The fear of the Founding Fathers, however, appears to
go much deeper than the fear of standing armies.  It was a
fear of the power of the central government.  To control the
potential for arbitrary power, therefore, the Founding Fathers
not only established a system of checks and balances, but
placed important powers regarding control and regulation of
standing armies in a popularly elected assembly.  As Hamilton
argued in Federalist No. 23:

A government, the constitution of which renders it
unfit to be trusted with all the powers which a free
people ought to delegate to any government, would
be an unsafe and improper depository of the national
interests.  Wherever these can with propriety be
confided, the coincident powers may safely accompany this.(11)

And as Matloff notes:

Those who mistrusted a powerful government argued
against a broad grant of authority not only in the
fields of taxation and commercial regulation, but,
and with especial force, in military matters as well.

Even those, like Hamilton, who wanted to give the
central government wide latitude in handling both
purse and sword were also somewhat wary of standing armies. They too were concerned over the
possible usurpation of political power by a military
force or its use by office-holders as an instrument
for perpetrating their personal power . . . In the
final compromise the problem of the military powers
of the central government was resolved through the
system of checks and balances built into the new
Constituion. (12)

Not only was a standing army viewed as necessary to the
Federal Government, but it was to be restrained and limited as
part of the total concept of limited powers of the Federal
Government. Although the fear of standing armies was natural
for a democracy, it was held that a democratic "standing army"
could be developed - one whose values and goals paralleled
that of the democratic political system. Not only was this to
be done by intermixing of regulars with civilian militia, but
also by instilling the army with democratic values - a love of
liberty, and by providing a proper balance between society
and the military.

This was well expressed by Josiah Quincy at the time of
the Coercive Acts.

No free government was ever founded or ever
preserved its liberty without uniting the characters
of citizens and soldier in those destined for defense
of the state. The sword should never be in the
hands of any, but those who have an interest in the
safety of the community. . . . Such are a well
regulated militia composed of the freeholders, citizen
and husbandman, who take up arms to preserve
their property as individuals, and their rights as
freemen. (13)

## A democratic intermix

Many Americans looked to Europe for the military model
for America's standing army, yet there developed a uniquely
American formulation. This was based on the experience in
the Revolution and the attitude of Americans toward the British regulars. According to the American model, in times of
crisis America would transform itself into a nation of free men
under arms and develop a citizen army; hence, there was little
need for a large standing army (indeed, there was little need
according to some, of an army). The only requirement was a
small cadre of professionals whose sole responsibility was to
guard the military stores and man fortifications, and provide
teachers and leaders for the citizen armies.

As some argued:

Had we a standing army when the British invaded
our peaceful shores?  Was it a standing army that
gained the battles of Lexington and Bunker Hill, and
took the ill-fated Burgoyne?  Is not a well regulated
militia sufficient for every purpose of internal defense?  And which of you, my fellow citizens, is
afraid of any invasion from foreign powers that our
brave militia would not be able immediately to re-
pel?(14)

But as Hamilton argued, the militia by itself was inef-
ficient and "War, like most other things is a science to be
acquired and perfected by diligence, by perseverance, by
time, and by practice."  (See note 9.)
     The experiences in the Revolutionary War reflect these
contending views.  For example, at the Battle of Guliford
Court House in 1781, General Nathaniel Green's Regulars saved
the day as they fought the British Regulars to a standstill.
This occurred after the American militia broke and left the
field in disarray.  On the other hand, Lord Burgoyne's invasion through Lake Champlain and the Hudson River route
was stymied by American irregulars.  Vermont farmers rushed
to arms and using what we would now call unconventional
tactics harassed the invading column to such an extent that
the invasion failed.  At the Battle of Cowpens in 1781, General
Morgan with 1,500 Continental Regulars and 3,000 militia was
attacked by 1,900 British Regulars under Lord Tarleton.  The
efficient use of the militia in conjunction with the American
Regulars routed Tarleton's forces.
     These experiences gave rise to the concept of democratic
intermix:  a nation of free men under arms, a citizen army,
and a regular establishment.  If used correctly and employed
according to their capabilities, the militia could give a good
account of themselves.  Yet, it was understood that in a face-
to-face struggle with the British Regulars, only American
Regulars could hope to achieve victory.  While there are
proponents of one or the other way, the two themes of a
citizen army and regular army became intermixed in our
political-military philosophy.
     Throughout the history of the United States, when faced
with crises with foreign powers, American reaction has been
to turn to a citizen army to augment the regulars.  The
National Defense Act of 1916, for example, provided for an
Officers and Enlisted Reserve Crops and a Volunteer Army in
times of war.  Some of the fundamental arguments today
regarding the military posture of American forces are based on
debates and issues familiar to those studying the early years of
the formation of the American Army.  The "total force" concept

is basically an attempt to augment the regular "forces-in-being" with a citizen force of reservists, reserve units, and national guard units. Similarly, the debates over selective service and the volunteer military have their philosophical roots in disagreement regarding citizenship obligations.

Aside from these tactical and strategic considerations, the intermixing had an implicit philosophical purpose. The influx of citizen soldiers would dilute the authoritarian tendencies of the regular military establishment. Thus, citizens with their love of liberty and social values attuned to a democratic system, could not be molded into regular soldiers, whose values were apparently anathema to democracy. Indeed, it was thought that the exposure of the regular establishment to citizen soldiers would maintain a democratic thread within the military institution. Interestingly enough, this remains a major argument in the current period for a "representative" military more reflective of the character and composition of American society.

There are a number of other arguments regarding the present state of American civil-military relations and military professionalism that have their roots in the debates and disagreements voiced during the American Revolution. In any case, during America's formative period, there was an overwhelming conviction that there had to be an American army and that such an army had to be compatible with democracy.

> The basic military lesson of the American Revolution lay in the importance to a democracy of a well-trained army, representative of the whole people, and a properly trained officer corps, drawn from the whole people - an army responsible to civilian authority and fully backed by it, capable of defending and expounding the principles for which the participants in the American Revolution risked their lives.(15)

## Democratic values and the military

Love of liberty, individuality, justice, human rights, and responsibility and accountability of officials to the people are part of the democratic value system. On the other hand, in a military system, the values and concepts stress obedience, loyalty, and discipline. Moreover, many believe that the values of a military system inherently place it in a confrontation with the purpose and public good of a democratic society. The purpose of the military - management of violence - is wedded to a concept of force and battle. At its most banal level, it means killing people. Reconciling this with liberty, justice, and worth of the individual has always been difficult and hardly achieved in a liberal democratic society, except in

clear crises where the very existence of the political system
was thought to be challenged.

The intermixing of the values of the military and society
is also reflected in the writings of de Tocqueville. Commenting on warlike classes in democratic armies, he observes:

> In every democratic army it will always be the NCO
> who is least representative of the pacific and orderly
> spirit of the country, and the private who best
> represents it. The private will carry the strength
> or weakness of national mores with him into military
> life; he will provide a faithful reflection of the
> nation. If the nation is ignorant and weak, he will
> let himself be drawn by his leaders into disturb-
> ances, either unconsciously or even against his will.
> If the nation is educated and energetic, this fact will
> keep him within the bounds of discipline.(16)

Part of the apparent conflict between democratic and
military value systems stems from the character and composition of the respective elites. De Tocqueville notes, for
example, that "because in democracies the richest, best-
educated, and ablest citizens hardly ever adopt a military
career, the army finally becomes a little nation apart, with a
lower standard of intelligence and rougher habits than the
nation at large. . ."(17)

The military view of human nature is thought to add to
the conflict between military and society. Military professionals tend to have a pessimistic view of the world - Hobbesian man. This tendency not only affects the professional's
view of democratic liberal society, but it makes him extremely
cautious in accepting political-social change. His conservative
outlook goes hand in hand with the view of human nature.
While not antidemocratic in spirit, the military professional
undoubtedly is more comfortable in a "law and order" society,
whose elite is unified and provides a coherent policy. Most
military professionals, therefore, presume that tension, conflict, and confrontation are indicative of an unstable system.
Any destabilizing elements or challenges to the existing
system, however legitimate in democratic ideology, are perceived as irrational and eroding of the law and order basis of
society. This, however, is counterbalanced to a degree by
the recognition that the military professional's claim to legitimacy and to professional status rests with society and that the
military institution must uphold and defend society and the
democratic value system. In this respect, the military professional education and socialization process stresses the
loyalty to elected officials and to the existing system.

In any case, the reconciliation of democratic values with
the military system has never been easy. At best, it has been

an abrasive reconciliation. The idea that the basis of national
security rests on "citizens" who come into the military as
temporary fillers and for short periods of time has been
anathema for the traditional regular soldier. This distaste is
prompted by the value system and attitudes that the civilian
brings with him. The traditional professional finds it difficult
to reconcile such values with obedience, discipline, and loyalty
to the regiment. In the modern context, value reconciliation
requires professional sensitivity to the political-social system,
the egalitarian impulses of society and to the worth of the
"individual." The difficulty in reconciling civilian and military
values is in no small measure the reason why a number of
professionals tend to view the integration of the military and
society as disintegrative to the military. The separation from
society and isolation of the military from the ills of society,
according to some, would considerably ease the problem of
developing a professional military institution.

    The true test of any military system is the strength of its
psychological as well as its material support from and in
society. Such support cannot be turned on and off as the
military or society see fit. It must be based on a continuing
and visible link between military and society. Values need to
be reinforced, relearned, and revitalized. This is a continuing process and cannot be solved by one-time commitments
or when a particular event or crisis occurs. The fact remains, however, that there is rarely to be found in American
military history a period in which relationships between society
and the military remained fixed in a position where society
totally dominated and the military was totally separate or
isolated.(18)

    Equally important, the nature and character of the
military profession and the shape of the institution were in no
small measure a function of the prevailing ideology and attitudes of society, and the changing nature of the political-
social-economic relationships within the political system.
Moreover, these linkages and relationships were nearly always
political in tone and dynamic and interacting – hardly a situation that one can simply label as civilian supremacy and
control.

    Even a cursory glance at some American historical high-
lights regarding military and society illustrates these points.
For example, at several points in our history, military service
and political activity were closely linked. As Kemble observes:

    On the political scene, military service remained
    almost a prerequisite for presidential candidacy until
    the mid-80s, and a reputation for the managerial
    skills acquired in the army was clearly an asset at
    the polls. Hancock, the Democratic candidate in
    1880, was acclaimed for his thorough military ef-

ficiency and if his West Point background was used with some effect against him in the campaign by followers of citizen-soldier Garfield, Congressman Garfield himself was on record as the regular army's staunchest defender.(19)

At some of the most dynamic and expansive times in American history, the military become deeply involved in the political-social system. Again, as Kemble observes:

Prior to the 70s regular army units had rarely been called upon to quell civil disorders. But between the first great wave of protests in 1877 and the Pullman strike of 1894, they were used repeatedly - in more than three hundred separate labor disputes, according to most accounts. State militias, immediately available to the governors, were employed even more.(20)

There are modern parallels, ranging from the involvement in civil rights riots in Chicago and Detroit in 1967-68 to environmental work, numerous reserve officers serving in Congress, and a variety of military interest groups; i.e., the Retired Officers Association.

## Civil-military relations in the modern environment

There has been much written on the changed nature of the military institution since the end of World War II. There seems little reason to repeat all of these well-known arguments. Yet, two points need to be made in support of an alternative model of civil-military relations. First, the changed and changing character of American society, both in terms of technology and political-social system has outmoded any model based on a "separateness" or absolute civilian control and supremacy of the military. Second, the nature of modern conflicts has eroded the concept that the battlefield belongs only to the military.

In a modern liberal democracy, the increasing sophistication of the populace and their expectation of equality have not only stimulated an egalitarian thrust in the political system, but also into its institutions including the military. As Abrams has noted with respect to England, ". . . there has developed a widespread social attitude which we might call the 'expectation of equal treatment,' an attitude very apparent among the young and one that flourishes despite continued existence of substantial material inequalities."(21) This is reinforced by van Doorn's observation regarding Western Europe that "The military are on the defensive in other ways as well. For their social environment expects the armed forces

to be geared as far as possible to the values and norms of
civilian society, which entails civilianization, democratization,
unionization and even politicization."(22)    These observations
are no less appropriate in describing American society.

In addition to the linkages between the military and
civilian systems, there are close linkages between the elite in
both systems.    As Janowitz and van Doorn observe, "In all
political systems the military and political elites are inter-
linked, socially and morally.    They often share the same
outlook and values, and they defend the same social order
against external and internal threats."(23)

Aside from these linkages, the military has an important
role in domestic politics and economics.    As most recognize,
for example, the military institution commands a large portion
of federal expenditures.    In so doing, it not only has an
impact on the American economic system, but it is also involved in the process by which the federal budget is formulated, passed, and implemented.    As a consequence, the
linkages between the military institution and other political
actors is formidable, be they in the form of reserve officers
serving as Congressmen, or associations espousing the military
cause.    Equally important, the demands of national defense
necessitates the development of some degree of military expertise on the part of elected national representatives.    Thus,
military considerations are now part of the mainstream of
public debate and public policy making.    Both civilian leaders
and military professionals have major roles to play in such
debates and processes.

Modern conflicts, regardless of their intensity or purpose, must have some support of society.    The Vietnam
experience demonstrated the close relationship between the
attitudes and values of society and the ability of the military
institution to engage in military conflict.    While there remains
a core of traditionalists both within the civilian and military
sector that regard conflicts as purely military problems, there
is a great deal of evidence to suggest that few "defense"
problems are purely military in scope.    Indeed, a number of
military men now recognize that there are no purely military
problems and accept the fact that the national security of the
state requires the material and moral support of the entire
country.

In the modern environment, therefore, to perceive a
distinctly separate military system is simply to disregard
compelling evidence from the past as well as the present.
Equally important, a separate military system invariably leads
to strategies that are sterile in their conception and rigid in
their execution.    The intermix between military and civilian
elites, the sharing of values, and the compatibility of intellectual discourse is basis for effective strategy and political-
military policy.    This also has a crucial impact on the rela-

tionship between civilian institutions and the military, bringing them together in a relationship that mitigates subordination but stimulates partnership.

## Summary

As we noted earlier, civil-military relationships were major issues for the Founding Fathers. They did not solve the "problem," but they laid the groundwork for future relationships between military and society. Whatever evolved in the subsequent periods of American history, the evidence does suggest that civil-military relations rarely was based on military isolation or separation, but rather on linkages and involvement with the political system. What determined the nature and character of the relationship was in no small measure the results of the interaction between society, the evolution of the professional military ethic, and the reshaping of the military institution in response to society's changes.
Kohn's observation regarding the formation period of American history serves as a signpost in this respect:

In the final analysis, the struggle over the military establishment possessed a significance far greater than the militarism of one wing of the Federalist party, or even the formation of national institutions after revolution. Only one set of issues (and rarely the primary ones before Congress or the public), the debates over the military nonetheless lay at the very heart of American political life during this era. Like most every important problem facing the new nation - economic policy, foreign relations, the opening of the West, the relationship of the people to government - national defense was in a very real sense new to Americans, and not susceptible to resolution within the context of their political heritage or their experience as provincials in the British Empire. Like most other issues, defense became submerged and entangled in the contest over the supremacy of national or state government. Like the others, it suffered distortion in the play of sectional self-interest and emerging partisanship. And like all the others, national revolutionary political leadership over the shape and future direction of the United States, not only as a society but also as a national entity.(24)

Assessing the posture and problems faced by the American political system in the post-Vietnam era, one is struck by the remarkable parallels between the struggles of the political leadership in the initial years of the American republic and what America faced in the past two decades and faces in the coming decade. In sum, these parallels represent the thrust of civil-military relations, regardless of periods of American military quiescence. They reflect the underlying relationships between military and society even when the outward manifestation of these relationships superficially presented an image of an isolated and separate military institution.

The underlying fear of an autonomous military perpetuating what may be values contradictory to democratic purposes is cause enough to draw the military closer to society. Equally important is the fact that no military can achieve legitimacy unless it does reflect society. Totalitarian systems breed totalitarian military systems; democratic systems breed a democratic military. While the values of the military need not be a perfect replica of society they must be supportive.

> The form of government, the traditions of the people, the nature of the country, and its geographical position in relation to other powers have had a profound influence upon American military institutions. In turn, those institutions are a reflection of the American culture and way of life. Indeed, the Army is essentially an institutional form adapted by American society to meet military requirements. The American military system has been developed so as to place a minimum burden upon the people and give the nation a reasonable defense without sacrificing its fundamental values. From the beginning the United States has sought to reconcile individual liberty with national security without becoming a nation in arms.(25)

## MILITARY PROFESSIONALISM

Apparent contradictions between society and the military, and the difficulty in determining specific boundaries between the profession and civilian professions, make it difficult to develop a clear concept of the military profession. While there may be generally acceptable definitions, these become frayed when applying them to specific roles in the political system, determining the extent of professional responsibility and accountability, and identifying educational and socialization processes. Compounding the problem is the multiplicity of relationships between military and society, and the variety of views held by society regarding the military profession.

Seeking the most clearly defined and coherent military professional posture, the military professional tends to adopt the most narrowly construed dimension which focuses primarily on military skills and competence. This has been supported by a body of opinion and scholarly assessments which tend to view the military as "separate" from society, with all that this implies. The self-definition and purpose of the military as perceived by professionals is closely integrated to the conceptual basis of military profession in a democratic system. The most prominent view rests on three features. The military profession is viewed as managers of violence and force in support of the state, the sole client relationship, and the unconditional servants of the state. Not only do such professional characteristics place the military squarely on the side of a centralized state structure, but they also condition the character and composition of the elite, and condition the environment and relationship with society. These in turn carry with them dilemmas and contradictions which are reflected in the moral and ethical basis for military professionalism - morality and ethics which, it might be added, must rest in the larger community; i.e., the liberal democratic society.

## Moral and ethical foundations: an overview

Proper moral and ethical conduct have been historically a part of military professionalism. In the modern era, it was the American involvement in the Vietnam War that generated a serious concern for the moral and ethical behavior of military men. The dilemmas posed to the profession by the necessities of war and survival, and the need for morality and ethical behavior in the context of a democratic value system are complex, difficult, and remain unresolved. As we learned in Chapter 10, the complexities of these matters and traditional professional perspectives create a condition which fosters the adoption of a moral free zone, moral expediency, and absolutist positions. That is, the military profession presumes that it's philosophical foundations rest on high moral and ethical criterion which in turn are based on absolute right and wrong. However, when involved in battle, these moral and ethical patterns become subordinated to success in battle. The battlefield becomes a moral free zone. As such, individual moral and ethical considerations also become irrelevant.

Because of institutional commitment and professional norms, it is presumed that the professional's institutional loyalty and adherance to the concepts of duty, honor, country, demand the subordination of individual autonomy and individual morality and ethics. Thus, the professional is placed in a position in which moral expediency and institutional criteria dictate moral and ethical behavior. Combined with other prevailing professional considerations, what the professional mold perpetuates is an officer who conforms, develops battlefield skills, subordinates his intellectual curiosity to technical matters, and falls back upon a moral free zone when faced with moral and ethical dilemmas.

The moral and ethical posture of the military profession, moreover, supports the concept of separation and isolation. It also provides a simplistic political posture in which the military is presumed to be apolitical, totally engrossed in the problems of military technology with little time for the broader issues of values, community, and political-social dimensions of professionalism.

It was thought that the military profession could not properly develop into a "professional" system, if there was continual attention to political-social issues and concern with developing a congruence with society, with its attendant political-social issues. This is reflected in modern writings of professional officers as well as civilian scholars in America. Isolation or separateness from society, it has been argued, will allow the military to develop the necessary discipline, obedience, and skills to perform its role.

This perspective logically leads to the articulation of the military profession as unconditional servants of society. Being isolated from society, concerned primarily with military skills, leading and managing a system that is based on obedience, discipline, and loyalty to the "regiment," many military professionals argued that they could be better prepared to take orders from society and accomplish the mission as dictated by society. There was little need for military professionals to be concerned with "politics" or moral and ethical norms outside of the institution. Moreover, such a perspective logically supported the view that military men are unconditional servants of the state.

As we have suggested, however, the moral and ethical foundations of military professionalism must be deeply rooted in the larger society. Regardless of how much military professionals strive to separate military from society, the philosophical underpinnings of the military system and its legitimacy are inexplicably linked with society. Moreover, since the end of World War II, it can be shown that the separation of military from society is not possible in terms of modern security considerations. Equally important, the evidence from earlier periods of American history (Indian Wars; Seminole Wars; the Philippines campaign; the Mexican intervention, and the variety of interventions in Latin America in the early 20th century), indicates that the separation of political-social elements from military professionalism is not historically correct. The separation or isolation myth has developed and has been perpetuated by the subtle alliance between political liberals and military traditionalists – an alliance that maintains a momentum in the current military thinking.

## The liberal-traditional alliance

The concept of the liberal-traditional alliance and the two major professional perspectives were discussed in Chapter 9, with respect to the educational requirements for military professionals. These observations are also relevant in examining civil-military relations, since they indicate professional attitudes with respect to society and the role of the military. In any case, the liberal-traditional alliance and prevailing professional perspectives reinforce the view that the military profession should be separate from society.

The American military profession has primarily followed the Uptonian tradition. Emory Upton in his book, The Military Policy of the United States, advocated a system based on the German model.(26)   Not only did this suggest the establishment of a general staff, but more important from the point of view of civil-military relations, it stressed that military institutions and the military profession stood above and separate from the political system. As one historian concluded:

> . . . Emory Upton did lasting harm in setting the main current of American military thought not to the task of shaping military institutions that would serve both military and national purposes, but to the futile task of demanding that the national institutions be adjusted to purely military expediency.(27)

The attitudes of younger officers during the early 20th century reflected an Uptonian orientation. The following quotation is illustrative:

> It is a self-evident proposition that a democracy based on the will of millions of people, expressed through devious and changing channels, cannot be as skillful or efficient in the conduct of military affairs as a monarchy headed by a wise and powerful chief. . . . National characteristics, which become governmental ones in a democracy like ours, make it impossible to organize and discipline an effective army from the point of view of military experts.(28)

While antidemocratic views have been significantly muted, the fact remains that there are few military men today that champion the kind of professional posture reminiscent of the views of Major General John Pope. Speaking to the Army of the Tennessee a few years following the Civil War, he stated:

> So long as the soldier remains one of the people; so long as he shares their interests, takes part in their progress, and feels a common sympathy with them in

their hopes and aspirations, so long will the Army
be held in honorable esteem and regard. . . . When
he ceases to do this; when officers and soldiers
cease to be citizens in the highest and truest sense,
the Army will deserve to lose, as it will surely lose,
its place in the affections of the people, and properly and naturally become an object of suspicion
and dislike. (29)

Similarly, more than a generation later, Colonel John
McAuley Palmer wrote, "A free state cannot continue to be
democratic in peace and autocratic in war. . . . An enduring
government by the people must include an army of the people
among its institutions." (30) In the main, however, views such
as those held by Pope and Palmer have had only a tangential
impact on reforming of civil-military relationships. While there
has been some attention to the broader dimensions of civil-
military relations, these have been primarily in terms of
reinforcement of a conflict and control perspective rather than
a new civil-military model.

## Summary

The same factors affecting civil-military relationships also
influence the character of the military profession. In this
respect, the Uptonian tradition still retains an important place
in the American military profession. Separateness and isolation, combined with civilian control and supremacy appear to
be the modern versions of this tradition. In such an environment, the idea of military profession is less difficult to
define and easier to implement. Simply put, civilians determine policy, dictate the general rules outlining military policy,
and leave the battlefield to the military. In such conditions,
the military simply carries out policy; they are not responsible
for it. There also exists a professional perspective that
recognizes the obscurity between military and political strategies, and sees the need for a close sensitivity to society and
the sharing of values of the political system. Moreover, to
develop this type of professionalism necessitates broadening of
the concept of military professionalism and a restructuring of
the socialization and educational processes within the profession. Such a reshaping of the military profession will have
a parallel impact on the relationships between the military and
society, eliminating for all practical purposes the concept of a
separate military sub-system.
The difficulties in reconciling these views and in developing a coherent military profession aimed at the modern
political system and security environment have created a gray
area in which the military profession remains mired, unable to
decide directions for the future. At the same time, this has

also affected the views regarding the proper relationship between military and society. Under such circumstances, it is part of human nature to fall back on well-known traditions: These provide a sense of security and direction in what may be viewed as a rather chaotic situation. Unfortunately, these traditional directions may not be relevant to the necessities of modern environment, which may demand imagination, initiative, and boldness.

## THE EQUILIBRIUM MODEL

The conflict and control model of civil-military relations has dominated scholarly perspectives, as we have seen. The intellectual tradition perceives a military that is apolitical and narrowly confined to the "barracks," reminiscent of the fear of standing armies earlier in our history. The traditional military professional view takes a similar position albeit for different reasons. A narrowly construed professionalism closely identified with military skills and weapons technology provides precise professional guidelines, tends to avoid controversial political-military issues, and is thought necessary for a coherent military system.

As we have shown, however, there is ample evidence supporting an alternative perspective. In brief, the historical patterns of the American political system and the evolution of the military profession are inexplicable. The intent of the Founding Fathers and the requisites of a democratic ideology, it can be argued, do not provide for a separate sub-system removed from society. The legitimacy and credibility of any military system rests with its linkages to society and the reflection of basic social values. While this is an imperfect reflection, there is nevertheless both a political-psychological as well as a formal link between the military and society.

What kind of model best represents this relationship? In its ideal form, the model presumes that the military profession (i.e. the officer corps) is an educated elite whose role in society is the organization, control, and application of force in pursuit of democratic values. Complementing this is the idea that the profession not only controls and supervises the military instrument in accordance with established policy, but that professional morals and ethics require a commitment to democratic ideals which necessitate a role in the political process for the achievement of goals that best serve the American system. This presumes an active role: engagement in public debate in which military expertise is relevant and which advocates in an enlightened way the priorities of the military - priorities which attempt to account for the total strength of the political system, based on political, economic,

and military synthesis. This political role, however, does not
envision the advocacy of a position to its ultimate military
solution.

The alternative model is one in which the relationship
between military and civilian is established by the proper
balancing of their political power and purposes: the equilibrium model. This is not a unique perspective in the social
sciences. It has been used, for example, in the study of
revolutionary change. It has also been used as a framework
for studying various aspects of social systems. It is used
here in its most simple form. Equilibrium is conceptually
applicable,

> . . . where it is possible to show that customs
> (norms), institutions, and the social activities re-
> lated to them (roles) dovetail in together in certain
> specified ways so that one provides a corrective to
> disruptive tendencies in another. It should also be
> possible to show how, if these functional relation-
> ships are lacking, a form of social life will break
> down; and also to show how a reacting tendency may
> go too far.(31)

In brief, the equilibrium model presumes that the various
sub-systems share the same values and agree upon the norms
of behavior. Moreover, in the case of the military and society, each maintains its own integrity and identity, but
political-psychological support to all individuals, regardless
of whether they are military or civilian, emanate from the
political-moral order. This is reinforced by the fact that the
military exists for the sole purpose of supporting the democratic political-social order. To do this properly, the military
must be committed to such a system, understand it, and reflect
its basic value structure within the military institution.

There are a number of other factors in the equilibrium
model that need to be considered. First, the model is based
on a concept of friendly adversaries, similar to the characteristics of the legal system. This presumes that adversaries
disagree with one another at times and use their political power
to pursue their priorities in accord with the democratic "rules
of the game," the established norms of behavior, and the moral
and ethical foundations of democratic ideology. Only in this
way is the political activity of the various sub-systems legitimized. For example, the military as a political institution
(among other things) pursues its priorities through a variety
of informal (unofficial) channels and processes which are
legitimate in the American political system. However, the
military's latitude in the official sphere is severely restricted,
as it should be in a democratic system. In either case,
however, in pursuing its goal as an institution, the military

will be interacting with other political actors whose legitimacy in the official sphere provides them more latitude. Thus, it is conceivable that the military institution may play a distinct secondary role in the official sphere, but a major role in the unofficial sphere.

Second, the relationship between the military and society is symbiotic; according to standard dictionary sources, it is a "partnership of dissimilar organisms which association, though at times harmful, is usually advantageous." The perpetuation of the liberal democratic system is based on the partnership between military and society and is valid not only at the most senior level of policy makers, but at a variety of levels and associations; i.e., the military professional elite with civilian elites. This partnership is predominantly one reflecting an educational and socialization intermix, where values, morals, and ethics of military and civilian elites are congruent. Additionally, the partnership between the military system and other political actors, although at times adversarial, is mutually advantageous in the pursuit of goals and in the perpetuation of the political system. In brief, conflict, tension, and a give-and-take relationship is not antithetical to democracy as some military men might presume. On the contrary, a number of social scientists argue that such a condition is a sign of a healthy democratic system as long as all political actors accept the advantage of being in one political system based on democratic ideology.

Third, the relationships in the equilibrium model are asymmetrical. That is, the military, although committed to defend the state, to democratic values, and the existing political system, does not have a major role in determining the norms or boundaries of the political power of political actors. This is done primarily by civilian institutions where public dialogue can legitimately occur. Moreover, policies regarding the limits of dialogue and dissent are primarily formulated through civilian institutions and by elected officials, not by military professionals. Thus, while the military cannot be isolated from the impact of policies, nor from the influence of political dialogue and value structures, it is the sole instrumentality (and in this sense isolated) when it comes to performing its primary role in war. Finally, the professional ethos accepts without qualification the fact that civilian policy makers are pre-eminent in the direction of the political system, even with respect to matters concerning the military.

Fourth, the military and civilian institutions and systems parallel each other; that is, while they are not the same, they are interconnected by a variety of relationships, values, and norms, as we have already noted. This parallelism occurs at every level of the military institution and between various elites. There is a multiplicity of relationship, but each political actor maintains its own identity and integrity. Yet, this is done within the context of a value system and ideology and provides the direction and legitimacy for the operation and existence of each sub-system. In this sense, there is no total autonomy for any sub-system. Although each sub-system differs, they evolve from the same political-social system and value base.

Fifth, equilibrium envisions a relationship which is dynamic, interacting, and self-adjusting. Both society and the military are perceived as seeking the same goals - the reinforcement and perpetuation of the democratic political system, although they may vary in the pursuit of these goals. Once this variance goes beyond acceptable standards for democracy, however, pressures are exerted by a variety of political actors to restore a reasonable congruence to the democratic axis. There are no absolutes in such a relationship, except the absolutism required to perpetuate and protect the democratic political system. The acceptable relationship between civilian and military sectors is determined by a variety of political linkages and influence. The critical mass of these relationships must be within the acceptable boundaries of democracy and must, in the final analysis, be supportive of the democratic system.

It would seem, therefore, that there is a pressing need to review the prevailing concepts of civil-military relations and military professionalism in order to determine their accuracy and relevancy in the modern era. The evidence suggests that there is ample cause to question what has become an intellectual and military tradition.

It would seem that any philosophical redirection of the military must come from open, reasoned, and multi-sided public dialogue.

As a start toward re-establishing this dialogue, we would all do well to learn a good deal more about our past civil-military relationships and about impressions and distortions they have left. We also need to chart our present position by sociological as well as historical and political triangulation, sighting on as many points as possible. In short, we need to examine the entire record. (32)

## A NEW PROFESSIONALISM

The shift to the equilibrium model of civil-military relations cannot be accomplished without a change in the intellectual interpretations of military professionalism and the broadening of civilian perspectives regarding the military elite. At the outset, there is a need to reduce the gap between ideals and

reality.  The ideal is to presume that the military is a professional organization in the purest sense; i.e., with no
political impact and no linkages to the political-social system.
Realities dictate that the system of democracy as well as all of
its sub-systems operate imperfectly.  Additionally, the realities
of the environment dictate a recognition that the military is
among other things a political institution and does have influence and access to the political process through a variety of
informal, as well as formal, channels.  Once having accepted
these realities, we can then turn to the question of what kind
of military professionalism and civilian environment is necessary to best operate in a democratic system.  For the military,
this is best accomplished by an enlightened advocacy posture
(This was discussed at length in Chapter 9).  In brief, the
domestic political-social system and the changed international
order require a military posture and professionalism that is not
wedded to traditional boundaries, but is steeped in broad
intellectual curiosity and evolves from political-social knowledge.

     The military professional therefore, cannot remain a pas-
sive and neutral cog in the operation of the political system.
The professional must be able to exercise intellectual judge-
ments and articulate such views based on an understanding of
military and civilian priorities within the context of democratic
society.  Moreover, this must be based on the acceptance that
the military is part of that system and that military professionals in a democracy must understand and nurture the values
that support a democratic system.  Such a professional perspective will shape a military posture that is not only attuned
to the needs of a democratic system, but is best prepared for
the challenges of the international system in the coming
decades.

     For the military profession to develop the proper per-
spective it must also develop the necessary educational and
socialization processes that foster a deeper understanding of
the American political-social system.  Similarly, the professional must recognize that there is a legitimate political dimension to the profession.  A dimension that not only integrates
political and military perspectives, but also appreciates and
understands to the fullest extent possible that the military
profession and the institution are, among other things, political.  Equally important, being political is a necessity in the
American democratic system, not for purposes of partisanship
and blatant advocacy, but in the sense of sophisticated and
enlightened perspectives regarding the military and democracy.

     For civilian elite and policy makers, the military must be
viewed as a true profession, one that is not shackled by
parochial intellectual perspectives.  This means that military
professionals should be reasonably expected to understand the
impact of military decisions on the political-social system, and

develop a deep understanding of the imperatives of democracy. For the civilian decision maker then, it is necessary to move away from the concept of "unconditional servants of the state," where robot-like military martinets are expected to accept without question even the most inappropriate policy and programs. Equally important, it means moving away from a view that military men are paid to do, not to think.

Society and the military alike can gain more from military professionals than military skills. The dimensions of civilian perspectives, the nature of democratic systems, and the strengthening of values through civic education, are major concerns that can be qualitatively reinforced by the contributions of an educated and enlightened military professional. But, this presumes that the profession is not outside of the political-social system; that it is in harmonious balance with society.

The evolving nature of security and the character of an industrialized democratic state cannot rest on the premise that internal systems are in a state of conflict and must be controlled. This is even less acceptable in light of evidence regarding the evolution of the American military and the nature of American democracy. The acceptance of the Uptonian military perspective has surely prejudiced the perceptions regarding civil-military relations. Yet, there has been an alternative that is particularly appealing. Colonel John McAuley Palmer, testifying before a Congressional Committee, observed that American military policy had to be based on a citizen army that was in "harmony with the genius of American institutions."(33) In 1941, Palmer published a book in which he concluded, "The forms of military institutions must be determined on political grounds, with due regard to national genius and tradition. The military pedant may fail by proposing adequate and economical forces under forms that are intolerable to the national genius."(34)

Participation in the political process and the maintenance of legitimacy requires the nurturing of values within and between sub-systems. This cannot be done intermittently, but requires a consistent pattern of policies and programs designed at developing a democratic ethic and in the case of the military, a professional military-civilian balance. Moreover, civil-military relations are not solely a reflection of the relationships between the Joint Chiefs of Staff, the President, the Secretary of Defense, the Service Secretaries, and Congress. Rather, they are a result of the variety of contacts and involvement between mliitary professionals and civilians in a variety of capacities and functions, and at a variety of levels. The characteristics of this "critical mass" of relationships and the images that emerge from these multiple interactions are what form civil-military relations in our system.

Palmer's view expresses the intent of democratic ideology and appears to be an accurate statement of the civil-military relationship as perceived by the Founding Fathers. The historical deterministic element in developing and assessing military professionalism and military institutions has distorted our view and has prejudiced our own perceptions of what the military profession means and what its role should be in a liberal democratic society.

A civil-military relationship based on an equilibrium model nurtured by a military professionalism stemming from education and enlightened advocacy may be an acceptable alternative to the prevailing views of civil-military relationships. Such an approach may not provide answers or eliminate the ills many tend to associate with military and society, but it may well provide the kind of environment stimulating imaginative inquiry and boldness in seeking new conceptual approaches in the study of military professionalism and civil-military relationships.

## NOTES

1. Leonard Dalton Abbott (Ed). Masterworks of Government. New York: McGraw-Hill Book Company, 1973, Volume 1, p. 25.

2. As quoted in C. Robert Kemble. The Image of the Army Officer in America. Westport, Conn.: Greenwood Press, 1973, p. 24.

3. Alexis de Tocqueville, Democracy in America. Garden City, N.Y.: Doubleday Anchor Book 1969, edited by J.P. Mayer, translated by George Lawrence, pp. 50-651.

4. See, for example, Kemble; Richard H. Kohn, Eagle and Sword; The Federalists and Creation of the Military Establishment in America, 1783-1802. New York: The Free Press, 1975; Maurice Matloff, American Military History. Washington, D.C.: Office of the Chief of Military History, US Army, 1968; Russell Weigley, History of the United States Army. New York: The Macmillan Company, 1967.

5. See note 30 and the discussion regarding homeostatic equilibrium.

6. Roy P. Fairfield (Ed), The Federalist Papers. Garden City, N.Y.: Doubleday Anchor, 1966, Second Edition. Quotes used in the paper from The Federalist Papers are taken from Fairfield. It is interesting to note the degree of attention given to the role of a standing army in the Federalist Papers. Eight of the Papers are specifically concerned with this issue, while a number of others deal with standing armies in the context of the powers of the central government.

7.  Kohn, p. 81.
8.  de Tocqueville, p. 651.
9.  Fairfield, p. 69.
10. Ibid., pp. 119-120.
11. Ibid., p. 62.
12. Matloff, pp. 105-106.
13. As quoted in Clinton Rossiter, The Political Thought
of the American Revolution. New York:  Harcourt, Brace and
World, Inc., 1953, pp. 126-127.
14. Weigley, p. 85.
15. Forest Carlisle Pogue, "The Revolutionary Trans-
formation of the Art of War," American Institute for Policy
Research, America's Continuing Revolution. New York: Anchor
Books, 1976, p. 316.
16. de Tocqueville, p. 654.
17. Ibid., p. 648.
18. An excellent study of this subject is in Kemble.
Tracing the evolution of the Army Officer's image in America,
the author clearly shows the interaction between the military
institution and society, and how the dynamics of society and
the professional ethic of the military interacted creating at
times deep antagonisms, and at others great sympathy and
pride.  The study of Weigley is also an excellent source in
this respect.
19. Kemble, p. 161.
20. Ibid., 120.
21. Philip Abrams, "The Late Profession of Arms," in
European Journal of Sociology, Volume VL, 1965, No. 2, p.
246.
22. Jacques van Doorn, The Soldier and Social Change.
Beverly Hills, Cal.: Sage Publications, 1975, p. 99.
23. Morris Janowitz and Jacques van Doorn (Eds), On
Military Ideology. Rotterdam:  Rotterdam University Press,
1971, Volume 3, p. xxvii.
24. Kohn, p. 296.
25. Matloff, p. 14.
26. Emory Upton. The Military Policy of the United
States from 1775. Washington, D.C.:  Government Printing
Office, 1904.
27. Weigley, p. 281.
28. Ibid.
29. Ibid., p. 222.
30. Ibid., p. 400.
31. Dorthy Emmet, Function, Purpose, and Powers.
London:  Macmillan, 1958, p. 26. This term as used in the
Social Sciences refers to the various actions and processes
within the political system and between parts of the political
system to maintain its identity or the identity of the various
parts, by reestablishing acceptable order or developing
counteractions to processes that would destroy the system or

parts of it if they exceeded more than a limited range. In sum, the political system and its parts seek to maintain their own integrity and legitimate relationships, even under the most trying circumstances. Thus, there always exists an environment in which change can take place and new actors and techniques can be absorbed in response to new pressures, forces, or changing environment. See the discussion in Chalmers Johnson, Revolutionary Change. Boston: Little, Brown and Company, 1966, pp. 53-58.

32. Kemble, p. 203.

33. Senate Committee on Military Affairs, Reorganization of the Army, Hearings before the Subcommittee on Military Affairs, Sixty-Fifth Congress, First Session.

34. John McAuley Palmer, America in Arms: The Experience of the United States with Military Organization. New Haven: Yale University Press, 1941, pp. 101-103.

# 13 Postscript: What Needs to be Done

Almost a decade has passed since I wrote my first essay on military professionalism. During that period of time the military profession and the institution have passed through difficult times, with more difficult times ahead. In reviewing the essays in this volume and what has occurred over the past years, however, I find little cause to change my views. Indeed, I am more firmly convinced that the problems facing the military profession are more philosophical and political than organizational or administrative. In this respect, the decade of the 1980s promises to be no less trying than the past decade.

My personal perspective on the military profession, with particular reference to the role of the military in a liberal democracy, stems from the Vietnam experience. All those who served in Vietnam and the generation of Americans who were engulfed in the Vietnam turmoil during the decade of the 1960s are probably still uneasy about explanations of our involvement and may well remain skeptical about explanations of what happened. The flurry of books on Vietnam that were published in the 1970s did little to resolve these problems. Many of these tended to rationalize one position or another, or disagreed on reasons for the involvement as well as the results.

I was particularly struck by the explanations provided by military men regarding Vietnam. I detected a deterministic approach; an acceptance of the American military role in Vietnam; and a conviction that the Vietnam issue was a passing phenomenon. Many professionals were convinced that the military institution would weather the storm and emerge like a "Phoenix" from the ashes of Vietnam, a better and more effective institution.

I am not a believer in the "Phoenix" theory. Yet, I take serious issue with those who saw in the Vietnam experience the collapse of the U.S. Army and its officers corps into chaos and anomie. To make such a charge is simply a superficial view of the problem, a lack of understanding of the character of counter-revolutionary conflict, and a focus on the effect rather than the causes of the American disillusionment and self criticism over Vietnam. The American military had serious problems as a result of its involvement in Vietnam, to be sure, but these in no small measure were a reflection of the domestic political and social turmoil, reinforced by the conventional and traditional posture of the American military, which hardly changed throughout the Vietnam experience. On the other hand, I cannot accept the view that the military "did its job" in Vietnam and therefore failures rest solely with the civilian leadership.

The complexity of the Vietnam issue does not allow simplistic finger point to any one event, institution, or set of political actors. In terms of the military profession, explanations and answers are more reasonably sought in a serious examination of the philosophical bases of the profession and its political-military dimension. The American military profession, reflecting a particular cultural orientation, is not prepared now, nor was it prepared in Vietnam, to adopt strategy and tactics to the demands of successful counter-revolution. This is not due solely to the profession itself, but also to the particular character of liberal democracy and the American political system (as was true with respect to the Vietnam War).

To return to the point made in the opening lines of this chapter, the problems of the military profession during Vietnam as well as in the current period stem from philosophical and political-military considerations. Military men are quick to point out however, that all of the theorizing and philosophizing about the profession are abstractions and meaningless without a specific plan of action. This "can do" attitude and action orientation of the profession are likely to create a great degree of sympathy for those who advocate specific recommendations for such issues as manpower levels, the number and type of maneuver battalions, the number and type of air squadrons, the infantry-armor mix, the replenishment and replacement procedures for units in combat, resource requirements, and weapons technology, among other things. These are important, to be sure. However, it is more important to study, analyze, and develop policies concerned with the philosophical and political-military dimensions of the military profession. These are the essential factors that establish the military mind-set and world view, and determine, in no small way, the quality of civil-military relations, military posture, and the moral and ethical patterns of the profession. In turn, these provide a particular military point of view on specific programs and policies.

As an illustration, two important considerations are military force structure and contingency plans. Force structure reflects the goals and missions in contingency planning, which in turn must be linked to strategy and political-military policy. Fundamental to this, however, is the fact that strategy and political-military policy manifest the character and nature of military professionalism and civil-military relations. Lest some argue that this is too facile an answer, let me hasten to note that the issues of military professionalism and civil-military relations are more difficult to examine and revise or change than to develop a shopping list of things that need to be done.

In other words, force structuring and contingency planning not only reflect the kind and quality of forces, their organizational structure, and combat orientation, but also detail the areas of probable operations and the political-social ingredients associated with military operations, ranging the entire length of the conflict spectrum. If the traditional military professional perspective retains its narrow focus, it is likely that "battle of the Central Plains" orientation with minimum consideration to non-European areas will dominate force structures and contingency planning. Additionally, these are likely to reflect a traditional distinction between military and civilian, and an artificial delineation between the military and the political. Thus, there is likely to be a "military" solution to even the most complex issues. Equally important such a perspective leads directly to the view that military men must simply carry out orders from above, uncritically and without intellectual reflection. Robot-like response and a moral and ethical "free" zone inevitably follow, to the denigration of the very concept of professional.

In sum, administrative and organizational considerations reflect the qualitative character of military professionalism and its political-military dimension. Thus, trying to analyze and answer questions about force structure and contingency planning, without addressing the philosophical bases of the profession is meaningless since it misses the fundamental point. Moreover, attempting to change or revise the basis of force structure and developing meaningful alternatives to the elements of contingency planning without changing or revising the philosophical and political-military aspects of professionalism is like putting old wine into new bottles - nothing really changes.

For those who are uncomfortable without specific points and programs, I would recommend a thorough reading and analysis of the farewell address by Major General Dewitt C. Smith upon his retirement as Commandant of the Army War College in June, 1980.(1) Although the entire address will not be repeated here, it is important to focus on several points made by General Smith.

In assessing our military posture, General Smith said, in part:

Our total defense is inadequate to face the threats and challenges of today, let alone those which may exist tomorrow.

In terms of manpower - of people, that is - I think our voluntary mechanism is strained at best. It is not serving the reserves well enough; it is not geared to the needs of swift mobilization; and it does not deal with the fact that an elite of well-to-do well educated and poorly motivated young Americans can, and do sit on their rear ends on prestigious campuses while the urban poor, the farm youngsters and the disadvantaged are enlisted to defend us. If that means we need the draft or national service, so be it.

Part of the answer to problems of national security and military posture according to General Smith includes the following:

Our nation's defense must be framed within a coherent national and military strategy based first on our finest national values, comprehensive policies, long-term goals, and an absence of expediency any place, in or out of uniform. A strategy cannot be safely or sensibly articulated within the bare bones of a budget; it cannot be found in the arid ground of "consolidated guidance."

General Smith went on to say:

that we have a professional obligation to be totally professional and to make soldiering a pleasure, to allow others to learn from honest errors, to provide priorities, to decentralize, and to eliminate make-work, over-commitment and over-supervision. And we have a further professional obligation to advocate these approaches strongly to our military and civilian superiors.

General Smith's commentary not only underscores the analysis and themes in this volume, but also reaffirms the serious challenges to the military profession. While there is no single answer to these issues, there is, in my view, overwhelming evidence that a major step in the right direction is the development of a military profession whose intellectual horizons and moral and ethical criteria evolve from educated

and enlightened military professionals. To be sure, an educated and enlightened military professional is not a cure-all of
replenishing units in combat for example. But an educated
and enlightened professional who has also mastered the technicalities of the military profession will be in a better position
to incorporate, digest, and weigh the alternatives presented
even in the most technical issues. Equally important, the
professional with the intellectual horizons associated with a
broader dimension of professionalism is likely to be in a better
position to understand the "whole" and anticipate the impact on
strategy and military policy. The engineering perspective
does have its place in the profession; i.e., identify the
problem, break it down to its essential elements, and seek a
solution. Nevertheless, there is an even greater place for
those who understand the "totality" of the issue and appreciate
the fact that there may be no solutions, that living adversity
and insoluble situations may be a military way of life.

   In any case, being a military professional has never been
easy. In the current environment it has become even more
difficult. Changes in the nature and character of military
professionalism and a more effective military system will not
occur in a deterministic fashion - as the Phoenix theory implies. Only through serious reflection about the character and
nature of military professionalism and a concerted effort to
change what needs to be changed and accept what cannot or
should not be changed, will military professionals be able to
make the military institution better and more effective. Having
said this, I must also stress that these matters do not rest
with the military institution alone. Civilian scholars, academicians, and decision makers have an equal responsibility.
The nature of the domestic political-social environment from
which the military evolves; i.e., values, beliefs, attitudes,
and the "democratic" nature of the system are in no small
measure the determinants of the character of the military
profession. It is such an environment that is susceptible to
the influence of civilian elite.

   It is ironic that one of the best statements regarding the
perceptions of civilian elite on the military profession should
appear in a work of fiction.

   It is a common prejudice advanced by the intelligentsia of every age that soldiering is a mindless
   profession undeserving of any moral respect, as
   though somehow the preservation of the estate of
   mankind is a minor effect to be left in the hands of
   fools and brutes.(2)

   This common prejudice is perpetuated by a military
profession that has failed to come to grips with the political-
social dimensions of modern conflicts and has yet to adequately

adapt to a highly industrialized, egalitarian, liberal democratic political system.

Finally, in reviewing all that has been said in this volume, and projecting this to the decade of the 1980s, I can only conclude that there is a long way to go for the military profession. This is particularly disconcerting because from all accounts, the decade of the 1980s is likely to be the most challenging: politically, socially, economically, and militarily. Out of all the political actors and sub-systems within the American political system, the military seems least prepared for the 1980s.

## NOTES

1. Major General Dewitt C. Smith, "Defense Unequal to Our Responsibilities," in Army Times, August 11, 1980, p. 21.

2. Don Pendleton, The Executioner #34, Terrible Tuesday. Los Angeles: Pinnacle Books, 1979, Frontmatter.

# Bibliography

Included in this bibliography are those works which I have found particularly useful in studying and examining military professionalism. These have been listed with other works which are aimed specifically at military professionalism, some having important input to the study of the subject although not primarily a work on military professionalism. I have not generally included publications of a policy nature or those aimed specifically at the Vietnam experience. Finally, only books or special issues of periodicals presented in book form are included. The reader is referred to the extensive notes with most of the chapters.

Abrahamsson, Bengt. Military Professionalization and Political Power. Beverly Hills, Cal.: Sage Publications, 1972.

Ackley, C.W. The Modern Military in American Society. Philadelphia, Pa.: Westminister, 1972.

Ambrose, Stephen E. and Barber, James A., Jr. (Eds.) The Military and American Society: Essays and Readings. New York: The Free Press, 1972.

Andreski, Stanislav. Military Organization and Society. (2nd ed.) Berkeley: University of California Press, 1968.

Bachman, Jerald G. and Blair, John D. Soldiers, Sailors and Civilians: The "Military Mind" and the All-Volunteer Force. Ann Arbor, Mich.: Institute for Social Research, November 1975.

Bachman, Jerald G., Blair, John D., and Segal, David R. The All-Volunteer-Force: A Study of Ideology in the Military. Ann Arbor, Mich.: University of Michigan Press, 1977.

Barnes, Peter. Pawns: The Plight of the Citizen-Soldier. New York: Alfred A. Knopf, 1972.

Betts, Richard. Soldiers, Statesmen and Cold War Crises. Cambridge, Mass.: Harvard University Press, 1977.

Bletz, Donald F. The Role of the Military Professional in U.S. Foreign Policy. New York: Praeger Publishers, 1972.

Bradford, Zeb B., Jr. and Brown, Frederic J. The United States Army in Transition. Beverly Hills, Cal.: Sage Publications, 1973.

Bramson, Leon and Goethals, George W. (Eds.) War: Studies from Psychology, Sociology, Anthropology. (Rev. Ed.) New York: Basic Books, 1968.

Brodie, Bernard. War and Politics. New York: Macmillan Publishing Co., Inc., 1973.

Brown, George W. Generals and the Public: Recent Policy-Making in Civil-Military Relations. Lawrence, Kan.: Governmental Research Center, University of Kansas, 1964.

Buchan, Alastair. War In Modern Society. London: C.A. Watts and Co., Ltd., 1966.

Calley, Lieutenant William L. Lieutenant Calley/His Own Story. New York: Viking, 1971.

Caraley, Demetrios. The Politics of Military Unification: A Study of Conflict and the Policy Process. New York: Columbia University Press, 1966.

Carey, Omer L. (Ed.) The Military-Industrial Complex and U.S. Foreign Policy. Pullman, Wash.: Washington State University Press, 1969.

Clotfelter, James. The Military in American Politics. New York: Harper and Row, 1973.

Coates, Charles H. and Pellegrin, Ronald J. Military Sociology: A Study of American Military Institutions and Military Life. College Park, Md.: Social Science Press, 1965.

Cochran, Charles L. (Ed.) Civil-Military Relations. New York: The Free Press, 1974.

Coffin, Tristram. The Passion of the Hawks. New York: Macmillan, 1965.

Cunliffe, Marcus. Soldiers and Civilians. Boston: Little, Brown and Co., 1968.

Davis, Vincent. The Admirals Lobby. Chapel Hill: The University of North Carolina Press, 1967.

de Tocqueville, Alexis. Democracy in America. Edited by
Mayer, J.P. Garden City, N.Y.: Anchor Books, 1969.

Derthick, Martha. The National Guard in Politics. Cambridge, Mass.: Harvard University Press, 1965.

Dixon, Norman F. On the Psychology of Military Incompetence.
New York: Basic Books, 1976.

Donovan, Colonel James A. (USMC, ret). Militarism, U.S.A
New York: Scribners, 1970.

Dupuy, Colonel R. Ernest (USA, ret). The National Guard:
A Compact History. New York: Hawthorn Books, 1971.

Ekirch, Arthur A., Jr. The Civilian and the Military. New
York: Oxford University Press, 1956.

Ellis, Joseph and Moore, Robert. School for Soldiers: West
Point and the Profession of Arms. New York: Oxford
University Press, 1974.

Foster, Michael B. Masters of Political Thought: Plato to
Machiavelli. Vol. I. Boston: Houghton Mifflin Co., 1941.

Gabriel, Richard A. and Savage, Paul L. Crisis in Command:
Mismanagement in the Army. New York: Hill and Wang,
1978.

Galloway, K. and Johnson R. West Point: America's Power
Fraternity. New York: Simon and Schuster, 1973.

Glick, Edward B. Soldiers, Scholars, and Society: The Social
Impact of the American Military. Pacific Palisades, Cal.:
Goodyear, 1971.

_____. Peaceful Conflict: The Non-military Use of the
Military. Harrisburg, Pa.: Stackpole, 1967.

Goodpaster, Andrew J. and Huntington, Samuel P. Civil-
Military Relations. Washington, D.C.: American Enterprise
Institute for Public Policy Research, 1977.

Gray, J. Glenn. The Warriors: Reflections on Men in Battle.
New York: Harcourt, Brace, 1959.

Hackett, Sir John. The Profession of Arms. London: Times
Publishing Co., 1962.

Halberstam, David. The Best and the Brightest. New York:
Fawcett, 1973.

Hanning, Hugh. The Peaceul Uses of Military Forces. New
York: Praeger, 1967.

Hauser, William L. America's Army in Crisis. Baltimore, Md.:
The Johns Hopkins University Press, 1973.

Hays, Colonel Samuel H. and Thomas, Lieutenant Colonel William N. Taking Command: The Art and Science of Military Leadership. Harrisburg, Pa.: Stackpole, 1967.

Head, Richard G. and Rokke, Ervin J. American Defense Policy. Baltimore, Md.: The Johns Hopkins University Press, 1973. (3rd ed.)

Herbert, Anthony B. Soldier. New York: Holt, Rinehart and Winston, 1973.

Hersh, Seymour, M. May Lai 4: A Report on the Massacre and Its Aftermath. New York: Random House, 1970.

Hofstadter, Richard. The American Political Tradition and the Men Who Made It. New York: Vintage Books, 1973.

Howard, M. (Ed.). Soldiers and Governments: Nine Studies in Civil-Military Relations. Bloomington, Ind.: Indiana University Press, 1962.

Huntington, Samuel P. The Soldier and the State: The Theory and Politics of Civil-Military Relations. New York: Vintage Books, 1957.

_____. Changing Patterns of Military Politics. Glencoe, Ill.: The Free Press of Glencoe, Inc., 1962.

_____. The Common Defense: Strategic Programs in National Politics. New York: Columbia University Press, 1961.

Janowitz, Morris. The Professional Soldier: A Social and Political Portrait. New York: The Free Press, 1971.

_____ (Ed.). The New Military: Changing Patterns of Organization. New York: Russell Sage Foundation, 1964.

Janowitz, Morris and Little, Lieutenant Colonel Roger W. Sociology and the Military Establishment. (rev. ed.) New York: Russell Sage Foundation, 1965.

Janowitz, Morris and van Doorn, Jacques (Eds.) On Military Ideology. Rotterdam: Rotterdam University Press, 1971. Colume 3.

Jones, W.T. Masters of Political Thought: Machiavelli to Bentham. Vol. 2. Boston: Houghton Mifflin Co., 1968.

Just, Ward. Military Men. New York: Knopf, 1970.

Karsten, Peter. The Naval Aristocracy. New York: The Free Press, 1972.

Keegan, John. The Face of Battle. New York: The Viking Press, 1976.

Kemble, Robert C.  The Image of the Army Officer in America: Background for Current Views.  Westport, Conn.:  Greenwood Press, 1973.

King, E.L.  The Death of the Army.  New York:  Saturday Review Press, 1972.

Kohn, Richard H.  Eagle and Sword:  The Federalists and the Creation of the Military Establishment in America, 1783-1802.  New York:  The Free Press, 1975.

Korb, Lawrence J.  The Fall and Rise of the Pentagon:  American Defense Policies in the 1970s.  Westport, Conn.:  Greenwood Press, 1979.

_____  (Ed.).  The System for Educating Military Officers in the U.S.  Pittsburgh, Pa.:  International Studies Association, 1976.

Lancester, Lane W.  Masters of Political Thought:  Hegel to Dewey.  Vol. 3.  Boston:  Houghton Mifflin Co., 1966.

Little, Roger W. (Ed.).  Handbook of Military Institutions.  Beverly Hills, Cal.:  Sage, 1971.

Loory, S.H.  Defeated.  New York:  Random House, 1973.

Lovell, John P.  Neither Athens Nor Sparta?  The American Service Academies in Transition.  Bloomington:  Indiana University Press, 1979.

Lovell, John P. and Kronenberg, Philip (Eds.).  New Civil-Military Relations.  New Brunswick, N.J.:  Transaction, 1974.

MacArthur, General Douglas.  A Soldier Speaks: Public Papers and Speeches of General of the Army Douglas MacArthur.  Edited by Vorin E. Whan, Jr. (Major, USA).  New York:  Praeger, 1965.

_____ .  Duty, Honor, Country.  New York: Rolton House, 1962.

Machiavelli, Niccolo.  The Prince.  New York:  Norton, 1977.  Translated and edited by Adams, Robert.

Maguire, Daniel C.  The Moral Choice.  Garden City, N.Y.:  Doubleday and Co., Inc., 1978.

Margiotta, Franklin D. (Ed.).  The Changing World of the American Military.  Boulder, Col.:  Westview Press, 1978.

Masland, John W. and Radway, Lawrence I.  Soldiers and Scholars: Military Education and Military Policy.  Princeton, N.J.:  Princeton University Press, 1967.

Matloff, Maurice.  American Military History.  Washington, D.C.:  Office of the Chief of Military History, United States Army, 1969.

Millis, Walter, Mansfield, Harvey C. and Stein, Harold. Arms and the State: Civil-Military Elements in National Policy. New York: The Twentieth Century Fund, 1958.

Millis, Walter. Arms and Men: A Study in American Military History. New York: Putnam, 1956.

Mills, C. Wright. The Power Elite. New York: Oxford University Press, 1956.

Mollenhoff, Clark R. The Pentagon: Politics, Profits and Plunder. New York: Putnam, 1967.

Moskos, Charles C., Jr. (Ed.). Public Opinion and the Military Establishment. Beverley Hills, Cal. Sage, 1971.

_____. The American Enlisted Man: The Rank and File in Today's Military. New York: Russell Sage Foundation, 1970.

Mylander, Maureen. The Generals: Making It, Military-Style. New York: The Dial Press, 1974. '

Oppenheimer, Martin, (Ed.). The American Military. New Brunswick, N.J. Transaction, 1971.

Paige, Glenn D. (Ed.). Political Leadership: Readings For An Emerging Field. New York: The Free Press, 1972.

Palmer, John McAuley. America in Arms: The Experience of the United States with Military Organization. New Haven: Yale University Press, 1941.

Peers, William R. The My Lai Inquiry. New York: Norton, 1978.

_____. The My Lai Massacre and Its Cover-Up: Beyond the Reach of Law? New York: The Free Press, 1976.

Rapoport, Anatol (Ed.). Clausewitz on War. Baltimore, Md.: Penguin Books, 1971.

Ridgway, General Matthew B. Soldier: The Memoirs of Matthew B. Ridgway. New York: Harper and Row, 1956.

Riker, William H. Soldiers of the States: The Role of the National Guard in American Democracy. Washington, D.C.: Public Affairs Press, 1957.

Rovere, Richard H. and Schlesinger, Arthur M., Jr. The General and the President, and the Future of American Foreign Policy. New York: Straus and Young, 1951.

Russett, Bruce M. and Stepan, Alfred (Ed.). Military Force and American Society. New York: Harper and Row, 1973.

Sabine, George H. and Thorson, Thomas L. A History of Political Theory. Fourth Edition. Hinsdale, Ill.: Dryden Press, 1973.

Sarkesian, Sam C. (Ed.). Combat Effectiveness: Cohesion, Stress and the Volunteer Military. Beverly Hills, Cal.: Sage Publications, 1980.

_____. The Professional Army Officer in a Changing Society. Chicago: Nelson-Hall, 1975.

Sarkesian, Sam C. and Gannon, Thomas M. (Eds.). Military Ethics and Professionalism. Special issue, American Behavioral Scientist, May/June 1976, Vol. 19, No. 5.

Schell, Jonathan. The Military Half: An Account of the Destruction of Quang Ngai and Quang Tin. New York: Knopf, 1968.

_____. The Village of Ben Suc. New York: Knopf, 1967.

Schilling, Warner R., Hammond, Paul Y., and Snyder, Glenn H. Strategy, Politics and Defense Budgets. New York: Columbia University Press, 1962.

Schmidt, Steffen W. and Dorfman, Gerald A. Soldiers in Politics. Los Altos, Cal.: Geron-X, Inc., 1974.

Schratz, Paul R. Evolution of the Military Establishment since World War II. Lexington, Va.: George C. Marshall Research Foundation, 1978.

Spanier, John W. The Truman-MacArthur Controversy and the Korean War. Cambridge, Mass.: Harvard University Press, 1959.

Stein, Harold (Ed.). American Civil-Military Decisions: A Book of Case Studies. Birmingham, Ala.: University of Alabama Press, 1963.

Stouffer, S.A., et al. The American Soldier: Adjustment During Army Life. Princeton, N.J.: Princeton University Press, 1949.

_____. The American Soldier: Combat and Its Aftermath. Princeton, N.J: Princeton University Press, 1949.

Swomley, John M. The Military Establishment. Boston: Beacon Press, 1964.

The Federalist Papers. Selected and edited by Fairfield, Roy P. Garden City, N.Y.: Anchor Books, 1966.

The Pentagon Papers (The Senator Gravel Edition): The Defense Department History of Decisionmaking on Vietnam. Boston: Beacon Press, 1971.

The Republic of Plato. Translated by Cornford, Francis Macdonald. New York: Oxford University Press, 1970.

Trager, Frank N. and Kronenberg, Philip S. National Security and American Society: Theory, Process, and Policy. Lawrence, Kan.: The University Press of Kansas, 1973.

U.S. Army War College. Study on Military Professionalism. USAWC, Carlisle Barracks, Pa., 30 June 1970.

U.S. Army War College. Army Tasks for the Seventies: The Decade of the Seventies: Perspectives and Implications for the United States Army. Carlisle Barracks, Pa.: USAWC, June, 1972.

U.S. Department of the Army. Leadership for the 1970s. Carlisle Barracks, Pa.: U.S. Army War College, 1971.

U.S. President's Commission on an All-Volunteer Armed Force. The Report of the President's Commission on an All-Volunteer Armed Force. Washington, D.C.: Government Printing Office, 1970.

Upton, Emory. The Military Policy of the United States from 1775. Washington: Government Printing Office, 1904.

Vagts, Alfred. A History of Militarism. New York: Meridian Books, 1959.

_____. Defense and Diplomacy: The Soldier and the Conduct of Foreign Relations: New York: King's Crown Press, 1956.

van Doorn, Jacques. The Soldier and Social Change. Beverly Hills, Cal.: Sage Publications, 1975.

_____ (Ed.). Military Profession and Military Regimes: Commitments and Conflicts. The Hague: Mouton, 1969.

_____ (Ed.). Armed Forces and Society: Sociological Essays. The Hague: Mouton, 1968.

Wakin, Malham M. War, Morality, and the Military Profession. Boulder, Col.: Westview Press, 1979.

Walton, Colonel George (USA, ret). The Tarnished Shield: A Report on Today's Army. New York: Dodd, Mead and Co., 1973.

Weigley, Russell F. (Ed.). The American Military; Readings in the History of the Military in American Society. Reading, Mass.: Addision-Wesley, 1969.

_____. History of the United States Army. New York: Macmillan, 1967.

_____. Toward an American Army. New York: Columbia University Press, 1962.

Westmoreland, William. <u>A Soldier Reports</u>. Garden City, N.Y.: Doubleday and Co., Inc., 1976.

Zumwalt, Elmo. <u>On Watch: A Memoir</u>. New York: Quadrangle Books, 1976.

# Index

# About the Author

Sam C. Sarkesian is professor of Political Science at Loyola University of Chicago. He served as Chairman of the Department from 1974-1980. He received his Ph.D. from Columbia University in the city of New York. Dr. Sarkesian served in the U.S. Army for over a 20 year period as an officer and enlisted man, performing duties with Special Forces, Airborne, and Infantry units in Germany, Korea, and Vietnam. He includes among his publications, The Professional Army Officer in a Changing Society (1975), Revolutionary Guerrilla Warfare (1975), Defense Policy and the Presidency: Carter's First Years (1979), Nonnuclear Conflicts in the Nuclear Age (1980), Combat Effectiveness (1980), and several other books and articles on similar subjects. He has served as Associate Chairman of the Inter-University Seminar on Armed Forces and Society and has lectured at various senior service schools. He received his B.A. from The Citadel.